CALVARY CATHOLIC CEMETERY

LEXINGTON, KENTUCKY

Transcribed Plus
Some Obits
A-Z

Compiled by

Teresa Mondelli

HERITAGE BOOKS
2010

HERITAGE BOOKS

AN IMPRINT OF HERITAGE BOOKS, INC.

Books, CDs, and more—Worldwide

For our listing of thousands of titles see our website
at
www.HeritageBooks.com

Published 2010 by
HERITAGE BOOKS, INC.
Publishing Division
100 Railroad Ave. #104
Westminster, Maryland 21157

International Standard Book Numbers
Paperbound: 978-0-7884-5268-0
Clothbound: 978-0-7884-8586-2

Abraham Hanood May 25, 1893 - Aug 20, 1943
Abraham Louis Mar 14, 1887 - Apr 20, 1964
Abraham Mike Aug 15, 1888 - July 1972
Abraham Moses 1870 - Apr 1910
Abraham Tofie Elias Jan 28, 1808 - Feb 22, 1917
Adams Charles F 1891 - 1948 Mary Norris 1897 - 1964

Nov 24, 1905 Leader
Ella E. Adams, 4 months, died in Fayette County, November
    23, of diphtheria, burial in Catholic Cemetery,
    November 24.

Adams J Q Nov 29, 1850 - Dec 24, 1910 wife Thresa S Nov
    22, 1900

Nov 25, 1900 Morning Herald
Services for wife of J Q Adams will be held at St Paul's
    Church this afternoon at 2 o'clock. Interment will
    occur in the Lexington Catholic Cemetery.

Dec 26, 1910 Leader
The funeral services of Mr. John Quincy Adams will be held
    at the residence, Monday afternoon. The internment
    will follow in the family lot in the Catholic Cemetery.

Adams Margaret Doyle died Jan 19, 1918
Adams Margaret S June 5, 1899 - Apr 9, 1947
Adams Mary Agnes Sept 20, 1909 - Apr 24, 1962 Leroy B Jan
    24, 1910
Adams Mary Sharkey 1878 - 1950
Adams Ruth W Feb 5, 1905 - Jan 7, 2001 John B Dec 24,
    1904 - Nov 16, 1985
Addis Glenn H June 7, 1911- Apr 23, 1982 Lucille L Oct 24,
    1910 - Mar 14, 2003

Aglar Anna H Sept 19, 1883 - Feb 2, 1953
Ahern H Julia died July 8, 1880 Lizzie died March 16, 1884
    aged 21
Ahern John W 1902 - 1939
Ahern Daniel April 7, 1876 his wife Mary 1830 - 1895
Ahern Neal died July 28, 1893 John 1863 - 1894 Daniel 1868
    - 1889
Albert Thomas 1894 - 1977
Allen Charles Fleece 1869 - 1946 and wife Maryetta Boarman
    1899 - 1977
Allender John Spalding June 15, 1931 - Feb 28, 2002 Mary
    Gentry Mar 21, 1931
Allender Matthew Spaulding Oct, 9, 1965 - May 19, 1983
Allender Waller R June 3, 1893 - Oct 12, 1983 Elisabeth P
    Nov 23, 1898 - Dec 19, 1994
Allgaier Ann Savilla 1818 - 1869
Allgaier Josephine (Under brush)
Allphin Jon 1874 - 1917 Doyle 1908 - 1919 Jane 1882 - 1903
Alma Marguerite 1886 - 1974
Amato Baldassaro 1863 - 1926 Vincenzina Papania 1865 -
    1960
Amato Christine Mangione Mar 11, 1902 - Apr 5, 1995
Amato Joseph 1894 - 1975 Mary Jane 1893 - 1949
Amato Kathleen Fitzpatrick Nov 23, 1892 - Aug 5, 1972
Jan. 16, 1920 Leader
The marriage of Miss Kathleen Frances Fitzpatrick to Mr.
    Matthew Joseph Amato was solemnized Wednesday
    morning at St. Paul's Catholic Church

Amato Matthew Joseph Sr. Aug 1, 1892 - Mar 13, 1992
Amato S J Sam 1892 - 1961 Christine M 1902 - 1995
Amato Samuel J Jul 31, 1892 - Jan 19, 1931
Amato Vincent Dec 1, 1922 - Feb 2, 1996
Ambrose Robert P Feb 21, 1916 - Oct 8, 1995 Elsie R Feb1,
    1921 - May 28, 1999

Ambrose David M 1886 - 19 Catherine M 1868 - 1949
Ambrose Mary C 1911 - 1934
Ambrose Moore Margaret 1890 - 1943
Amos Audra K Aug 6, 1895 - Oct 19, 1976
Anderson Anna Mae McKenna Mar 31, 1899 - July 17, 1979
Anderson Anne B 1890 - 1963
Anderson Beatrice McAvoy Sept 17, 1898 - Apr 21, 1980
Anderson Bobbie Burke May 15, 1909 - Sept 23, 1992
Anderson Charles M July 23, 1933
Anderson Dorothy N. Barkman Aug, 1915 - Aug 12, 1992
        Widow of Robert L Barkman
Anderson George K Nov 27, 1902 - Mar 24, 1975
Anderson George W 1874 - 1944
Anderson Helen Margaret Jan 30, 1939 - Aug 28, 2008
Anderson Henry M 1884 - 1950
Anderson John Gund Dec 27, 1916 - Oct 2, 1977 Jane Alice
        July 19, 1919 - Apr 17, 2000
Anderson John Siegfried May 22, 1871 - June 28, 1967
Anderson Lena Huller 1881 - 1972 George W 1874 - 1944
Anderson Lillian D 1921
Anderson Mannie C 1939
Anderson Wesley J July 30, 1906 - Jan 22, 1979
Anderson William B 1920
Andreen Scott J Aug 11, 1969
Andrews Frank Nov 1, 1922 - July 5, 1986 Olga July 24, 1923
Angel Nancy Feb 26, 1948 - Nov 18, 1949
Angel Nora Welch 1882 - 1977
Angelucci Ersilia Jan 1, 1895 - May 3, 1981
Angelucci Joseph Oct 9, 1885 - July 7, 1960
Angelucci Joseph Matthew Apr 27, 1964 - Nov 23, 1988
Angelucci Philip J 1919 - 2004 Mary Ann D 1925 - 2005
Angelucci Phillip Oct 27, 1888 - Sept 18, 1971 Lucia Tenaglia
        Dec 13, 1890 - May 25, 1987
Aug 1, 1919 Herald
Phillip Angelucci, tailor, files application to become U. S.

3

citizen. Came here in 1911.

Oct 1, 1915 Lexington Herald
DeLuxe Tailoring Co. Announces Opening
Phillip Angelucci is in charge of the Woman's Department
and Andrew Bucci, is in charge of the men's
department. Mr. Angelucci was recently connected
with J. B. Luck, who discontinued business a short
time ago and Mr. Bucci has been for several years
associated with the Standard Woolen Mills.

Dec 3, 1915 Lexington Herald Advertisement
Deluxe
Ladies and Gents' Tailors
Union Bank & Trust Co. Building
BUCCI & ANGELUCCI
Competent Home Tailors

Feb 11, 1917 Lexington Herald
Angelucci to New York
P. Angelucci, of Deluxe Tailors, leaves this morning for New
York, there too meet his wife and children, envoyaged
from Rome, Italy.

Anglin J J
Nov 2, 1881 Lexington Transcript
John J. Anglin weds Mollie McCormick at St. Paul's
November 10.

Anglin Jennie Dowd 1891 - 1965 wife of John T Anglin
Anglin John 1798 - 1862

Anglin John T 1890 - 1939
Anglin Margaret Ryan 1874 - 1957

Aug 16, 1902 Morning Herald
The funeral for T C Anglin will take place at St. Paul's
    Cathedral at 9 o'clock Monday Morning. The
    interment will be in the Lexington Catholic Cemetery.

Anglin William P
Aug 12, 1904 Leader
W. P. Anglin, aged 38, one of the best known and most highly
    esteemed citizens of the county and a prominent
    trotting horse breeder, died at his home, on the
    Nicholasville Pike, about one mile from this city
    Friday afternoon.

Aug 14, 1904 Leader
William P. Anglin, died at his late residence on the
    Nicholasville Pike Friday afternoon. The funeral
    services will take place at St. Paul's Catholic Church
    this afternoon, Rev. J. P. Barry officiating.

Anglin William P 1893 - 1936
Anton Mollie Joseph Dec 1, 1903 - Jun 23, 1931 wife of
    Louise Anton
Antone Louis Jan 19, 1891 - Aug 14, 1967
Antone Sally T Nov 3, 1908 - June 29, 1985
Archdeacon Carrie Smith Dec 14, 1882 - Feb 20, 1963
Archdeacon Ernest I Apr 27, 1904 - Sept 10, 1969 Florence
    Breiner Aug 16, 1911 - Feb 18, 2003
Archdeacon James William Oct 29, 1911 - Nov 10, 1986
Archdeacon John Joseph Sept 24, 1920 - May 6, 1943
Aredan Sue Mary July 10, 1939 Infant daughter of Norbert
    and Mabel Aredan
Armstrong J A July 16, 1884 - Dec 5, 1946
Armstrong Mayme McGarvey July 22, 1886 - Apr 12, 1959
    wife of J A Armstrong

Armstrong Sarah K 1872 - 1914
Dec 14, 1914 Leader
Following a brief illness of pneumonia, Mrs. Sarah Kelly
Armstrong, wife of Thomas M. Armstrong, a well -
known C. & O. railroad engineer, died at St. Joseph's
Hospital this morning.

Dec 15, 1914 Leader
The funeral services of Mrs. Sarah K. Armstrong will take
place at St. Peter's Catholic Church Wednesday
morning.

Armstrong Thomas N 1866 - 1948
Arvin Andrew B 1938 - 1984 Mary Jo 1939 - 1988
Asbridge Gabriel Wilson July 28, 2005
Ashby Joseph 1911 - 1986
Atkins Samuel W May 28, 1914 - Sept 3, 1971 WWII
Atwell Aline L Apr 25, 1923
Augur Daniel W born in Cincinnati May 30, 1855 - Died June
24, 1882
Ausherman Marjorie Moran Feb 1, 1921 - Aug 2, 1997
Ausherman Robert J Jan 13, 1921 - Oct 22, 1976
Austin Robert J Aug 13, 1907 - 1977 Rosalind A Jan 9, 1910 -
Sept 13, 1992
Ayer Forrest W Nov 14, 1889 - July 16, 1970 May Ginocchio
Feb 14, 1886 - Sept 30, 1972
B - - Mary T July 26, 1900 - Aug 31, 1910
Baker Auval Jack 1870 - 1948
Baker Jack 1912 - 1996
Baker Loretta Hale June 1, 1907 - Nov 8, 1989
Baker Mary M 1875 - 1964
Baker Paul Standafer May 27, 1934 - Oct 9, 1978
Baldwin Alma Hite June 10, 1932 - June 22, 1968
Ballard Bland Aug 31, 1898 - Dec 8, 1986 Rosanna
McGarvey Oct 19, 1891 - Feb 7, 1964

Ballard Eugene T Apr 25, 1927 - Aug 19, 1998 Edith E May
8, 1926 - May 5, 1998
Ballard James Lou May 24, 1924 - Jul 10, 1984 PVT US
ARMY WWII
Ballard Joseph A Aug 27, 1920 - Apr 26, 1997 CAPT US
ARMY
Ballard Joseph Aloysius Aug 27, 1920 - Apr 26, 1997
Margaret Mary June 22, 1919
Ballard Joseph Russell 1905 - 1966 Elizabeth O'Daniel 1905
Ballard - Hite James Lou May 24, 1924 - July 1984 Joe M
Mar 12, 1933 - Aug 9, 2008 Donna Jean Feb 20, 1953
Betty B Jan 31, 1929 - Sept 19, 2008 Phillip J Dec 20,
1954
Banahan Angela Marie Mar 21, 1937 - Oct 26, 1995
Banahan Barry Oct 3, 1893 - Mar 26, 1955
Banahan Dan D 1875 - 1943
Banahan Francis 1818 - 1891
Banahan James E Oct 26, 1925 - Dell Crain Oct 10, 1917 -
Oct 16, 1992
Banahan James B EOW Feb 23, 1935 Killed in the line of
duty
Banahan James J 1886 - 1948
Banahan James P 1854 - 1926 Hannah A 1859 - 1949
Oct 30, 1883 Lexington Transcript
James Banahan weds Hannah Anglin.

April 14, 1889 Leader
James P. Banahan, the Clerk of the Recorder's Court, was born
in Woodford County, January 22, 1854. He came to
Lexington about 23 years ago. Six years ago Mr.
Banahan married Miss Hannah Anglin.

Banahan John F 1885 - 1929
Banahan Lucy C 1834 - 1898
Banahan Mary Ada Mar 2, 1964

Banahan Mary Carroll Mar 7, 1897 - Nov 19, 1977
Banahan Steve E Sr. 1899 - 1979
Banahan W Anglin 1892 - 1945
Banks William R Oct 9, 1919 - Jan 10, 1972
Banta James L 1895 - 1964 Della Hickey 1893 - 1978
Banta James L Jr. Nov 21, 1925 Glema McNeal Feb 29, 1928
Banta James L Kentucky Co 159 Depot Brigade WWI
Banta Joseph F July 7, 1927 - Mar 7, 2005 Louise W July 27,
    1930 Wed Feb 14, 1953
Banta Joseph Frank July 7, 1927 - Mar 7, 2005 TEC 5 US
    ARMY WWII
Barbieri A Jerry June 6, 1915 - Feb 26, 1998 Annette G Mar
    20, 1916 Married Apr 7, 1940
Barker David L 1900 - 1953
Barker Dawn Lavin May 27, 1969 - Aug 1, 2007
Barker Katherine L 1908 - 1968
Barkman John H Feb 1921 - Apr 2001 SGT US ARMY WWI
Barkman John O Sept 14, 1887 - Mar 16, 1973
Barkman Margaret Elizabeth Schulte Nov 26, 1886 - Jan 7,
    1975
Barkman Mary Catherine Egalite Feb 23, 1922 - Jan 24, 2002
Barkman Robert L 1918 - May 6, 1973 KY FIRST LT ARMY
    AIR FORCES WWII
Barlow Carolyn J 1917 - 2006 Claude 1913 - 1970
Barlow Claude Jun 12, 1913 - May 31, 1970 KY PFC FIELD
    ARTY WWII
Barnes Henry C Apr 12, 1897 - Oct 29, 1995
Barnes Nell Burke Punch died 1965
Barrett Lucy Brophy 1913 - 1982
Barry Albert A 1895 - 1968 Minerva R 1900 - 1947
Barry James
Jan 29, 1909 Leader
After simple, but solemnly impressive funeral services, held
    Friday morning at St. Paul's Church and attended by
    the largest concourse of people ever gathered in this

historic edifice on a similar occasion, all that was mortal of Rev. Father James P. Barry, for over twenty years the venerated and beloved pastor of that church was laid to rest in the Lexington Catholic Cemetery, in the tomb prepared by his direction nearly ten years ago as the repository of his body.

Barry John F 1848 - 1940 Mary Ellen 1847 - 1934
Barry Michael W 1872 - 1947 Sarah E 1879 - 1951
Barry Mr. and Mrs. Richard born in Ireland
Barry Thomas illegible
Bartholomeu Unknown Feb 22, ?? - June 14, 1887
Barton Hugh A 1894 - 1982
Barton James W 1898 - 1993 Anne M ? - 1978 Gillian L 1934
        - 1998
Barton Jennie V 1890 - 1975
Barton Joseph Jr. 1940 - 1948
Barton M Lillian 1896 - 1976
Barton Rose Cecilia 'Bertie' 1892 - 1986
Battle Howard L July 29, 1930 - July 14, 2002 Daisy A Aug
        18, 1935 Wed May 9, 1960
Battle M J
Bauer George A 1887 - 1946
Bauer Joe July 15, 1865 - Nov 19, 1899 his wife Katie Aug
        27, 1870 - May 25, 1903
Bauer Madeline Joyce 1894 - 1928
        May 3, 1914 Leader
The marriage of Miss Madeline A. Joyce and Mr. George
        Bauer was quietly solemnized at St. Paul's Patronage
        Wednesday, April 29th.

Baur Bernard H May 8, 1916 - Aug 13, 1972 WWII Helen B
        Dec 13, 1919 - Nov, 11, 2007
Beagle James R May 31, 1962 - Oct 31, 1962
Beargie James Clair 1966 - 1976

Beatty Katherine McKenna 1886 - 19
Beatty Mary Reagan 1886 - 1960
Beatty Russell Lowell 1892 - 1963
Beatty Veronica McKenna 1894 - 1925
Beaven our children Sarah Marie and Natalie Hill
Beaven Richard Hill May 23, 1954 married Aug 11, 1973
    Donna Hughes Apr 21, 1954 - Nov 2, 1997
Beaver Robert G Mar 17, 1922 - May 14, 1974
Beck Fred L 1914 - 1980 Helen M 1914 - 1998
Becker Frank E Nov 3, 1927 Patricia Flynn Oct 31, 1931
Becker Frank 1868 - 1930 Kate 1872 - 1951
Becker John P Feb 22, 1968 - Oct 3, 2001
Becker Joseph Sept 20, 1901 - May 6, 1970 Clara Keller Feb
    18, 1902 - Mar 24, 1968
Beckum Frances J 1912 - 1989 Charles H 1908 - 1986
Beckum James T 1930 - 1984
Begley Judy Nov 19, 1936 - Oct 26, 2007 Bill Dec 5, 1937
Bell Nellie Houlihan 1890 - 1944
Benckart Ann Mary died Nov 27, 1937

Nov 30, 1913 Leader
The marriage of Miss Lilye Benckart to Mr. Robert Carter
    Shinn of Washington, D. C., and New York City, was
    beautifully celebrated the afternoon of Thanksgiving
    Day at the home of the bride's parents, Mr. and Mrs.
    Matthew Benckart, on North Limestone.

Benckart Anne Gertrude Apr 26, 1926 - June 22, 1993
Benckart Frederick John Aug 25, 1889 - Feb 1, 1970
Benckart Gertrude Harrington Jan 9, 1896 - Aug 16, 1947
Benckart John E 1861 - 1900
Benckart Joseph Sept 1870 - June ?
Benckart Margaret Katherine Feb 11, 1924 - Feb 12, 1970
Benckart Mather died Nov 25, 1917
Bernard Terrill A May 26, 1946 Michael G Dec 14, 1948

Bernier Chester A 1904 - 1983 Bernice A 1908 - 1976
Berry Michael Wayne Apr 13, 1965 - Aug 15, 1969
Berryman Clinton E 1882 - 1961 Mary Burke 1873 - 1958
Bethel Mary M June 16, 1883 - May 17, 1958
Bettez Muriel S 1925 - 1963
Bickers Homer G 1924 - 2004 Evelyn C 1930 - 2007
Bickers Homer G Jan 23, 1924 - Mar 3, 2004 WWII
Bietz Charles G Jan 22, 1865 - Apr 22, 1925
Birge Velna 1867 - 1934
Birmingham John W Feb 14, 1924 - Aug 11, 1977 WWII
Birmingham John W Feb 14, 1924 - Aug 11, 1977 Frances D
    Apr 21, 1921 - June 12, 2006
Bishop Anne Lee Reister May 12, 1914 - May 13, 1984 wife
    of Edgar E Bishop
Bishop Edgar William Jan 2, 1912 - Jan 27, 1995
Bishop Marta A Nov 14, 1926 - May 14, 2009
Bishop Mary Connie Aug 3, 1947 infant daughter of Edgar
    and Anne Lee Bishop 7 hours old
Bivin William Frank 1871 - 1948 Margaret Henry 1875 - 1951
Black Jeffrey A June 13, 1947 - Jan 16, 1998
Blackwood Robert 1916 - 1935 Margaret 1917
Blake Edmond 1814 - 1904 Mary 1818 - 1895
Blakeman Jean Mar 10, 1929 - Jan 3, 1989
Blanchet Louis P July 22, 1884 - Feb 24, 1968 Margaret Flynn
    Sept 1, 1890 - May 16, 1995
Block Alvin H Jr. Sept 20, 1912 - Dec 10, 2000 Frances
    Houlihan Mar 27, 1914 - Dec 28, 1998
Block Timothy Brian May 27, 1970 - Dec 14, 1997
Blount John Gregory 1925 - 1948
Board John W 1871 - 1936
Board Mary E 1901 - 1976
Board Mary M 1867 - 1955
Board Ruth D 1904 - 1973
Boarman Sutzer Margaret 1837 - 1927
Boatwright Josephine Mar 7, 1895 - Jan 20, 1961

Bockhoop Patricia K 1906 - 1915 Many hopes lie buried here
Bockhoop Sallie S
Bocko Andrew J May 15, 1896 - June 11, 1965 Anna P June
    29, 1902 - July 28, 1986
Bodine Jack B Apr 1, 1922 Jean A Apr 1, 1928 married Mar
    3, 1973
Bogaert Victor Mar 7, 1859 - Mar 7, 1950 Caroline Reyners
    Mar 30, 1854 - Oct 1895 daughter Henriette Jul 5,
    1882 - May 188?
Bogaert Flora S 1903 - 1969
Bohan Margaret Julia Wharton Hillenmeyer May 30, 1924
Bohannon Mary Louise Feb 14, 1906 - Aug 1, 1915
Bohannon Neal Oct 12, 1884 - Feb 4, 1951
Bohne Catherine Stafford July 17, 1911 - Dec 14, 1986
Bohne Margaret Shannon Aug 24, 1879 - Aug 21, 1958
Bohne Mary Ann Jan 6, 1922
Bohne Robert Fraser Jul 12, 1907 - Apr 1, 1987
Bolen Owen died Jan 24, 1890
Bologna Samuel F Oct 28, 1916 - Nov 12,1996 Frances Apr
    11, 1920 - May 31, 2002
Bona Anthony 1843 - 1921
Bona Charles Joseph Louis Florence Joseph May
Bona Isabelle 1850 - 1916
Bonfield James Jul 2, 1860 - Jan 30, 1926
Bonfield Joseph Erwin Jan 7, 1897 - Oct 8, 1977
Bonfield Pat Gantley May 11, 1913 - Nov 23, 1988
Bonner Linda Jannlin Nov 14 - 16, 1958
Bonnyman George died Mar 20, 1904 Sarah A died Aug 16,
    1902
Bonnyman George Jr. died Nov. 10, 1949
Boome Honora 1879 wife of Ed
Borland Mary Margaret Minihan Oct 31, 1900 - Mar 2, 2001
Borne Katherine A Mar 27, 1975 - Apr 10, 1975
Bosau A J Frederick died Mar 31, 1920
Bosau Ann K Feb 1, 1898 - Mar 29, 1988

Bosau Dorcas Levy July 4, 1915 - Feb 12, 2004
Bosau Elizabeth Grace died Dec 16, 1987
Bosau George F Feb 4, 1897 - Jan 2, 1975
Bosau Gertrude Frieda died Oct 4, 1979
Bosau Marie Marguerite died June 26, 1984
Bosau Mary Barbara died June 21, 1944
Bosau Raymond J Mar 3, 1907 - Sept 30, 1996
Bossi Federico Dec 14, 1913 - Dec 19, 1967
Bottom Louise Perrin
Botts Anne Hanly Mar 13, 1831 - Sept 13, 1912
Boulanger Charles Edward Jan 4, 1922 - Apr 15, 1953 Mary
    Hegare Jul 5, 1923 - Dec 31, 2005
Bour Madeleine Nov 18, 1888 - Apr 22, 1959
Bourgeois Joseph Z Mar 13, 1879 - Dec 7, 1959
Bowlin Dorothy C 1913 - 1931
Bowman Elizabeth R 1858 - 1924 James A 1852 - 1918
Bracken Aug 18, 1862 - July 24, 1875
Bracken Bridget died Dec 15, 1872 wife of Michael Bracken
Bracken Sallie C 1868 - 1907
Bradley Agnes Cecelia Jan 21, 1878 - Jan 1?,1926
Jan 17, 1926 Herald
Bradley Agnes Lasserre Aug 29, 1872 - Mar 24, 1957
Bradley Alice died Feb 3, 1902
Feb 6, 1902 Leader
Mrs. Alice Bradley, wife of Mr. Barney Bradley, died at their
    family residence, Wednesday afternoon, aged 65 years.

Bradley ?astha Nov 18, 1823 - Feb 9, 1856 and infant son
    Lawrence
Bradley Barney died Apr 3, 1902
Bradley Billie Jane Murphy Oct 14, 1918 - Apr 12, 1989
Bradley Edward J 1881 - 1946 Cora Parker 1885 - 1952
Bradley Edward Riley Dec 12, 1859 - Aug 15, 1946
Bradley Emmett Sept 10, 1900 - Aug 13, 1982
Bradley Francis M 1870 - 1937

Bradley Frank A 1877 - 1951 Mattie Woodward 1867 - 19
Bradley James
Bradley James 1867 - 1920
Bradley James Charles son of Paul and Rosa Bradley
Bradley James Douglas Aug 30, 1908 - July 6, 1984
Bradley James 1828 - 1901 Sarah 1829 - 1879 Frank 1865 -
      1899 Susie 1875 - 1901 Wm J 1874 - 1904 John 1857 -
      1926 James 1859 - 1930
Bradley Jas 1816 - 1872 Ellen 1834 - 1915
Bradley John F 1870 - 1944
Bradley Joseph J Dec 23, 1903 - Jan 5, 1980 Leo M July 20,
      1903 - Nov 8, 1978
Bradley Katherine died Apr 12, 1935 At Rest
Bradley Margaret 1857 - 1903 At Rest
Oct 3, 1903 Leader
The funeral services of Ellen Margaret, infant daughter of Mr.
      and Mrs. J. F. Bradley, will be held at the family
      residence, Sunday afternoon.

Bradley Martha June 7, 1851
Bradley Patrick Mar 17, 1808 - Oct 12, 1880
Bradley Peter 1882
Bradley Peter died July 23, 1885
Bradley Rosa McNamee died May 16, 1910
May 17, 1910 Leader
Mrs. Rosa Bradley, widow of Mr. Paul Bradley, died at the
      home of her daughter, Mrs. John Conners, Ludlow,
      Ky., Monday morning aged 83 years. The funeral
      services will be held at Ludlow and the remains will be
      brought to Lexington for interment in the family lot in
      the Catholic Cemetery.

Bradley Rose died Nov 23, 1930 At Rest
Bradley Thomas F Dec 20, 1911 - Feb 26, 1999
Bradshaw James H Jr. May 1, 1928 - Sept 8, 2008 Katherine C

Apr 22, 1931
Brady David F Feb 24, 1920 - Dec 19, 2003 Margaret K Dec
    19, 1923
Brady Francis Whitney Jan 3, 1893
Brady Nellie O Aug 14, 1888 - June 29, 1982
Brain Alice 1902
Bramlett Katie King Christopher Apr 9, 1885 - Mar 21, 1966
Bramlett Steven Lee May 27, 1958 - Dec 31, 1977 Joanne E
    July 14, 1932 Fred A Dec 2, 1928 - July 5, 1989
Branddenburg Hugh G 1908 - 1944
Brandenburg Hugh F 1934 - 2006 Hugh G 1908 - 1944
Branigan Robert 1911 - 19 James T 1884 - 1953 Marie H
    1879 - 19
Brannon Mary Margaret 1893 - 1990
Brannon Thomas R Jr. 1897 - 1975 John R Sr. 1911 - 1978
Bransom Henry Earl Aug 7, 1919 - Dec 9, 1968
Breezing Belle 1859 - 1940
Sept 15, 1875 Lexington Daily Press
A marriage in high life is reported between Miss Belle
    Breezing and Mr. James Kinney. The ceremony was
    performed at the residence of the bride's mother. It was
    brief but most significant, and performed in a manner
    so touching that it drew tears from the eyes of those
    who witnessed it.

Brenan Sarah 1896
Brennan Bernard died Aug 9, 1899
Brewer Mary McCoy 1873 - 1948
Bricken J Noland Jan 30, 1882 - Sept 26, 1962 Jessie Crawley
    Oct 1, 1890 - Dec 1967
Bricken John M Mar 22, 1919 - Jan 31, 1974
Bricken Joseph Noland Jr. June 19, 1917 - Mar 8, 1981 WWII
Bricken Mary Colbert Apr 8, 1915 - Feb 4, 1987
Bringardner Fred 1882 - 1940
Bringardner Laura 1888 - 1981

Bringardner Theresa July 9, 1927 - July 31, 1986
Brittingham George Lee 1888 - 1973
Brittingham Nell Gleeson 1888 - 1967
Broadus Paul K Jan 3, 1929 - Oct 4, 1980 Lois H Apr 7, 1930
    - Nov 14, 2008
Broadus Paul K Jan 3, 1929 - Oct 4, 1980 WWII
Broadus Stephen Pierce Dec 19, 1959 - Jan 8, 1960
Broagwelaw Keith Jan 22, 1848 - 1887
Broagwelaw Lilian
Brophy Ann 1904 - 1996 Ida Shade Mar 13, 1873 - Aug 27,
    1932 Michael J Oct 24, 1860 - Sept 1931 Leo J Oct 24,
    1907 - Dec 2000
Brophy Joseph Andrew Mar 22, 1913 - Oct 6, 1979

Feb 18, 1910   Leader
The funeral services of Mrs. Susan A. Brothers will be held at
    St. Peter's Church Saturday morning and the interment
    will follow in the family lot in the Catholic Cemetery.

Brophy Paul J (Father) Aug 1906 - Aug 27, 1985 ordained
    June 10, 1933
Brown Dr Aubrey J July 3, 1913 - Jan 6, 1968 Helen Molloy
    Nov 10, 1912 - Oct ?, 1990
Brown George Francis Mar 25, 1862 - Nov 6, 1955 Elizabeth
    Squires Jan 31, 1864 - Mar 31, 1941
Brown George W 1902 - 1951 Mary E 1906 - 1970
Brown Harold G Sept 1934 - Mar 2000 Louise I July 6, 1940
Brown Harold Gene Sept 4, 1934 - Mar 2, 2000
Brown J Ardath Aug 17, 1894 - Sept 23, 1942
Brown James Cronin 1904 - 1955 Mary Colbert 1914 - 1996
Brown James Kenton May 28, 1931 - May 28, 1977 Patricia
    Wilson Nov 17, 1936 - June 23, 1977
Brown Joseph Christian Sept 22, 1993
Brown Kathryn Lynch 1886 - 1980
Brown Malcolm 1873 - 1937 Mary S 1873 - 1951

Brown Mary Garland Dec 26, 1901 - Aug 16, 1972
Brown Mary H 1839 - 1910
Brown Robert Francis Nov 8, 1951 - Nov 27, 1982 Patricia
    Lynn Nov 8, 1956
Brown William C Jr. Feb 5, 1963
Browne Eliza S died Apr 8, 1881
Browne John died June 26, 1858
Bruin Alice 1902
Bruin George Oct 9, 1874 - Feb 1, 1955 Susie Jan 4, 1880 -
    July 26, 1963
Brumwell Unknown
Brumwell Margaret A 1845 - 1939
Brumwell Thomas 1871 - 1957
Bryant James A Mar 6, 1931 Ann McCarthy May 13, 1930 -
    Jan 10, 1993
Buchanan Donald E Dec 5, 1917 - Jan 16, 1985
Buchanan Donald E Dec 5, 1917 - Jan 16, 1985 Alta Ross
    Aug 17, 1916 - Nov 18, 2006
Buchanan J Allan 1924 - 1978
Buchanan James A Oct 30, 1953 - June 1, 1975
Buchanan James Allan WWII
Buchanan Jim 1953 - 1975
Buchanan William C Jan 15, 1892 - Mar 1, 1967 Alyce C Sept
    10, 1891 - Aug 1, 1973
Buchanan Zestre 1861 - 1889 Mary Keithley 1916 - 1920
Apr 7, 1920   Leader
Mary, the 3-year-old daughter of Mr. and Mrs. Frank Keithley,
    died at Wilmington, Delaware, on Tuesday afternoon.
    The body will be brought here for burial in the family
    lot in the Catholic Cemetery.

Apr 11, 1920   Leader
Mr. and Mrs. Frank Keithely will arrive here Monday morning
    with the body of their daughter, Mary Virginia, who
    died on Tuesday at Wilmington, Del. Burial will take

place in the Buchignani family lot in the Catholic
Cemetery.

Buchignani Brent Louis July 14, 1940
Buchignani Candito 1833 - 1890
Sept 17, 1890 Leader
Candito Buchignani, father of Eugene, Hannibal, Caesar and
    Miss Attilia Buchignani, died this morning at 9
    o'clock, at his home on the old Frankfort Pike, of
    softening of the brain, in 58th year.

Buchignani Catherine 1903 - 1936
Buchignani Eugene Jr. 1893 - 1916
July 5, 1916   Herald
4 young people of Lexington drown in Kentucky River about
    5 miles up river from Frankfort: Anne Embry, Paris;
    Francis Champ, Paris; Eugene Buchignani, Lexington;
    Curral Dale, Lexington. Eight rescued.

Buchignani Eugene Sr. 1856 - 1911
Dec 10, 1911   Leader
After an illness of a complication of diseases, prolonged
    through many months, Mr. Eugene Buchignani, 55
    years of age, and one of the most highly respected
    citizens of Lexington, died at St. Joseph's Hospital
    Sunday morning.

Buchignani Eugenia 1863 - 1957
Buchignani Eusepia 1832 - 1899
Buchignani Flora June17, 1833 - June 16 1850
Buchignani Hannibal 1858 - 1915
Dec 29, 1915   Herald
Hannibal Buchignani dies, age 57, well - known merchant
    here for 30 years.

Buchignani Harold Sr. 1900 - 1945
Buchignani Hugo 1888 - 1953
Buchignani John J Mar 16, 1887 - Oct 12, 1962 WWI
Buchignani Leo J Aug 15, 1889 - Oct 15, 1952 WWI
Buchignani Louise B 1889 - 1954
Buchignani Louise N 1907 - 1916
Buchignani Marguerite 1891 - 1986
Buckley Hannah 1866 - 1951
Bullock Everett B 1893 - 1973
Bullock Julia Coyne 1892 - 1963
Bundy James E Aug 26, 1886 - May 3, 1959
Bunton Florence Anne Aug 18, 1923 - Aug 12, 1999
Burch Henry Lyman May 2, 1869 - Aug 27, 1940 Agnes
        Glenn Feb 22, 1873 - Apr 12, 1953
Burch James M died May 18, 1956
Burch Nora Heafey died Oct 17, 1949
Burger Joseph Aug 1870 - Sept 1916 and Elizabeth
Burk George 1867 - 1957 Emma 1872 - 1929
Burk Samuel Aug 10, 1854 - Jan 5, 1931
Burke Annie 1872 - 1947 William F 1873 - 1941 Mary Hanley
        1917
Burke Dorothy L 1918 - 1929
Burke Dudley J Jan 21, 1904 - Feb 20, 1986
Burke Earney 1861 - 1931
Burke Elizabeth L Apr 13, 1859 - Feb 27, 1941
Burke James Jan 11, 1873 - Mar 8, 1941 Catherine Conley
        Burke Dec ?, 1880 - May 31, 1953

Feb 13, 1909 Leader
The body of John Burke, who died Friday, has been taken to
        the home of his brother, William Burke. The funeral
        services will be held at St. Paul's Church Sunday
        afternoon, the burial following in the Catholic
        Cemetery.

Burke John G Mar 13, 1856 - May 31, 1925 Mamie G Dec 6,
    1860 - Apr 2, 1936
Burke Louis Joseph 1893 - 1985 Julia Fister 1894 - 1960
Burke Louis Jr. 1922 - 1951
Burke Patrick 1870 - 1931
Burke Rose O'Neill Dec 24, 1908 - Oct 23, 1983
Burke W M 1862 Annie 1862 - 1916 W E 1887 - 1918
Burkhart Carrie Ellen Jan 4, 1908 - Feb 19, 1948
Burkhart William L May 21, 1911 - May 8, 1964 Anne E Oct
    17, 1906 - Jan 9, 1976
Burns Betsy Glenn Dec 24, 1944 - Jan 7, 1945 our baby sister
Burns James 1882
Burns Kathryn K June 10, 1903 - Sept 6, 1995
Burns Mary Conroy died Feb 20, 1941
Burns Mary L 1866 - 1929
Burns Rodman Oct 18, 1917 Evelyn Kincaid Mar 8, 1919
Burns William Cary Aug 16, 1900 - Feb 24, 1963
Bush Ann Powell Dec 26, 1930 - Feb 2, 2002
Bush Billy June 3, 1905 - Nov 27, 1973
Bush Cecelia H Feb 4, 1900 - Mar 18, 1997
Bush Curtis Jan 25, 1893 - Dec 10, 1956
Bush James L Sept 20, 1898 - Sept 20, 1944
Bush Josephine Kennedy Jan 28, 1893 - Apr 1, 1985
Bush William Curtis Jan 13, 1934
Butler Bernard Jan 14, 1889 - Feb 27, 1908
Mar 1, 1909 Leader
The funeral services of Bernard Butler, son of Mr. and Mrs. J.
    E. Butler of Witney Avenue, took place at St. Paul's
    Catholic Church Monday morning

Butler J E 1852 - 1935 Lizzie Lee 1858 - 1921
Butler Ronald J June 11, 1937 - May 16, 1978
Byrne James M 1897 - 1940

Byrne Rev Andrew died June 10, 1886

June 12, 1886   Lexington Transcript
Funeral services held for Father Byrne, chaplain of St.
    Joseph's hospital. Ten priests present.

Byrnes Christopher F 1876 - 1919

Byrnes Christopher Mar 25, 1828 - Aug 13, 1890
Oct 19, 1890   Leader
Christopher Byrnes, died at 8:30 o'clock Saturday night, of
    consumption, in his 63rd year.

Byrnes Christopher F WWI 1899
Byrnes Edward J 1857 - 1931
Byrnes Ellen Shea June 15, 1836 - Mar 25, 1916
Byrnes James M Mar 26, 1865 - 1916
Nov 19, 1916   Herald
James M. Byrnes, veteran printer, dies at 62.

Byrnes James M 1897 - 1940
Byrnes John D Dec 11, 1860 - June 28, 1886
Byrnes Katherine C 1877 - 1930
Byrnes Louis F 1910 - 1962
Byrnes R E 1889
Byrns Bridget K 1862 - 1900
Caden Alice 1879 - 1951
Caden Ann M 1860 - 1944
Caden Anna Pohlmeyer

July 5, 1903 Leader
The burial of Annette, the infant daughter of Mr. and Mrs.
    John Caden, will take place at the Catholic Cemetery
    this morning.

Caden Delia 1868 - 1925
Caden Elizabeth 1869 - 1936

Caden James R died July 14, 1863 Rosa B died Nov 25, 1882
    Charles Albert died July 11, 1883
Caden John 1857 - 1918
May 10, 1880   Lexington Transcript
John J. Caden weds Katie Hanley.

Caden Kate 1886
Caden Mamie F 1866 - 1939
Caden Margaret R died 1955
Caden Owen 1850 - 1905
Apr 21, 1905   Leader
Mr. Owen Caden died at his home on the Bryan Station Pike
    Friday morning. Besides his wife he leaves nine
    children.

Caden P K died Apr 13, 1880 wife died Apr 2, 1912
Apr 2, 1912   Leader
Mrs. Margaret Caden, widow of Mr. Patrick Caden, died
    Tuesday morning at the residence of her daughter.

Caden Sue D died 1956
Caden Susan McGurk 1830 - 1926
Cahill Catherine Mar 31, 1881 - Feb 26, 1975
Cahill David died Sept 14, 1933
Cahill Ellen Shinners died Jan 7, 1916
Cahill James
Cahill John D Oct 1, 1879 - Aug 8, 1959
Cahill Lillie Oct 8, 1875 - Nov 24, 1960
Cahill Margaret May 1841 - Apr 26, 1926
Cahill William J D Dec 20 1876 - Sept 1, 1934
Cain William Noel M D 1896 - 1958 Sally G 1913 - 1991
Calhoun Maggie Dec 9, 1873 - Sept 11, 1945
Calk David 1960 - 1987
Callinan Cornelius 1829 - 1901
Calvard John S 1909 - 1979 Frances J 1911 - 2002

Calvert Frances McCormick 1893 - 1939

Campbell Ann K Jan 1, 1930 - Oct 30, 1981

Campbell Jack D Aug 5, 1910 - Nov 12, 1984 Mary Lillian
     Apr 1914 - July 4, 2001 J Dan May 18, 1940 – Feb 5,
     1985

Campbell John died Nov. 11, 1883

Campbell John J 1880 - 1948 Jane C 1881 - 1954

Campbell Louise O Sept 26, 1886 - Nov 1, 1975

Campbell Margaret Coyne

Canan Bernadette B Nov 14, 1894 - Nov 5, 1980

Canan James J Jan 23, 1894 - July 26, 1971

Canan John July 5, 1851 - Oct 10, 1905

Canan John Thomas Jan 10, 1886 - Sept 9, 1964

Canan Mary Eliz Aug 3, 1861 - Dec 1944 James J Sr. Sept 10,
     1855 - June 1942

Canan Mary Ford Aug 6, 1889 - July 2, 1910

Canan Terance Francis Aug 2, 1897 - June 14, 1968

Nov 8, 1914 Leader

Mrs. Annie Candioto, aged 61 years, died at her residence,
     yesterday afternoon, after an illness of three months.
     The funeral services will be held at St. Paul's Catholic
     Church on Tuesday morning. Interment in the Catholic
     Cemetery.

Candioto Charles F May 20, 1943

Candioto Joseph 1889 - 1940

Candioto Mildred K 1891 - 1948

Canning Edward Dec 2, 1862 - Mar 10, 1922

Canning Edward died May 13, 1873

Canning Sarah Q died Apr 2, 1877

Canning Timothy L Mar 24, 1864 - Oct 5, 1934

May 7, 1902

William Canning, section foreman at Ewing, Fleming County,

formerly of Lexington, died Tuesday morning. His body will arrive here Thursday morning on the Maysville train and will be interred in the Catholic Cemetery.

Canoen Daniel 1823
Cantrell G W 1889 - 1939
Cantwell Grace M Sept 5, 1919 Tipton Mary C Aug 30, 1888 - Sept 23, 1970
Canty Doris Mary Baby
Canty Doris Smith WWII
Canty Patrick J Margaret D Jan 9, 1912 Jesus grant us a safe journey home
Capitano Pietro 1876 - 1951
Caravan John May 9, 1872 - May 13, 1892
Cargs Antonio 1837 - 1902
Carlin Charles Feb 24, 1896 - Oct 13, 1966 Mary Morgan Dec 1900 - Dec 4, 1981
Carlin Elizabeth H 1868 - 1940 Phillip H 1865 - 1948 Stella K 1907 - 1972 Albert 1897 - 1975 Anna M 1910 - 1992
Carlin Ralph P May 14, 1892 - Dec 23, 1967
Carlucci Vincenzo Aug 7, 1890 - 1972 Teresa
Carmichael William R Jr. May 4, 1937 - Nov 26, 1997 Margaret R Feb 9, 1938
Carmichael William Russell Sept 1902 - May 1958 Katherine Byrnes 1903 - Oct 1987
Carollo Benedict 1818 - 1848 Bernard A 1874 - 1947 Mary 1894 - 1978
Carollo Benedict 1918 - 1978 Marjorie 1920 - 1979
Carollo Joseph A May 24, 1895 - Apr 18, 1969 Leora L Sept 4, 1896 - Oct 27, 1990
Carr Elizabeth L 1902 - 1910
Carr Frank B 1862 - 1939 Elizabeth L 1869 - 1942
Carr Frank B Jr. 1905 - 1982 Marie 1909 - 2002
Carroll Anne 1870 - 1878

Carroll Bee S 1867 - 1896
Carroll Bridget C 1836 - 1902
Carroll Catherine C May 17, 1901 - Sept 21, 1980
Carroll Ellen C died Oct 17, 1939
Carroll James Sr. 1796 - 1869
Carroll James W 1861 - 1919
Carroll Jas Co. E 10 Ky. Inf.
Carroll John 187?
Carroll John 1865 - 1868
Carroll Lucy 1878 - 1880
Carroll Margaret F 1861 - 1930
Carroll Margaret S 1872 - 1940
Carroll Mary and James
Carroll Mary C 1863 - 1865
Carroll Mary J 1876 - 1929
Carroll Michael F died Jan 31, 1921
Carroll Michael 1883 - 1960 Margaret 1893 - 1968
Carroll Patrick 1830 - 1884
Carroll Patrick M 1816 - 1884
Carter Kate Paul Jan 20, 1876 - Feb 20, 1953
Carter Minnie Cole died Nov 29, 1969
Carter Patrick 1825 - 1898
Casazza Joseph A Nov 22, 1826 - Feb 12, 1888
Casey Julie Ann Sept 17, 1973
Caskey Catherine Hogarty Nov 20, 1890 - Feb 20, 1986
Cassell William H 1876 - 1950
Cassidy James Peter July 26, 1905 - Mar 20, 1976
Cassidy Philip died June 26, 1929
Castelli Amerigo May 12, 1911 - Apr 18, 1963
Catherine 1873 - 1952 Magee area
Catterall John Leslie 1905 - 1972 Mary Lancaster 1917 - 2000
Cavanaugh Jessie A 1890 - 1973
Cavanaugh Patrick 1854 - 1904 his mother Mary 1829 - 1897
        Pray for us
Caywood Edward Feb 1, 1896 - Oct 1, 1949 WWI

Caywood Joseph B Dec 22, 1942 - Mar 26, 1982
Caywood Josephine Dec 1899 - July 190?
Caywood Mary Agnes Quinn June 1, 1893 - Dec 29, 1955
    wife of Walter T
Caywood Nellie J May 13, 1905 - Apr 21, 1989 Grandson
    James D Nickell Feb 25, 1949 - Nov 4, 1993 wife of
    Edward
Caywood W F 1858 - 1928 Katherine 1955
Caywood Walter T Apr 7, 1891 - Sept 16, 1950
Caywood William F 1905 - 1963
Cements John Jos Dec 27, 1894 - 1895
Chambers Jane died Aug 28, 1882
Champion Gertrude Caywood 1926 - 1991
Chapman David Edward Feb 28, 1950 - July 6, 1988 Sally
    Mudd Dec 6, 1951
Chapman Fred 1900 - 1937
? Charles Elmore Feb 25, 1884 - Jan 7, 1935 Mary Catherine
    Nov 11, 1896 - Aug 29, 1961
Chasteen Emma Klair died May 18, 1959 wife of Wm. Bert
Chasteen Josephine Geran May 3, 1921 - Apr 22, 1983
Chasten John Thomas May 14, 1921 - June 1, 1987 WWII
Chawk Bridget B 1872 - 1914
Chenault Charles Withers
Chenault Charles Withers Aug 3, 1889 - May 10, 1962
    Josephine Jeter Aug 2, 1893 - Nov, 27, 1978 William
    Anderson June 27, 1922 - May 14, 2006
Chenault Josephine Jeter
Chenault Martha F 1905 - 1972
Chenault William Anderson
Chesher Joseph C 1895 - 19 Katherine T 1900 - 1938
Chevalier Frances 1820 - 1904 aged 84
Chevalier Jennie died Jan 25, 1901
? Children Mary 1855 - 1888 Eliza 1885 - 1889
Chism Hendricks Angela Nov 9, 1919 - May 17, 1998
Chowning J Arthur Oct 5, 1899 - Aug 27, 1969 Clara Streiff

Dec 8, 1910 - Oct 9, 1979
Christopher Joseph Dec 27, 1859 - Apr 28, 1917
Chumley Ann Cory Douglass Oct 15, 1992
Chumley Henry L 1911 - 1982
Chumley Margaret F 1913 - 1995
Clague Joanne Sept 30, 1950 - Mar 20, 2001
Clague John P July 15, 1901 - Apr 13, 1988 Frances S May
    26, 1908 - Sept 8, 1978
Clair Hugh James Oct 2, 1895 - June 25, 1964 Lucille Hudson
    Feb 17, 1902 - Feb 14, 1983
Clancy Evelyn June 21, 1909 - July 21, 1996
Clancy Jane G died Feb 25, 1973 Nellie
Clancy John C 1866 - 1932
Clancy John H 1880 - 1946 Clara G 1884 - 1960
Clancy Nell Scully passed to immortality Aug 2, 1939
Clancy Nettie C June 18, 1887 - Dec 31, 1975
Clancy Thomas J Feb 10, 1922 - Apr 21, 1977
Clancy Timothy C passed to immortality May 4, 1944
Clancy W G died Nov 28, 1967 Beatrice C Dec 28, 1951
Clark Agnes S July 4, 1897 - June 17, 1962

May 2, 1909 Leader
Mrs. Catherine Clark, wife of Mr. Thomas Clark, died at St.
    Joseph's Hospital late Saturday afternoon, aged fifty-
    three years. The interment will follow in the family lot
    in the Catholic Cemetery.

Clark Ellen
Clark James
Clark James Jan 18, 1908 - Nov 9, 1936
Clark James T
Clark John B 1897 - 1956 Christine O 1902 - 1992
Clark John Francis Aug 5, 1872 - July 19, 1948
Clark Julia G
Clark Lillie Stivers Nov 23, 1882 - Sept 29, 1943

27

Clark Margaret
Clark Martin
Apr 30, 1906   Leader
Martin Clark, 30, died April 29 at Mill and Water Streets of
    gun shot wound. Burial in
The Catholic Cemetery.

Clark Mary wife of Wm
Clark Mary Frances Mar 14, 1906 - Nov 14, 1960
Clark Paul L June 16, 1904 - June 19, 1958 Isabel B Sept 26,
    1906 - Feb 24, 1981
Clark Stanley M Apr 26, 1985 Elsie E July 12, 1971 Jane H
    Hines Dec 5, 1993
Clark Stanley Morton June 20, 1891 - Apr 26, 1985 WWI
Clark Thelma Richard July 18, 1919 - Sept 14, 2007
Clarke Augustine Bennett and wife Sarah E. Coffee
Clarke Catherine died Nov 1900 wife of James
Clarke Emily Frank 1925 - 2006 Grover Cleveland 1921 -
    2003
Clarke George 1847 - 1931
Clarke Gus Edward Aug 20, 1888 - Apr 8, 1984 Lucille
    McKinivan Aug 20, 1900 - July 5, 1993
Clarke James died June 22, 1874
Clarke Michael July 15, 1850 - Mar 1874 Augustine Jan 1852
    - Oct 7, 1893
Clarke Thomas Feb 23, 1855 - June 17, 1941 Mary July 19,
    1857 - Oct 1942
Clarkson Charles J 1883 - 1953 Flava M 1887 - 1967
Clarkson Helen E 1910 - 1981
Clarkson James S 1848 - 1886
Clarkson Sarah H 1856 - 1946
Clarkson Susie P 1885 - 1945
Claussen Lavern D July 2, 1916 - Feb 23, 1991 Ruth
    Anderson Dec 28, 1909 - Dec 7, 1987
Cleary Elizabeth died Dec 1887

Jan 3, 1906 Leader
The burial of Mrs. Mary Cleary, who died at her home in
  Richmond, Ky., yesterday, will take place in Lexington
  Catholic Cemetery.

Cleary William died 1887
Cleveland Anne Diamond Dec 23, 1897 - Sept 5, 1990
Cleveland Teshe Clinton June 17, 1895 - May 10, 1971
Clohesey Katherine 1873 - 1962
Clohesey Mary Ellen 1874 - 1955
Cloud Grace Cecelia Dec 21, 1937 - Apr 6, 1941 daughter of J
  H and Edna E
Cloud Harry D Oct 3, 1879 - May 11, 1941 Mary Ann S Nov
  14, 1888 - Oct 10, 1977
Cloud Josephine Dion Mar 21, 1884 - July 1, 1971 wife of
  Rufus B
Cloud Rufus B Mar 24, 1876 - May 26, 1939
Clugston Hannah M died Jan 5, 1899
Codlin Stella Dehore 1909 - 1985
Coffee Elizabeth died 1883
Colbert Johanna 1884 - 1955
Colbert John 1876 - 1961
Colbert Katherine T 1880 - 1953 wife of Richard master
  commissioner of Fayette circuit court
Colbert Richard J Jr. Aug 21, 1918 - Dec 24, 1992 mayor of
  Lexington from 1960 - 1964
Colbert Rosa McGlone 1830 - 1932 wife of William Colbert

Colbert William 1844 - 1910
Jan 13, 1910   Leader
Mr. William Colbert, died at his home, Thursday morning. His
  death, which resulted from rheumatic heart failure, was
  sudden and very unexpected. Besides his wife, he
  leaves a large family of children.

Coleman John Allen 1864 - 1931
Coleman John F 1891 - 1953
Coleman Marg B July 11, 1867 - Feb 23, 1943
Coleman Thomas J Jan 6, 1889 - Apr 3, 1975 Esther Flood
    Feb 10, 1899 - Apr 23, 1982
Collier Rose Jewell Ruh 1928 Please pray for us
Collins Ann Louis 1924 - 1980 Mary Lillian White 1904 -
    1993
Collins Cornelius 1884 - 1922
Collins Elizabeth Mary 1888 - 1966
Collins Freda C 1895 - 1948
Collins John
Collins Margaret 1851 - 1913
Collins Mary Trainor Fallon 1908 - 1983
Collins Patricia Nov 10, 1926 - Aug 28, 2000 Korea
Collins Shirley S Aug 16, 1938
Collins Thomas 1844 - 1907
Collins Thomas E Sr. 1887 - 1946
Collins Josie 1877 - 1939
Concannon Ann Donnelly Feb 22, 1893 - Dec 3, 1969
Concannon John E 1888 - 1962
Concannon Lawrence J 1895 - 1958
Concannon Martin J 1852 - 1935
Concannon Martin J Dec 6, 1892 - May 28, 1973
Concannon Martin J Mar 16, 1929 - Apr 2, 2000
Concannon Mary Scott 1859 - 1943 wife of Martin J
Concannon Robert J 1903 - 1940
Cone Carl Bruce Feb 2, 1916 - Feb 2, 1995 Mary Louise
    Regan Mar 30, 1913 - Oct ?

Feb 28, 1910 Leader
The funeral services of Mrs. Caroline Vance Conley, who died
    at the residence of her daughter, Mrs. J. H. Keefe,
    Saturday night, took place at St. Paul's Catholic

Church Monday afternoon, burial following in the Catholic Cemetery.

Conley Catherine V 1834 - 1910
Conley Cecelia Aug 10, 1843 - Jan 21, 1929
Conley Michael J Feb 22, 1880 - Apr 27, 1938
Conley Patrick J Mar 10, 1874 - July 2, 1936
Conlin Annie
Connelly Barbara wife of Claude W Murphy
Connelly Dudley J 1891 - 1943
Conner Ella 1861 - 1936
Conner Frank 1894 - 1955 Ann T 1890 - 1990
Conner Infant Aug 31, 1941 daughter of Ann and Jack
Connor Anna Louise 1900 - 1992
Connor Annie 1881 - 1919
Connor James 1858 - 1902
Oct 20, 1902 Leader
James Connor, proprietor of Reed Hotel, died at St. Joseph's
    Hospital, after an illness extending considerably over a
    year, and a critical illness of about six weeks. Mr.
    Connor was born in Bourbon County forty - three
    years ago, but at an early age moved to Nicholas
    County, where he was reared. He came to Lexington
    sixteen years ago and has been proprietor of the Reed
    Hotel for the last fifteen years.

Jan 26, 1898 Herald
Jeremiah Connor for years the watchman at the Rose Street
    Crossing has died.
The Funeral will take place from the St. Paul's Catholic
    Church Thursday at 9 o'clock with interment in the
    Catholic Cemetery.

Sept 15, 1908 Leader
Mrs. Mary Connor died at her home Tuesday, aged 68 years.

The funeral services were held at St. Paul's Church
Tuesday morning and the interment followed in the
family lot in the Catholic Cemetery.

Connors Christopher T 1966 - 1968
Connors W. Edward 1888 - 1957 Lorence Rainger 1888 -
    1981
Conrad Joseph A July 2, 1921 - Mar 16, 1985
Conrad Marian L Garvin Nov 13, 1922 - Aug 12, 1999
Conroy Frank died Apr 1, 1942
Constantine Jerry J Sept 18, 1906 - May 6, 1982 Catherine A
    Nov 2, 1906 - July 5, 1995
Conway Catherine died Jan 2, 1892
Conway Catherine 1859 - 1932
Conway Charley Mar 11, 1855 - Feb 1, 1904
Conway Frank 1857 - 1890
Conway James died Dec 18, 1891
Conway Mary illegible
Conway Michael died Apr 10, 1875
Conway O Connell Clara 1885 - 1924 wife of Thomas
Cook E T (Bud) 1898 - 1966
Cook Helen G 1901 - 1992
Cook Kelley Elizabeth 1903 - 1952
Coons Anita Hanly 1895 - 1960 wife of Claude J. Coons
Coons Claude J Aug 29, 1890 - Sept 17, 1973
Coons Louis Bletz Nov 24, 1891 - May 18, 1971
Cooper Robert J 1932 - 1979 Laura E 1935
Corman Eugene 1930 Preston 1937
Corman Luther F Sept 9, 1922 - Mar 24, 2004 Rebecca R Apr
    19, 1929 - Aug 12, 2000 married Dec 21, 1957
Cornell Robert C Dec 14, 1917 - Aug 16, 2000 Jane Murphy
    Sept 20, 1918 - May 8, 2003
Cornette Clare Dooley 1920 - 1970
Corrigan 1900
Corrigan Thomas J died 1946 Kathryn S 1894 - 1959

Costello James V May 27, 1914 - Nov 4, 1985 Josephine Nov
8, 1916 - Oct 25, 1989
Costello John 1856 - 1916 Mary A O'Hara 1855 - 1929
Costello Katherine Agnes Sept 12, 1891 - Mar 1, 1982
Costello Margaret Francis Mar 21, 1895 - Nov 26, 1971
Couch Robert 1840 - 1919
Coughlin Francis W 1897 - 1949
Coughlin Jeremiah Dec 25, 1819 - Jan 19, 1894 Ellen Mar 17,
1833 - Oct 30, 1888
Coughlin Jerry 1851 - 1928
Coughlin Laura 1862 - 1942
Coughlin Mary Norton 1906 - 1985 wife of Francis W
Cowart Catherine Caskey Dec 30, 1917 - June 18, 1977
Cowart William Mar 24, 1950
Cowling Mary Mar 18, 1922
Cowgill Ann Caskey July 3, 1919 - Aug 21, 1989
Cowgill John Hardwick Oct 26, 1941 - Mar 8, 1968
Cowgill William Caskey Aug 17, 1948 - Dec 22, 1964
Cox Barbara Kunz Nov 8, 1931 - Oct 13, 1983
Cox Infant daughter of Fred and Carolyn Aug 12, 1957
Coyne Annie
Coyne Elizabeth C 1878 - 1976
Coyne Elizabeth O'Day 1858 - 1921
Coyne Ella I died Dec 29, 1947
Coyne John M 1876 - 1956
Coyne John Joseph
Coyne Joseph A 1893 - 1965
Coyne Mary Alice 1885 - 1957
Coyne Michael 1843 - 1912
Feb 12, 1912   Leader
The funeral services of Mr. Michael Coyne will be held at St.
Paul's Catholic Church Tuesday morning.

Coyne Peter 1825 - 1903 Mary 1843
Jan 24, 1903   Leader

Mr. Peter Coyne, aged 78, died at his home, this morning of paralysis.

Coyne Peter W

Sept 20, 1905 Leader
The remains of Thomas Coyne, who died at Knoxville, Tenn., Monday, arrived Wednesday morning via the L. & N. train, accompanied by his brother, Patrick Coyne. The burial took place in the family lot of the Catholic Cemetery after the arrival of the train.

Coyne Thomas F 1888 - 1974
Coyne William P 1882 - 1940
Cramer Anabel Luigart 1896 - 1967
Cramer Ann N 1926 - 1994 wife of Hugh J Cramer
Cramer Gladys Gormley 1897 - 1983 wife of Hugh R Cramer
Cramer H Cable 1894 - 1975
Cramer Hugh J 1923 - 2005
Cramer Hugh R 1890 - 1957
Cramer Judson P May 4, 1925 - Feb 1, 2007
Cramer Margaret B Timmins 1925 - 2008
Cramer Mary Francis July 21, 1919 - Feb 14, 1993
Cramer William 1897 - 1966 Margaret 1906 - 1987
Crantz Thomas J 1919 Rose Ryan 1917 - 1979
Craven William A May 8, 1936
Cravens Gertrude 1902 - 1912
Cravens Thomas D 1861 - 1926 Mary E 1869 - 1950
Crawley Catherine McGurk 1867 - 1935 Michael E 1869 - 1947
Crawley John E WWI
Craycraft James K Jan 8, 1940 - Dec 12, 1993
Creech Lucille Hoelich May 2, 1908 - Dec 31, 1993 wife of Ollie J
Creekbaum Alice E July 23, 1880 - Dec 3, 1958

Croghan Charles E Nov 2, 1877 - Mar 1, 1911
Croghan James F 1840 - 1927 SERG Co. A 6 Ky Vol Cav
Croghan Katie R Aug 21, 1875 - Oct 15, 1967
Croghan Nettie C 1882 - 1970
Crombie Margaret 1870 - 1929
Cronan Mary 1819 - 1891
Cronan Patrick Herbert 1841 Michael Cronan 1851 husband
    of Mary Burke
Cronan T 1847 - 1875
Cronin Anna 1898
Dec 30, 1898   Leader
Miss Annie Cronin, daughter of Mr. and Mrs. James Cronin,
    died last night at the residence on East Fourth Street,
    after a lingering illness of consumption.

Cronin Father 1883 - 1927
Cronin Johanna Oct 15, 1866 - Oct 9, 1889
Oct 9, 1889   Leader
At 9 o'clock this morning Miss Hannah Cronin, aged 23 years,
    died at the home of her father, James Cronin.

Cronin Mother 1918
Cronlin Margaret illegible
Cronlin Margaret 1880 - 1883
Cronlin Mary L 1874 - 1922
Cronlin Rev Jas R 1862 - 1922
Crouch Henry Jan 16, 1878 - Sept 19, 1925
Crowe Daniel J 1873 - 1934 his wife Anna F 1874 - 1958
Crowe Sarah Aug 16, 1877 - Nov 17, 1904 daughter of Wm &
    Margaret
Nov 18, 1904 Leader
Miss Sarah Crowe, aged 32, died at St. Joseph's Hospital
    Thursday night of tuberculosis. Her funeral services
    will take place at St. Paul's Catholic Church Saturday
    morning, burial in Catholic Cemetery.

Crowe William 1835 - 1911
Crowley Timothy 1835 - 1890 and wife Katherine O'Neill
     1838 - 1925
Cummins Frank J July 14, 1906 - Feb 21, 1964
Cummins Mayme Sweeny Jan 20, 1865 - Jan 21, 1942
Cummins Richard P Jr. Feb 23, 1902 - May 27, 1944
Cummins Richard Sr. Feb 8, 1863 - Dec 14, 1945
Curnutte David Morris Oct 20, 1935 - Nov 27, 1997 Guilkey
     Barbara
Curran Ruby N Lane Mar 31, 1928 - Aug 19, 2001
Currie William P Jr. WWII
Currie William Patrick Aug 6, 1867 - Sept 12, 1945 Elizabeth
     Murray Jan 10, 1872 - Oct 17, 1952
Curry Catherine B 1868 - 1908
Curry Charles 1825 - 1886
Curry Francis B Nov 23, 1897 - Mar 24, 1940
Curry Frank 1862 - 1898
Curry John C Mar 29, 1855 - July 7, 1908
July 9, 1908 Leader
Jack Curry, the noted Kentucky trainer, who died Tuesday at
     Kansas City, was laid to rest in the Catholic Cemetery
     here at noon Thursday.

July 9 1908 Lexington Herald
The body of Mr. J C Curry will arrive here Thursday at 11:10
     p. m. over the Chesapeak and Ohio road. The funeral
     will be from the train and interment in family lot in
     Catholic Cemetery.

Curry Joseph H May 3, 1894 - Dec 31, 1925
Curry Margaret 1900 - 1928
Curry Mary 1820 - 1880
Curry Mary C 1866 - 1943
Curry Rev William B 1880 - 1947

Curry Robert B Dec 28, 1887 - Nov 30, 1975
Curry Robert E May 6, 1861 - Aug 10, 1946
Curry Sarah 1858 - 1938
Curtis Horace S 1900 - 1935
Curtis John J Dec 1, 182? - Aug 28, 1883
Curtis Mary E 1900 - 1989
Curtis Newton 1859 - 1933
Curtis Ruth A 1879 - 1964 William E 1885 - 1935
Dacci Mayo E Apr 26, 1927 - July 29, 1956 Gladys T Nov 6,
    1929 - Apr 8, 1976
Dacci Romeo Apr 12, 1894 - June 25, 1981 Marie S Apr 21,
    1900 - Oct 21, 1986
Dacci Infant died 1923 Infant died 1934 sons of Romeo and
    Marie
Dailey Cornelius B Aug 16, 1883 - May 12, 1978 Mollie M
    died May 29, 1967
Dalton Annie L Nov 7, 1868 - Jan 16, 1946
Dalton Frank X June 21, 1928 - 1902
Apr 23, 1902 Leader
Mr. Frank Dalton, of this city, received a telegram last night
    that the body of Charles Govan would be here tonight
    at 10 o'clock. The funeral will take place Thursday
    morning at his late residence on the Maysville Pike.
    The burial will take place in the Catholic Cemetery.

Dalton Richard, Bridget, Annie Dalton, Louis Fili, Alice
    Dolton Benckart, Mary Fili, F R
Dalton and Joseph Ann Murray

Aug 23, 1909   Leader
Louis Fili, who died at the home of Joseph Benckart on
    Saturday night was buried in the Catholic Cemetery
    Monday morning, the funeral services over his body
    being held at St. Peter's Catholic Church.

Dalton Stanley John born Mar 31, 1935 Patricia Nunan born
    Nov 4, 1934
Daly Alice 1859 - 1943
Daly B Francis died Jan 21, 1907
Daly James M died June 6, 1893 Edward P died June 18, 1875
Daly Mary C Feb 7, 1941
Daly Patrick 1822 - Mar 2, 1878 Mary Oct 11, 1902
Daly Patrick died June 1, 1888 Ellen died May 28, 1909 at last
    I rest with thee, with thee in Christ, shall rise again
May 30, 1909 Lexington Herald
The Funeral services of Mrs. Ellen Daly will be held at St.
    Paul's Catholic Church Saturday morning at 9 o'clock
    and the interment will follow in the family lot in the
    Catholic Cemetery.

Danahy Johanna 1879 - 1964
Daniel George H 1915 - 1969 Pauline 1914
Daniel Martha Ann Sept 12, 1954 daughter of George H and
    Pauline
Darnaby Elizabeth Haney 1880 - 1918 wife of John
Daugherty Chester Cecil July 19, 1897 - Aug 13, 1965 Mary
    Catherine Jan 4, 1900 - Sept 27, 1987
Daugherty Eliz S died July 12, 1935
Daugherty James W 1863 - 1957 his wife Sarah B Monahan
    1868 - 1946
Daugherty Joseph A Oct 11, 1906 - Aug 28, 1957 WWII
Daugherty Mary E died Jan 23, 1966
Daugherty Thomas died June 21, 18?
Daughtery Charles Edward July 21, 1870 - Nov 10, 1953
Daughtery George W
Daughtery Jess L Sept 10, 1902 - Jan 16, 1924
Davenport Thomas B 1959 - 1989 Louis Ward 1955 - 1967
David Margaret B 1906 - 1982
Davidson Charles C Aug 8, 1928 - June 10, 1992 Dorothy K
    July 16, 1934

Davidson Oscar H Apr 8, 1906 - Sept 2, 1974 Ellen Duffy Dec
    25, 1919 -
Davis George W Oct 25, 1939 - Mar 2, 1978
Davis Mary Ann Bruin June 22, 1897 - May 27, 1968 Wife of
    Emerson C
Davis William B 1916 - 1970 Mary B 1917 - 1981
Davis William H died 1948 WWII
Davis William J Aug 13, 1906 - Apr 4, 1960 Katherine G June
    10, 1910 - Dec 4, 1980

Jan 18, 1909 Leader
The funeral services of Mrs. Edna C. Deckert, wife of Mr. O.
    C. Deckert, who died at St. Joseph's Hospital Saturday
    night will take place at St. Paul's Catholic Church
    Tuesday morning and the interment will be in the
    Catholic Cemetery.

Deboor Ethel L Nov 25, 1959
Deboor Irvin died Sept 12, 1898 Julia Shea died Oct 29, 1940
Deboor Marianna Devereux 1896 - 1985 wife of Matthew J
    Deboor
Deboor Matthew J 1895 - 1967

Jan 26, 1905 Leader
The funeral services of Frank De Breason will be held at St.
    Paul's Church Friday afternoon. Interment will be in
    the Catholic Cemetery.

Decker Mildred G 1906 - 1985 Frank S 1895 - 1956
Defilippo Ester Juanita Mar 13, 1938 - Oct 14, 1972 Michael
    Angelo Mar 12, 1934 - Feb 14, 1985
Defilippo Michael born Oct 17, 1882

Feb 9, 1903 Morning Herald
The funeral of Mr. John Dehore, who died at his home, will be

conducted from St Paul's Catholic Church, at 3 o'clock this evening. The interment will take place in the Catholic Cemetery.

Dehore Thomas 1830 - 1904 Catherine 1841 - 1928
Dehore Thomas Christopher 1871 - 1929 Mary Wehrle
    Benckart 1871 - 1936

Feb 24, 1909 Lexington Leader
The funeral services of Mr. George Deigman of Greendale
    will be held at St. Paul's Church Thursday morning.
    The interment will be in the family lot in the Catholic
    Cemetery.

Deignan Elizabeth Horgan 1871 - 1946
Deignan Elizabeth M 1869 - 1952
Deignan George 1867 - 1939
Deignan Katherine 1868 - 1956
Delaney Elizabeth Baker died Jan 22, 1922
Delreo Prince Frank 1914 - 1983
DeMarco Anona E Mar 8, 1909 - Aug 26, 1962
DeMarco John F July 31, 1906 - Jan 20, 1980
Demma Frank 1899 - 1910
Demma Vincent 1894 - 1982 Teresa 1894 - 1949
Dennis Ron Lee Aug 28, 1950 Terry Davis Apr 16, 1954 -
    Aug 8, 2008
Dennison Fred R Aug 12, 1891 - Jan 6, 1962
Dennison Luigart Flora 1894 - 1978
Desolier Edward Jan 8, 1899 - Sept 17, 1959 WWI & WWII
Devereux Ella Flynn 1863 - 1942 wife of Patrick B Devereux
Devereux Father and Mother
Devereux Gretchen A 1935 - 1994
Devereux Infants of P B and E S
Dec 31, 1901 Morning Herald
The six-day-old child of Mr. and Mrs. P. Deveraux, who died

Sunday, was interred in the Catholic Cemetery yesterday afternoon.

Devereux James B 1958
Devereux John R 1895 - 1979
Devereux Lauretta Brady 1903 - 1969 wife of Thomas F
Devereux Margaret Gurried 1908 - 1953 wife of John R
Devereux Marie Browning Sept 16, 1927 - Mar 6, 2002

July 30, 1906 Leader
The funeral services of Mary Joseph Devereux took place at
    the family residence, Saturday afternoon, the
    internment taking place in the Catholic Cemetery.

Devereux Patrick B 1858 - 1927
Devereux Patrick B Nov 4, 1926 - Aug 3, 2003
Devereux Rosemary Monaghan 1939 wife of James B
    Devereux
Devereux Thomas F 1893 - 1981
Devereux Thomas F Jr. 1934 - 1997 Susan S 1933 - 1983
Devers Richard Allen Oct 21, 1995
Devore George died 1910
March 25, 1910 Leader
The body of Mr. George Devore, who was killed in a railroad
    wreck near Richmond, arrived in Lexington Thursday
    afternoon and was interred immediately thereafter in
    the Catholic Cemetery.

DeWaegenaere Hubert 1883 - 1951
DeWaegenaere Margaret McKenna 1887 - 1963 wife of
    Hubert
Di Breason Mary O'Brien 1867 - 1889
Diamond Beatrice Gilchrist June 1860 - Dec 26, 1925
Diamond James H Jan 4, 1883 - Aug 20, 1941
Diamond John June 1850 - July 27, 1920

Diamond Lt Edward A Nov 20, 1890 - Jan 9, 1948
Diamond Sarah A May 20, 1887 - Dec 30, 1909
Dickerman William L 1882 - 1950 Maude Shaw 1892 - 1971
Dickey Susan Keenan wife of Howard
Diek Mary Francis died June 21, 1927
Dieruf Nicholas J May 20, 1982 - Apr 8, 2004 Iraq
DiMeo Chris L 1920 - 1987 WWII
DiMeo Chris Leonard Sept 24, 1920 - Mar 10, 1987 Dolores
    Martha Mar 22, 1932 Angels can do more
Dinand John Ferdinand Oct 21, 1880 - Oct 5, 1966
Dineen Bridget
Dineen Edith Price died May 17, 1991

Jan 22, 1906 Leader
Helen Dineen, 5 days, died at Ludlow, January 13, of
    congenital cardiac. Burial in Catholic Cemetery.

Dineen John died Feb ?
Dineen Mary
Dineen Mary Whalen died Dec 9, 1892
Dineen Michael died Apr 5, 1870
Dineen Timothy
Dineen William J died June 10, 1972
Dinelli Eremenia L Nov 3, 1885 - Nov 19, 1972
Dinelli John I April 27, 189? - July 19, 1930 WWI
Dinelli Mary Isola 1865 - 1953
Dinelli Maude E May 31, 1882 - Apr 26, 1976
Dinelli R Eugene 1892 - 1892
Dinelli Sylvester 1839 - 19?7
Dinelli Sylvester May 6, 1895 - May 1, 1972
Dinh Nguyen Thang 1970 - 1976
Dixon Lura Spicer Aug 17, 1919
Dixon Thomas C Apr 22, 1931 Ruth Ann June 5, 1931
Dodd Anna E 1902 - 1990
Dodd Anna M 1873 - 1960

Dodd Charles P 1868 - 1948 Ida Turner 1868 - 1945

July 28, 1908 Leader
The infant daughter of Mr. and Mrs. Charles P. Dodd died
    Tuesday morning at their home. The internment will
    take place from the home Wednesday. She will be
    buried in the Catholic Cemetery.

Dodd James A died May 23, 1948
Dodd James Joseph 1905 - 1976
Dodd James R 1839 - 1929
Dodd Jessie 1899 - 1922
Dodd Kate Lenihan Dec 3, 1876 - Jan 17, 1952 William John
    Apr 17, 1877 - Nov 10, 1955
Dodd Margaret M 1876 - 1959
Dodd Martha McGuddy 1908 - 1946
Dodd Mary J 1843 - 1920
Dodd William Joseph Feb 3, 1914 - Oct 23, 1963 Anita Keller
    Oct 1, 1916 - May 6, 2005
Dolan John died Oct 23, 1903
Dolan Marquerite Oct 29, 1908 - Oct 28, 1975
Dolan Michael B Dec 17, 1903 - Aug 31, 1985
Dolan Michael B Jr. June 20, 1932 - June 20, 1992
Dombrowski
Donahoe Forrest E Apr 20, 1917 - Dec 23, 2005 WWII
Donahoe James B 1878 - 1974
Donahoe John J died Jan 6, 1887
Donahoe Kathryn B 1878 - 1964
Donahue 1859 - 1907
Donahue Bridget died Jan 27, 1870
Donahue Catherine died Aug 14, 1877 James R died Nov 4,
    1883
Donahue Ellen Moran Nov 1828 - Nov 13, 1856
Donahue John M died July 8, 1870 Catherine Ryan died Mar
    1888

Donahue Patrick 1892 - 1976 Erma 1900 - 1985
Donnelly George (Father) May 19, 1900 - April 21, 1978
    ordained June 6, 1957
Donelly Willie 1888 - 1891
Donlan James A 1861 - 1940
Donlan Margaret Heafey
Donlan Nora C 1884 - 1959
Donlan Patrick Bridget Maria
Donlan Thomas Aug 7, 1874 - Mar 17, 1922
Donlon Thomas May 12, 1888 Killed in the line of duty
Donnell H C 1872 - 1923
Donnell Hallie G 1876 - 1922
Donnellly James L 1869 - 1951 Elizabeth F 1881 - 1971
Donnelly Bernard died 1887 Maggie Cahill died 1891 Rose
    Hickey died 1895 Susan B died 1894 Nancy D Bunnell
    died 1898 Susan died 1887
Donnelly Bess Lee Nov 15, 1887 - Jan 25, 1974
Donnelly Charles E July 25, 1893 - 1907
Donnelly Edward 1853 - 1925 Patrick H 1869 - 1942 William
    B Bonnell James T 1861 - 1913 John B 1871 - 1949
    Fannie Bonnell Tatman
Donnelly Felix illegible
Donnelly Felix P 1853 - 1917 Margaret G 1859 - 1927
Donnelly James B 1857 - 1913 Mary H 1859 - 1943
Donohue Jeremiah 1887 - 1972 Mary Doyle 1892 - 1945
Donohue Victor July 29, 1930 - Jan 24, 1997
Donovan Charles 1844 - 1911 Margaret 1854 - 1944
Apr 4, 1911 Leader
The funeral services of Mr. Charles Donovan, who has for
    many years been an employee of the Queen &
    Crescent railway as a flagman at the South Broadway
    crossing of the road, was held Tuesday morning at the
    St. Paul Catholic Church, followed by interment in the
    Catholic Cemetery. Mr. Donovan died at his home on
    Monday morning.

44

Donovan Jerry A Dec 31, 1889 - Mar 22, 1952
Donovan John J Feb 15, 1934 - Nov 27, 1999 Deanna J May
    8, 1940 - July 15, 2003
Donovan John Luke
Donovan Katherine died 1921
Donovan Margaret N 1892 - 1965
Donovan Raxana White Sept 22, 1907 - Dec 26, 1993 John I
    Oct 27, 1898 - Sept 11, 1988
Donovan Timothy L 1878 - 1922
Dooley Infant son Thomas and Judy Nov 23, 1963
Dooley Nell Hogan 1887 - 1978 Margaret Marie 1912 - 1984
Douds Benjamin R Jan 17, 1914 - Feb 25, 1977
Douds Mary Regina Mar 16, 1909 - June 30, 1994
Dougherty John W Katherine G 1874 - 1928
Douglas James William 1868 - 1959
Douglas John 1836 - 1922
Douglas John 1861 - 1904
Douglas John T 1898 - 1979 John B Knight 1926 - 1980
Douglas Jon and Martha
Douglas Margaret A died Mar 18, 1902 James M Jr. Nov 22,
    1870 - June 15, 1898
Douglas Margaret McGlone 1873 - 1936
Douglas Mary Margaret 1900 - 1968
Douglas Mattie Elizabeth 1903 - 1973
Douglas Sallie 1867 - 1930
Douglass Infant Dec 19, 1942 son of Anne S and Prentiss P
Dowd Kathleen 1896 - 1918
Dowd Aimee Clohesey Apr 22, 1891 - May 13,1981 wife of
    John S Dowd
Dowd Ann 1816 - 1885
Dowd Bee
Dowd Catherine 1870 - 1936
Dowd John S
Dowd John S Jan 29, 1893 - Feb 8, 1964

Dowd John S Jr. Aug 26, 1921 - April 18, 1926

Dowd Joseph A 1901 - 1929

Dowd Martin

Dowd Martin 1815 - 1884

Dowd Mary June 5 - 20, 1927 Infant daughter of John S and
    Aimee C. Dowd

Dowd Michael 1864 - 1906

Feb 1, 1906 Leader

The loving friends of Michael Dowd laid him to rest in the
    Catholic Cemetery Thursday morning. Mr. Dowd was
    one of the most popular men in Lexington. He was a
    member of the City Council and his death was the
    result of an accident.

Feb 1, 1906 Leader

Michael E. Dowd, 42, died January 30 at St. Joseph's Hospital
    of fractured skull. Burial in Catholic Cemetery.

Sept 28, 1914   Leader

The body of Mrs. Sallie Dowd, formerly of Paris, who died in
    Indianapolis on Saturday, will arrive here for burial
    tomorrow morning. The funeral will be held at St.
    Peter's Catholic Church. The interment will follow in
    the Catholic Cemetery.

Dowd Thomas

Dowling Edw 1845 - 1925

Dowling Edw T 1882 - 1926

Dowling Edward 1845 - 1925 Frances L 1852 - 1912

Apr 26, 1920   Leader

A telegram today announced the sudden death of Mrs.
    Elizabeth B. Dowling 68 years old, widow of Bernard
    Dowling, former well known Lexington citizen, at her
    home at Southgate, a suburb of Newport. Interment in

the family lot in the Catholic Cemetery.

Dowling Frances Cronan 1852 - 1912
Feb 4, 1912   Leader
Mrs. Frances Cronin Dowling, fifty - nine years old, wife of
    Mr. Edward Dowling, died at her home, on Saturday
    afternoon after a protracted illness. Interment in the
    Catholic Cemetery.

Dowling Herbert R 1886 - 1965
Dowling John J 1880 - 1891
Dowling M L 1850 - 1920
Dowling Margaret 1884 - 1958
Dowling Marie Riordan 1890 - 1973
Dowling Mary 1922
Downing Myrtle Luke Dec 15, 1917 - Jan 31, 1973 WWII
Doyle Anna White July 31, 1896 - Apr 23, 1981
Doyle David 1854 - 1909
Doyle Dominic 1871 - 1924
Doyle Edwin D Nov 26, 1918 - Apr 24, 1973
Doyle Elizabeth C 1884 - 1978
Doyle James died Apr 9, 1913 Catherine died Feb 2, 1911
Doyle John 1870
Doyle John died July 18, 1889
Doyle John B and Jane
Doyle John L June 13, 1885 - Mar 26, 1943

Apr 28, 1908 Leader
The funeral services of Mr. John T. Doyle were held at St.
    Paul's Church Tuesday morning and the internment
    will be in the family lot in the Catholic Cemetery.

Apr 9, 1903 Leader
The funeral of Mrs. Katherine Doyle, who died at her home on
    Jefferson Street Tuesday night, was held this

afternoon. Burial in the Catholic Cemetery.

Doyle Luke B Oct 1, 1874 - Dec 24, 1910
Dec 26, 1910   Leader
The funeral services of Mr. Luke Doyle will be held at St.
   Paul's Catholic Church Monday afternoon. The
   internment will be in the Catholic Cemetery.

Doyle R died Oct 1902
Doyle Robert J Mar 4, 1928 - Mar 19, 1982
Doyle William E 1912 - 1914
Drinovec Anton 1895 - 1985
Driscoll James Howard Jul 18, 1922 - Mar 16, 1988
Driscoll James P Feb 27, 1882 - July 4, 1938
Driscoll John 1825 - 1901 Margaret 1827 - 1892
Driscoll Margaret Claire June 8, 1889 - Dec 11, 1970
Drummy James died Feb 28, 1889
Drummy Margaret died Dec 9, 1903
Drummy Mary C died 1948
Drummy Mary Ready 1871 - 1963
Drummy Nicholas E died June 9, 1894
Drummy Thomas T
Drummy William Joseph 1872 - 1936
Drury John L 1909 - 1997 Regina J 1912 - 2004
Duff Leona Warren May 30, 1903 - Jan 3, 1990
Duff Mary 1840 - 1906
Duffy Anna Omelia Sept 30, 1924 - Feb 8, 1929 Herbert Oct
   3, 1934 - Oct 3, 1934 Cousins
Daughter Duffy Ellen Apr 5, 1893 - Jan 22, 1972 mother
   Bridget Barrett Sullivan Duffy died Mar 23, 1913
   daughter Elizabeth Sullivan died Apr 4, 1912
Duffy Hallie P Dec 24, 1892 - Apr 15, 1989
Duffy Joseph F 1931 - 1952
Duffy Robert E Sr. Feb 16, 1885 - June 14, 1971
Duffy Thomas Francis Sr. July 26, 1889 - Aug 23, 1966

Gertrude Cracraft Mar 18, 1895 - Mar 24, 1989
Dunlap Christopher Sally Jan 24, 1908 - Sept 25, 1992
Dunlap John Jenning Aug 17, 1915 - Mar 18, 1983
Dunleavy Margaret B 1829 - 1911
Dunleavy Michael 1837 - 1913
Dunn Catherine V May 17, 1911 - Nov 9, 1974
Dunn John E Nov 22, 1908 - Dec 25, 1987
Dunn Roger P 1924 - 1977
Dunne Catherine Helen 1902 - 1995
Dunne Helen Dinniene 1877 - 1934
Dunne Mary Anne 1904 - 1981
Dunne Patrick 1862 - 1938
Duns Richard Apr 8, 1882 - Oct 16, 1967 Ella Kennedy Mar
    10, 1891 - May 26, 1982
Durbin Ruth Aug 5, 1901 - Feb 27, 1918
Durkin John J Mar 31, 1854 - Feb 12, 1906
Durkin Joseph Hartley 1880 - 1937
Dwyer Mary L Apr 24, 1870 - Nov 15, 1967
Dwyer Mary Nell June 13, 1950 - May 28, 1977
Dwyer Rosemary Mulholland June 28, 1920 - May 28, 1977
Dwyer Sheila Ann Nov 22, 1953 - May 28, 1977
Dyrcz Walter A June 8, 1924 Sally A July 16, 1924
Eberthardt Betty Gentry 1929 - 1991
Eberhardt Daniel L 1923 - 1995
Eberhardt Mary Ellen May 14, 1958 - Nov 26, 1965
Eckert Charles C 1824 - 1917
Edger Maud Miller Nov 6, 1887 - June 23, 1968
Edmond 1878 - 1949 Magee area
Edwards Marie Rothan 1906 - 1967
Effinger Charles 1841 - 1906
Egalite Albert F Aug 6, 1887 - Nov 27, 1930
Egalite George Farrell Apr 11, 1886 - May 9, 1967
Egalite Henry J Sept 30, 1889 - June 26, 1977
Egalite Henry J Jr. July 30, 1925 - June 30, 1955
Egalite Jacob June 12, 1858 - Dec 19, 1920 Margaret F Aug 9,

1858 - Dec 19, 1945
Egalite Jacob A Aug 30, 1891 - July 8, 1968
Egalite Kathern Weisenberger Apr 19, 1887 - Feb 14, 1973
    wife of Henry J
Egalite Leo A 1890 - 1938

Feb 18, 1914   Leader
Martha Lucille Egalite, the one-month-old daughter of Mr.
    and Mrs. F. K. Egalite, died at the home of her parents
    yesterday. The interment took place this morning in the
    family lot of the Catholic Cemetery.

Egalite Mary C 1893 - 1948
Egalite Sophia 1853 - 1908 George 1853 - 1908
Egalite Ted H 1907 - 1974 Elizabeth 1914 - 1973
Egalite William A Sept 30, 1918 - July 22, 1975
Egan James Oct 10, 1918
Egan Margaret 1864 - 1947 wife of Jas Egan
Eggart Daniel Mar 10, 1821 - Jan 20, 1886
Egloff Paul T 1908 - 1939
Egman Josephine 1878 - Dec 25, 1951
Elam Agnes Hunt died Feb 8, 1944
Elam Florence Agnes died Sept 20, 1988
Eldridge Louise Mischler 1887 - 1937 Gollie Thomas 1885 -
    1959
Elfers Raymond J May 30, 1902 - Oct 5, 1986 Elizabeth R
    Aug 25, 1902 - Dec 20, 1985
Elgin Charles W June 6, 1839 - Dec 5, 1905
Dec 18, 1905 Leader
Charles W. Elgin, 65, died December 15 at St. Joseph's
    Hospital of consumption. Burial in Catholic Cemetery
    December 17.

Elkins Harold Mar 9, 1935 - Feb 2, 2009 Mary Hungate Nov
    20, 1941

Elkins Harold Mar 9, 1935 - Feb 2, 2009 US NAVY
Ella Margaret Sept 26, 1889 - May 8, 1978 Maybe Ward
Ellie Unknown
Elliott Garland H Nov 12, 1877 - Sept 19, 1946
Ellis Charles June 20, 1877 - June 21, 1953
Ellis Maggie E June 22, 1867 - Jan 22, 1974
Ellis Sarah McNamee 1867 - 1902
Ellis Thomas Paul May 2, 1919 - Aug 11, 1942
Elovitz Anthony 1882 - 1970 Regina Triplett 1891 - 1962
Elovitz Frank F June 29, 1914 - Feb 25, 1988 Irene Horvath
    June 1, 1915
Elsh Elizabeth probably Welsh
Ernandez Pasquala Gullen born in Spain Nov 7, 1880 - Oct 7,
    1985 wife of Juan Ernandez Sr.
Erena Anthony J 1921 - 1974 Marie A 1922 - 2009
Erskine Catherine died 1895
Erskine James 1850 - 1910
Erwin Mary E Aug 1862 - May 29, 1912
Esenbock Alma Barton 1902 - 1970
Esenbock August 1843 - 1905
Esenbock Lee Roy 1888 - 1953
Esenbock Lucian lee June 2, 1913 - Jan 27, 1960
Esenbock Mary Frances McCarthy May 14, 1915 - Feb 15,
    1996 wife of Lucian L
Esenbock Michael S 1915 - 1976 Elizabeth N 1913 - 1983
Esenbock William D 1932 - 1989 Mary Ann 1931 - 1995
Esenbock William R Nov 15, 1924 - Feb 14, 1974 John Leo
    Oct 25, 1892 - Feb 29, 1931 Ethel Fain Aug 180? Nov
    5, 1979
Estes Jesse J 1888 - 1927
Estes Mary E 1888 - 1957
Ethorbin Ruth Aug 5, 1901 - Jan 27, 1918
Ethridge Margaret A May 15, 1944 - Dec 1, 1991
Eustage Daniel E Nov 7, 1897 - Mar 30, 1970 Emily Martin
    July 22, 1896 - Dec 16, 1978

Evans John 1890 - 1918

Evans John Richard Jr. June 6, 1916 - Mar 5, 1942

Evans Ruth M 1904 - 1978

Ey Rudd Lillian Apr 28, 1903 - Nov 30, 1990

Ey William Charles 1893 - 1979 husband of Lillian Rudd

Eyl Ann Beatrice Apr 30, 1900 - Dec 1, 1982 WWII

Eyl Beatrice G May 22, 1877 - Oct 24, 1949

Eyl J Edward Jan 23, 1863 - Aug 8, 1951

Eyl James E 1893 - 1977 WWI

Eyl Joseph M Dec 29, 1897 - Aug 10, 1919

Eyl Mary Bell Mar 26, 1903 - July 25, 1990

Eyl William C Apr 4, 1895 - Mar 9, 1984 WWI

Fahy Catherine A 1902 - 1986

Fain Lucien Conrad Aug 17, 1915 - Feb 27, 1991 Pauline
    McCray Jan 27, 1922

Falconer David Grey Dec 14, 1837 - Mar 8, 1926 Co. B 79
    NY Inf

Falk - Krom Margaret E Falk Oct 14, 1893 - Sept 8, 1989
    Kervyn T Krom Feb 7, 1919 - Nov 23, 1976 Elizabeth
    C Krom Sept 1, 1918 - Jan 9, 2005

Fallon Anna 1903 - 1903

Nov 30, 1903   Leader

The funeral services of Anna, the 4 - months child of Mr. and
    Mrs. L. J. Fallon, will take place tomorrow afternoon,
    burial in the Catholic Cemetery.

Fallon Bernard A 1884 - 1944

Fallon Esther

Fallon Harold 1900 - 1973

Fallon Louis J 1896 - 1935

Fallon Luke 1890 - 1903 Joseph 1882 - 1883

Fallon Luke J 1859 - 1913 his wife Anna Strohmann 1862 -
    1913

Fallon Nell Trainor 1882 - 1968

Fanatico Cailey July 23, 1998 - July 23, 1998 Jesus loves me

Farley James Wm 1896 - 1960 Kathryn 1900 - 19
Farley Ralph WWII
Farley Richard A Dec 12, 1923 - Oct 30, 1976
Farrell Edward P Sept 11, 1861 - May 13, 1908 Pray for him
May 14, 1908 Leader
The funeral services of Mr. Edward P. Farrell, who died
    Wednesday afternoon, after a long illness, will be held
    at St. Paul's Catholic Church Friday morning at 9
    o'clock and the interment will follow in the family lot
    in the Catholic Cemetery.

Farrell Jane M Nov 27, 1865 - Nov 2, 1954 Pray for her
Farrell Mary B
Farrell Patrick died Oct 29, 1891
Farris Emma R Ellis 1854 - 1903 wife of R C Farris
Dec 24, 1903 Leader
Mrs. R. C. Farris died at her residence, Fourth and Chestnut
    Streets, this morning of general debility, aged 48 years.
    She was the daughter of the late Benjamin Ellis of
    Bardstown, Kentucky. Her husband, Mr. Clark Farris,
    a well-known turfman, and her daughter, Mrs. George
    Holmes, have the sympathy of a large circle of friends.

Fash Margaret 1860 - 1918
Fawn McKenna Mary Aug 15, 1862 - June 7, 1913
Fawn William Oct 11, 1854 - Dec 13, 1911
Fealy John 1828 - Aug 26, 1899 Mary died Oct 7, 1894
Featherstone Sue 1872 - 1931
Feck August Aug 15, 1829 - Jan 14, 1895 Mary July 4, 1834 -
    Feb 7, 1919
Feck Jesse O 1901 - 1937
Feck John Feb 15, 1868 - Oct 30, 1908 Robert Traugott Sept
    19, 1897 - Dec 8, 1913
Feck Lizzie May 23, 1863 - Oct 20, 1888 Mary Traugott Apr
    4, 1858 - May 17, 1898

Feckt Frank Oct 15, 1867 - May 19, 1937 Elizabeth Aug 17,
        1882 - Dec 22, 1946
Feehan Mary Sharkey Dec 11, 1907 - Sept 19, 1980
Feeley Bridget Kane 1887
Feeley D A 1866 - 1891
Feeley Daniel 1881
Feeley Ella McManus Jan 26, 1866 - Aug 21, 1988
Feeley John L Nov 25, 1857 - Feb 28, 1925 Mary Lilly Oct 1,
        1897 - July 9, 1898
Feeny Anne C 1861 - 1934
Feeny Mary Murray 1842 - 1918 wife of Michael
Feeny Michael 1837 - 1914
Oct 1, 1914   Leader
The funeral services of Mr. Michael Feeney who died last
        night, will be held at St. Paul's Church Friday morning.
        The interment will be in the family lot in the Catholic
        Cemetery.

Feeny Patrick Henry 1847 - 1925 Mary G 1851 - 1933
Feese Helen Grant Dec 27, 1889 - May 20, 1985
Ferguson John D
Ferguson Louise Maguire
Finch Margaret Mary 1908 - 1977
Finerty Martin July 27, 1882
Fingham William M Oct 15, 1886 - June 25, 1947 Ella Burke
        Sept 28, 1886 - Mar 4, 1980
Finn Lulie Embry 1864 - 1961
Finn Mary Bernadette Feb 15, 1882 - Mar 20, 1982
Finn Mary D 1889 - 1932
Finn Patrick E Mar 17, 1862 - Mar 26, 1926
Finnegan James J Nov 21, 1921 - Jan 13, 1982 Yvonne N Oct
        9, 1923 - Aug 24, 1995
Finneran Agnes Haney 1893 - 1921
Finneran Alfred E Apr 28, 1928 - Apr 10, 1979
Finneran Alfred Edward Apr 28, 1928 - Apr 10, 1979 Korea

Finneran Bernardine Lannon 1903 - 1994
Finneran Cecilia P Jan 10, 1922 - Jan 9, 2005
Finneran Edward A Dec 12, 1883 - Aug 10, 1962 Nell Haney
      Jan 20, 1894 - Dec 1, 1962
Finneran Genevieve F Mar 5, 1921 - Apr 6, 1989
Finneran Helen C born July 31, 1913
Finneran James T Dec 5, 1914 - Apr 28, 1984
Finneran John Lannon 1929 - 1930
Finneran Lucille G Oct 16, 1909 - Nov 16, 1982
Finneran Thomas F Aug 30, 1879 - Jan 18, 1942 Mary G
      Feeny Sept 20, 1876 - Oct 10, 1938
Finneran William J 1886 - 1951
Finneran William J Jr. 1915 - 1975
Fired Mary C 1899 - 1993
Fired Valentine 1855 - 1953
Firth John J 1881 - 1959
Fischer Otto 1852 - 1936 Annie 1863 - 1937
Fister Agnes Scully Jan 27, 1916 - Jan 9, 2002
Fister Anna M 1851 - 1902
Fister Cecelia C 1940 C Vincent 1919 - 1981 Elizabeth S 1921
      - 2002
Fister Cecil Ray 1970
Fister Charles John 1890 - 1969
Fister Daniel Alfred 1928 - 2000
Fister Donald Joseph 1928
Fister Edward Nicholas Nov 20, 1908 - Apr 15, 1995 Ann
      Kevin Aug 30, 1910 - May 22, 1998
Fister Elizabeth Decker 1888 - 1986
Fister Ferdinano 1886 - 1898
Fister Florence C July 25, 1909 - Feb 22, 1978
Fister Francis A 1914 - 1915
Fister Fred M
Fister Fred Marion 1878 - 1948
Fister Hubert R Sr. Sept 25, 1926 - Aug 7, 1997 Pauline
      Gregory May 31, 1923 - Dec 1, 1994

Fister James 1877 - 1885
Fister James Paul May 27, 1918 - Jan 25, 1939
Fister John B 1846 - 1919
Fister John F Mar 26, 1925 - July 7, 1985 Rosalie Dec 31,
     1921
Fister John W 1909 - 1910
Fister Joseph and John Apr 28-29, 1930 twins of Charles and
     Mary
Fister Joseph N 1881 - 1952 Carrie A Wolfe 1883 - 1935 John
     Ferdinand 1908 - 1910
Fister Joseph N Jr. Apr 25, 1913 - Dec 5, 1989 Louise
     Vannoy June 27, 1918 - Jan 26, 2005
Fister Julius C Dec 9, 1912 - Mar 7, 1972 Irene Willes Nov
     13, 1913 - Aug 28, 1966
Fister Leo Libert Oct 22, 1920 - Apr 1969 Betsy Robards Feb
     19, 1918 - Dec 23, 2003
Fister Louis Jan 3, ? - Aug 30, 2005 Nancy
Fister Louis A Dec 31, 1912 - May 17, 1995
Fister Mac Dalene Van Ness Apr 29, 1926 - Apr 9, 1938
     Andrew Eugene Oct 16, 1923 - Nov 1982
Fister Magdalen S 1884 - 1983 John P 1882 - 1967
Fister Margaret Ann 1926 - 1995
Fister Margaret Mary Apr 3, 1916 - Jan 24, 1989
Fister Marian Elizabeth 1923 - 1926
Fister Martha Gibson 1920
Fister Mary Frances Rebel 1888 - 1961 wife of Charles J
Fister Mary Hutchison 1930
Fister Mary McLafferty 1930 - 1981
Fister Nettie Stuntebeck 1879 - 1942
Fister Ray A April 6, 1915 - Aug 18, 2005 Helen M Jan 21,
     1920 - Nov 24, 2007
Fister Richard Edward 1917 - 1983
Fister Robert Benjamin 1920 - 1955
Fister Robert Francis Oct 4, 1920 - Jan 13, 1985
Fister Stanley Edward July 23, 1931 - July 29, 1936

Fister Sylvester F Jan 29, 1919 - July 18, 1990 Mary Elizabeth
     May 23, 1920
Fister Sylvester F Jr. May 21, 1940 - July 21, 2004
Fister William Marion 1888 - 1956
Fitch Frank 1915 - 1938
Fitch John William 1909 - 1986 Jane Marrs 1909 - 1991
Fitch Mary C 1905 - 1975 Thomas Fay 1907 - 1972
Fitch Mary E 1879 - 1957
Fitch P Preston 1885 - 1971
Fitch Robert 1841 - 1934
Fitch Walter L Jan 23, 1920 - July 29, 2003 Margaret M Sept
     14, 1918
Fitzgerald David died Jan 26, 1891
Fitzgerald J 1826 - 1896 his wife Catherine 1834 - 1863
Fitzgerald Joseph E 1911 - 1993
Fitzgerald Mollie 1857 - 1942
Fitzgerald Thomas 1891
Fitzpatrick D F 1886 - 1923
Fitzpatrick Garrett Sr. Martin Garrett Jr. Mary E John T
     Murphy
Fitzpatrick Mary Ann Mar 13, 1942 - July 12, 1943 Samuel
     Henry Mar 31, 1908 - Oct 31, 1945 William H Oct 2,
     1870 - July 29, ?
Fitzpatrick William Feb 2, 1824 - Dec 9, 1901 John Oct 1,
     1868 - Oct 6, 1868 Margaret May 20, 1865 - Aug 12,
     1869
Flad Anna 1849
Flad Father 1841 - 1890
Flad John 1880 - 1934
Flad Lawrence 1872 - 1940
Flad Mathas 1868 - 1940
Flad Mother 1839 - 1911
Flairty Robert 1911 - 1959 Mae 1913 - 1959
Flannery Rachel Dec 14, 1936 - Oct 2, 2007
Floyd Byrditt R 1908 - 1970 Effie M 1902 - 2000

Floyd Lee Edwards 1909 - 1962 husband of Opal Joy
    Rickman
Flynn Daniel W Aug 1, 1874 - Dec 29, 1989 Ada C Apr 3,
    1888 - Mar 27, 1971
Flynn Dock C May 11, 1928 - Mar 4, 1977
Flynn James July 19, 1874 - Aug 19, 1949 Annie Barrett May
    25, 1878 - Jan 20, 1947
Flynn James J 1851 - 1923
Flynn James W WWII
Flynn James William Nov 6, 1913 - Apr 29, 1971 Margaret
    Lee Parke Nov 13, 1915 - July 23, 2004
Flynn John Lewis 1884 - 1909
Flynn Lenore F Koonz Mar 1918 - Jan 17, 1959
Flynn Mary E 1855 - 1936
Flynn Mary Vivian Oct 23, 1923 - Dec 30, 1979 daughter of
    Thomas and Myrtia
Flynn Maurice Oliver 1867 - 1922 Annie Goforth 1870 - 1951
Flynn Michael Burke Oct 29, 1919 M Jean Wood July 6, 1920
    - June 11, 2009
Flynn Myrtia Snowden Dec 3, 1904 - Apr 14, 1969 wife of
    Thomas D
Flynn Pauline S July 7, 1920 - Jan 8, 1976 Jerome T Oct 5,
    1915 - Dec 9, 1992
Flynn Richard 1842 - 1900
Oct 14, 1900 Morning Herald
The funeral for Flynn - who was killed by an engine Friday,
    took place at St. Joseph's Hospital yesterday afternoon
    at 8 o'clock. Burial in Catholic Cemetery

Flynn Stephen E Feb 2, 1900 - June 3, 1955 Mary R Apr 16,
    1909
Flynn Susan D 1885 - 1960 Thomas K 1875 - 1949
Flynn Thomas D Dec 29, 1902 - July 2?, 1963
Flynn Thos N
Flynn Will E 1882 - 1971

Fockele Helen Carol May 15, 1961
Fogle Eugena M 1898 - 1973 Eugene C 1851 - 1923 Margaret
    N 1870 - 1914 Gertrude F 1899 - 1976
Foley Anne Frances Oct 16, 1923
Foley Anne Lavery Oct 21, 1885 - Oct 24, 1979
Foley Bernard L Aug 3, 1920 - Jan 27, 1946 WWII
Foley D P 1864 - 1932
Foley Daniel 1847 - 1898
Foley Ella 1859 - 1909
Foley Ellen Fox and baby
Foley Ellie 1877 - 1961
Foley Hannah died Oct 14, 1878
Foley Jo B R.N. died May 31, 1947
Foley John Mar 25, 1830 - Feb 1, 1896
Foley John W Jan 27, 1906 - June 1957 WWII
Foley Joseph 1910 - 1973
Foley Lucy A 1902 - 1969
Foley Margaret C 1867 - 1948
Foley Nannie V July 2, 1879 - Apr 5, 1885
Foley Shanahan Mary Nov 6, 1895 - Nov 10, 1921
Foley Timothy B 1887 - 1969 Emma I 1897 - 1973 Mary K
Foley William J 1874 - 1910
Foley William J July 4, 1881 - Mar 12, 1954

Jan 15, 1913   Leader
The funeral of the late William Foley was held Wednesday
    morning at St. Peter's Church, preceding interment in
    the Catholic Cemetery.

Follier William M 1834 - 1920 SADLR Co. C 11 Ky Cav
Ford Gwendolyn E 1924 - 2000
Ford Harold B Jan 18, 1919 - Mar 27, 1976 Gewndolyn T Mar
    21, 1924 - Jan 2, 2000 married June 1943
Ford Harold B 1919 - 1976
Foree Joe K Jr. 1898 - 1964 Mary Smith 1901 - 1973

Forman William G Sept 15, 1918 - Oct 9, 1985 Mildred D Apr
    25, 1916
Forman William Lee Nov 27, 1883 - Mar 22, 1919 Mary Mae
    May 8, 1884 - Apr 26, 1923
Forrest Karl Charlotte
Forster Elsie Mercer 1895 - 1969
Foster Bettie Fall 1875 - 1960
Foster Clint Lannom 1871 - 1917
Foster Elizabeth Conlon 1881 - 1928
Foster Mary Ann Roche Dec 20, 1926 Robert Warren Aug 1,
    1925

Dec 8, 1905 Leader
Mary Annett, the infant daughter of Mr. and Mrs. Fred D.
    Foster, died at their home, Thursday afternoon, aged
    nine days. Interment was in the family lot in the
    Catholic Cemetery, Friday morning.

Foster Mary R 1908 - 1981
Fotsch Alice Gertrude Nov 12, 1895 - July 18, 1959 dau of B
    B and T B Fotsch
Fotsch Anna Marie Sept 1894 - Feb 21, 1987 George Bernard
    Aug 10, Dec 20, 1887 - 1940
Fotsch Anna Theresa Feb 16, 1891 - Feb 9, 1912 dau of B
    Band T B Fotsch
Fotsch Bernard B June 5, 1856 - July 18, 1929
Fotsch George B Dec 1949
Fotsch Theresa Benckart Nov 6, 1857 - June 20, 1914 wife of
    Bernard B Fotsch

Mar 1, 1915   Leader
The funeral of Mr. Harry Price Foushee will be held at St.
    Paul's Catholic Church Monday morning. Burial will
    be in the family lot in the Catholic Cemetery.

Fowler William Bryan 1888 - 1951 Mollie Mary 1884 - 1975
Fox Bridget Apr 8, 1885
Fox Eugene H May 5, 1922 - Jan 23, 1985 Rosemary E Jan 7,
   1929
Fox Kate James P 1868 Michael
Fox Michael 1875
Fox William June 8, 1951 Manuel Jan 28, 1959
Foyle ? 1918
Frakes Marian Welch Oct 30, 1954 - Mar 1, 1999
Fraley Harlan 1915 - 1982 Ruel 1955 - 1976 Frances 1912 -
   1980
Frank Emma May Tutt Oct 25, 1895 - Sept 25, 1975
Franklin Edward Oct 17, 1886 - Oct 8, 1944
Franks Catherine 1902 - 1945
Franks Catherine Hauck 1902 - 1945
Franz Lena Schneider Nov 22, 1888 - Oct 2, 1977
Franz Michael 1885 - 1964 Lena S 1888 - 1977 Joseph A
   1920 - 2001 Helen E 1917
Franz Michael Feb 16, 1885 - June 20, 1964
Franz William Apr 30, 1921 - Oct 3, 1969 Wilma Bowman
   Nov 7, 1921
Fraser Norman Leslie Dec 19, 1916 - Apr 3, 1963
Fraser Rita Madigan Sept 14, 1918 - Jan 7, 2000
Freckman Louise H Jan 20, 1884 - Apr 4, 1964
Freckman Marie T 1838 - 1907
May 27, 1907   Leader
The burial services of Mrs. Marie Freckman, mother or
   Deputy Sheriff Ben Freckman, were held Sunday
   afternoon at St. Paul's Church, Rev. Father Delaney
   officiating, followed by burial in the Catholic
   Cemetery.

Frediani Attila Buchignani 1865 - 19212
Freeman Richard L 1901 - 1966 Coletta D 1902 - 1974
Freeman William R July 13, 1928 - June 11, 1996 Betty Jo

Dec 7, 1930 - Dec 18, 1996
Freman Conley Rudolph Sept 4, 1953 - Sept 16, 1953
Fried Anne Hannibal 1863 - 1950
Fried Sienna 1886 - 1974
Fritz Ann Rita 1923 - 1939 daughter of Mary and George
Fritz Barbara K 1894 - 1989
Fritz Charles 1887 - 1955 son of Elizabeth Long and John
    Fritz
Fritz George F 1921 Santina G 1922
Fritz George Francis 1884 - 1937
Fritz John Carroll 1879 - 1943
Fritz John 1852 - 1931 Elizabeth 1854 - 1931 Emmett 1885 -
    1924 brother
Fritz Joseph Leon Nov 23, 1923 - Jun 20, 1999
Fritz Kathleen Reagan wife of Charles
Fritz L William 1916 - 1957
Fritz Lawrence Leo 1892 - 1955
Fritz Louis W Sr. 1887 - 1963
Fritz Margaret Elizabeth July 5, 1919 - Sept 10, 1998
Fritz Margaret Henry 1879 - 1944
Fritz Mary Brannon 1889 - 1946
Fritz Robert J 1927 - 1949
Fruhauf Alexander 1901 - 1974 Karoline 1905 - 1963
Frye Paul Joseph Oct 30, 1942 - Nov 26, 1992
Fucci Dominic A 1928 - 1987 Betty A 1931 – 2008
Fugazzi Anne 1891
Fugazzi Clarence A 1883 - 1933
Fugazzi Constantine 1854 - 1924
Fugazzi Elizabeth Nunn Dec 24, 1915 - June 4, 2008
Fugazzi Frances Granducci 1874 - 1938 wife of Constantine
Fugazzi Fred E III Feb 26, 1915 - Apr 12, 1990
Fugazzi Fred Sr. 1858 - 1922
Fugazzi Fred Jr. 1892 - 1937 A.E.F. 1917
Fugazzi Irene Joyce 1892 - 1932
Fugazzi Louis Arzeno 1864 - 1936

Fugazzi Marie Heine 1890 - 1959
Fugazzi Rose Mary 1922
Fugazzi Ruby 1886 - 1927 William 1920
Fugazzie Irene 1896 - 1913
Fugett John Robert 1886 - 1966 Beatrice Grant 1883 - 1961
Fuller Lillian M Mar 21, 1903 - June 18, 1994
Furlong area James R 1903 - 1913 Carolyn 1920 - 1925 James
    R 1916 - 1949
Furlong Dennis A 1907 - 1990 Anna C 1907 - 1999
Furlong Dennis Andrew Apr 9, 1874 - May 7, 1957
    Genevieve McGrath Oct 5, 1894 - Apr 20, 1964
Furlong Kathleen Rennick 1875 - 1942
Furlong Michael P 1870 - 1921 Margaret Feeney 1871 - 1931

Feb 23, 1908 Lexington Leader
The funeral services of Mr. Michael Furlong will take place
    from the home of his son, Mr. Robert Furlong. The
    services will be held at St. Paul's Church Monday
    morning. The interment will follow in the family lot in
    the Catholic Cemetery.

Furlong Nellye Feeney 1874 - 1942
Furlong Patrick 1835 - 1908 Ardeielar 1847
Furlong Patrick Joseph 1866 - 1955
Furlong Philomena 1904 - 1960
Furlong Robert F 1876 - 1944
Furt Thos died June 16, 1880
Fury Mary Gilmore 1867 - 1934
Fury Mary Gilmore 1867 - 1934
Fury Thomas Gilmore May 26, 1897 - Sept 5, 1967 Avel
    Powell Nov 3, 1902 - Dec 23, 1984
Gadd Joseph Carroll Aug 27, 1906 - Jan 2, 1964
Gadd William Floyd Oct 2, 1936 - Apr 25, 2009

Sept 28, 1902 Morning Herald

The funeral services of Mr. Thomas Gagan will be held at St.
Paul's Church this afternoon at 3:45 o'clock. The
interment will be in the Catholic Cemetery.

Gallagher Eugene J Mar 11, 1925 - Aug 27, 1962
Gallagher James E July 24, 1922 - Feb 26, 1991
Gallagher Leonard G Feb 28, 1929 - Jun 1, 2008
Gallagher Margaret S July 23, 1899 - Oct 25, 1980
Gallagher Thomas S July 4, 1930 - July 15, 2000 Betty A Apr
21, 1935
Galligan Kate H died Sept 26, 1887
Galloway Catherine Kirby Aug 14, 1889 - Aug 15, 1968
Galvin Ann Margaret Feb 17, 1997
Galvin Anna Dowd 1888 - 1958
Galvin Billie F 1928 - 1930
Galvin Evelyn Young 1913 - 1976 wife of J J
Galvin J J
Galvin James Patrick Oct 25, 1929 - May 29, 2007 Katherine
Ruth Galvin July 7, 1932
Galvin John J 1874 - 1945
Galvin John J Jr. 1917 - 1985

Mar 18, 1913   Leader
The funeral services of Mrs. Mary Galvin, who died suddenly
Saturday morning at her home on Chestnut Street,
were held Monday morning at St. Peter's Church,
followed by interment in the family lot in the Catholic
Cemetery.

Galvin Raymund A 1921 - 1973
Gangany Thomas died Aug 22, 1883
Gannon Mary Ann O'Connor died Nov 9, 1861
Gannon Roger Jan 3, 1819 - Jan 3, 1899

Nov 12, 1909 Leader

The body of Roger D. Gannon, the Fayette county man who
was murdered in Oklahoma City, Okla., sometime
Saturday night was buried in the Catholic Cemetery in
this city Friday morning. The funeral services were
held at St. Peter's Catholic Church.

Garcia Eudocio Dec 25, 1903 - Mar 23, 1980 Celia R Mar 12,
1906 - Apr 15, 1974
Garland ? died Dec 5, 1897 his wife Catherine Apr 25, 1904
Garland Annie Bonnyman 1867 - 1936 wife of Peter J
Garland Bridget F Feb 2, 1866 - Sept 19, 1924
Garland Catherine 1836 - 1904
Garland Laurence J Aug 12, 1896 - Sept 2, 1965
Garland Leonard A Jan 7, 1895 - Jan 19, 1965
Garland Mary M Apr 23, 1967
Garland Peter J 1867 - 1942
Garland Richard 1840 - 1897
Garland Richard J 1873 - 1920
Garland Richard L May 17, 1898 - Feb 4, 1955
Garland William A Nov 28, 1868 - May 9, 1924
Garstka Matthew A 1920 - 2006 Eleanor 1926 - 2004
Gary Dudley Bailey Apr 17, 1916 - Sept 12, 1963
Gaston Teddy M Jr. 1962 - 1980
Gavanaugh John 1888
Gavanaugh Ann Apr 29, 1893 wife of John
Geary Constance Clark July 2, 1880 - Apr 19, 1942 Edward
A June 15, 1877 - Oct 9, 1947
Geary Edward A June 15, 1877 - Oct 9, 1947 SP AM WAR
Geary John A June 24, 1841 - Jan 24, 1931 Ellen Dec 25,
1949 - May 2, 1920

May 5, 1920 Leader
Following a protracted illness, Mrs. Ellen Ahern Geary,
prominent lumberman of this city, died at her home, on
Sunday night. Mrs. Geary, who was born in Cincinnati,

but had been a resident of Lexington for many years. Burial will be in the family lot in the Catholic Cemetery.

Geary John D died 1878 Mary died 1890
Geiger Hannorah Welsh 1864 - 1956
Geis G J "Jack" Aug 30, 1933 - July 1, 2005
Gentry Hood 1900 - 1977 Helen Jacobs 1905 - 19629
Gentry Olin 1900 - 1990
Gentry Pauline McCarty 1902 - 1970
George E 1904 - 1930 Lusse area
George John P May 1, 1917 - Jan 29, 1990 Jessie M May 12, 1926 wed Feb 19, 1946
George John Philip May 1, 1917 - Jan 29, 1990 WWII
Geran Helen 1914 - 1964
Geran John L 1887 - 1958 Anna B 1890 - 1974
Geran John L Jan 11, 1917 - Nov 3, 2001
Geran John L Jan 11, 1917 - Nov 3, 2001 WWII
Geran Katherine J 1891 - 1981
Geran Mary Ann 1855 - 1918
Geran Michael 1854 - 1938
Giatani Mary H Joseph 1869 - 1953
Giblin Thomas F Feb 10, 1883 - Sept 5, 1973
Gibson Robert B Jan 18, 1938 - June 13, 1991 Elaine M Aug 16, 1938 - Mar 30, 2006
Gilbreath William O May 2, 1919 - Dec 12, 1995 Frances S Mar 14, 1921 - Dec 28, 1998
Gilchrist Alma Lee Mar 31, 1916 - Apr 30, 2000
Gilchrist Charles E 1886 - 1946
Gilchrist Edward C 1912 - 1990
Gilchrist Jennie Sharkey 1888 - 1949
Gilchrist Mae 1913 - 1991
Gilchrist William 1916 - 1917
Gilfoy Paul Eugene Mar 8, 1934 - Mar 11, 1951
Gill James M 1875 - 1900 Thomas J 1873 - 1934

Feb 23, 1900 Morning Herald
James M Gill passes away Thursday after a long illness
The Funeral services will be held at St. Paul's Catholic Church
Saturday morning at 9 o'clock. The remains will be
interred in the Catholic Cemetery.

Gill Katherine A 1883 - 1948
Gill Michael 1837 - 1912 Catherine 1853 - 1939
Sept 27, 1912 Leader
The funeral services of Mr. Michael Gill, who died
Wednesday afternoon, will be held Saturday morning
at St. Paul's Church. The burial will follow in the
Catholic Cemetery.

Gill William E 1877 - 1905
Gillet William James 1919 - 1997 Burneda C Anderle 1919
Gilliam Nellye Furlong June 8, 1903 - Oct 25, 1991
Gilman Charles B 1848 - 1922
Gilman Mary 1852 - 1933
Gilmore Mary J 1888 - 1906
Aug 10, 1906 Leader
The body of Mrs. Mary Gilmore arrived Friday morning from
Flemingsburg, Ky. The burial took place in the
Catholic Cemetery upon the arrival of the train.

Gilmore Thomas J 1839 - 1924
Gilroy 1850 - Mar 2, 1873
Gilroy Bernard J July 18, 1918 Battle of Soissons Co. K 9th
Inf
Ginocchio illegible
Ginocchio Alphonse Laggrio 1903 - 1957
Ginocchio Elvira Buchignani 1892 - 1981
Ginocchio Frances Anthony 1846 - 1919 Ollie L 1884 - 1975
Ginocchio Francis Joseph 1898 - 1974
Ginocchio Frank Salvini 1893 - 1987

Ginocchio John Sept 21, 1888 - Nov 14, 1947
Ginocchio John A Aug 6, 1843 - Mar 9, 1924 Philomenia G
        Dec 28, 1862 - May 21, 1934
Ginocchio John Bernard 1886 - 1973
Ginocchio Laura E Sept 18, 1879 - Mar 24, 1971
Ginocchio Lillian Mahoney 1892 - 1943
Ginocchio Louis Martin 1889 - 1966
Ginocchio Louis Martin 1929 - 1991
Ginocchio Martin H 1931
Ginocchio Mary Jo 1928 - 1975
Ginocchio Rose Lagorio 1867 - 1950
Ginocchio Sue S 1933 - 2005 wife of Martin
Ginoochio Susan Hall 1899 - 1979
Giurgevich John A Oct 29, 1924 - Aug 30, 1980 WWII
Giurgevich Loraine M Nov 3, 1923 - Oct 7, 1947
Glancy Annie 1801 - 1885 Thomas 1884 - 1920
Glancy Margaret born Nov 14, 1880
Glass Everett 1900 - 1946 Gussie 1902 - 1983
Glass Frank D Dec 3, 1895 - Dec 28, 196? Helen Laughlin
        1896 - 1978
Glass Harry E 1906 - 1970 Clara P 1912 - 1990
Glass James Leo Jan 13, 1925 - May 8, 1938
Glass Owen J 1869 - 1926 Katherine 1878 - 1935 James A
        1898 - 1930

Dec 28, 1909 Leader
The funeral services of Edmond Gleason will be held at St.
        Paul's Catholic Church Wednesday morning followed
        by interment in the family lot in the Catholic
        Cemetery.

Godfrey George J WWII
Godfrey Thomas Lee Feb 17, 1892 - May 5, 1959 WWI
Godfrey William S WWI
Goerg Augusta 1869 - 1966

Golbout Alfred died Mar 1, 1919
Golden Edward Aug 20, 1892 - Apr 1957 WWI

Aug 25, 1904 Morning Herald
The funeral Services of Mr. John Golden Sr. will take place
    from the St. Paul's Catholic Church this morning at 9
    o'clock. The burial will be in the Catholic Cemetery.

Golden Katherine B Feb 7, 1887 - Jan 31, 1973
Golden Pat S 1887 - 1937
Golden Theodore 1881 - 1946
Golden Timothy J
Gona Donald J 1927 - 1990 Evelyn T
Goodin James Nov 1845 - July 1876
Goodlett Ruth Smith July 9, 1949 - May 1, 1995
Goodman Mary S 1871 - 1965 Thomas 1872 - 1965 Joseph P
    1915 - 19 Frances 1913 - 1930 Thomas 1908 - 1918
Goodpaster Claude W Oct 19, 1927 - Nov 2, 2004 Heidy F
    Dec 22, 1925
Goodpaster Helene Marie Langlois Mar 6, 1918 - Nov 7, 1968
    wife of Howard T
Goodpaster Howard T Mar 12, 1917
Goodpaster Opal Joy Nov 9, 1911 - Sept 15, 2003 wife of
    Howard T
Goodwin Wm E 1864 - 19 his wife Katie B McFadden 1864 -
    1925
Gorham Adam Ryan Nov 25, 1990
Gorham Ben W 1892 - 1937
Gorham Carl Joseph 1925
Gorham Mary C 1893 - 1979
Gorham Mary Kathleen Mar 7, 1950 - Mar 21, 1952
Gorham Mary Kearney 1927 - 1980
Gorham Nell Sheehy 1889 - 1972
Gorham R Allen Nov 9, 1928 - May 28, 1977 Mary Ann Jan
    29, 1931 - May 28, 1977

Gorham Robert Julian Jan 8, 1927 - Sept 22, 1990
Gorman Ann C 1919 - 1963 Daniel C 1943
Gorman Daniel 1862 - 1899
Gorman Hugh 1858 - 1879
Gorman Mother 1925 - 1898
Gorman Patrick J 1860 - 1936
Gormley Charles G
Gormely Hugh June 21, 1864 - July 19, 1924 Katie Gormley
     Apr 186? - July 21, 19?

June 23, 1909 Leader
The funeral of Mrs. Kate Gormley, who died at Versailles,
     will be held Thursday morning at St. Leo's Church in
     Versailles, and the body will then be brought here for
     burial in the Catholic Cemetery.

Gormely James died 1821
Gormely James Feb 6, 1857 - Dec 13, 1873 Mary Elizabeth
     Aug 2, 1868 - Apr 23, 1873
Gormely Margaret
Gormely Pat Jr. 1881 - 1918
Gormely Patrick J 1873 - 1953 Marie McGarvey 1885 - 1919
Gormely Thomas
Gormely William 1838 - 1908 Ann 1829 - 1913
Gormely William M Mar 9, 1905 - May 8, 1874
Gormely William T Sr. Sept 1, 1876 - June 20, 1950
     Katherine F Nov 20, 1888 - Nov 16, 1958
Gormley Berla I Isaacs Feb 27, 1900 - June 22, 1975 wife of
     Roger
Gormley Bridget Clarke 1868 - 1938
Gormley Charles
Gormley Charles J 1871 - 1940
Gormley Henry T Feb 19, 1885
Gormley J J
Gormley James 1821

70

Gormley James 1866 - 1937

Gormley James B Oct 12, 1895 - Jan 13, 1960

Gormley James Nov 11, 1819 - Mar 4, 1871 Alice McIntyre
    Mar 25, 1832 - Sept 23, 1883

Gormley Julia E

Gormley Lillie A 1888 - 1941

Gormley Mary 1869 - 1919

Gormley Orpha Shattuck 1869 - 1969 wife of Philip J.
    Gormley

Gormley Patrick 1845 - 1926

Gormley Patrick J 1869 - 1950 Mary E 1866 - 1930

Gormley Philip J 1869 - 1927

Gormley Roger Nov 4, 1885 - Dec 2, 1958

Gormley Sarah 1846 - 1906

Gormley Thomas died Dec 30, 1866

Gormley Thos died 1862

Gormley William J 1901 - 1980

Gormley William M Mar 9, 1905 - May 8, 1974

Gott Christine S Egalite 1898 - 1928 wife of Edwin J

Gott Edwin J 1892 - 1936

Gott Mary Ann Oct 31, 1920 - Sept 24, 2001 Carolyn Jan 7,
    1923

Gott Nell O'Day 1891 - 1958

Grace Michael Augusta Mar 12, 1868 - Aug 9, 1930 Margaret
    Mulcahy July 17, 1873 - Jan 26, 1961

Govan Charles J Apr 20, 1902

Apr 23, 1902 Leader

Mr. Frank Dalton, of this city, received a telegram last night
    that the body of Charles Govan would be here tonight
    at 10 o'clock. The funeral will take place Thursday
    morning at his late residence on the Maysville Pike.
    The burial will take place in the Catholic Cemetery.

Grady Bridget 1854 - 1888

Grady Father 1819 - 1908

Grady John 1859 - 1896
Grady Maggie 1865 - 1888
Grady Mother 1826 - 1900
Grady Patrick 1856 - 1902
Grady Thomas 1860 - 1937
Graham James A Dec 28, 1919 - Aug 26, 1983
Graham Shirley C Jan 26, 1923 - June 21, 2000
Grant Family
Grant Frank B June 10, 1897 - Feb 3, 1965 Anna Winans Feb
        3, 1906 - July 6, 1985
Grant Helen Feeney Mar 26, 1866 - Oct 31, 1941 Edward E
        Aug 15, 1864 - Dec 19, 1932
Grant James Carey June 20, 1913 - Apr 25, 1993 Margaret
        Mar 4, 1991 - Feb 5, 1997
Grant John 1862 - 1920
Grant Joseph M Jan 23, 1895 - Aug 7, 1972 Nora Reynolds
        Feb 11, 1903 - Oct 3, 1989
Grant Jude Patrick Aug 30, 2007 - Sept 22, 2007
Grant Margaret 1885 - 1934
Graves Family 1896 - 1958
Graves George Dewey July 23, 1898 - Mar 29, 1964 Marie A
        Helmes Aug 11, 1899 - Sept 13, 1980
Gray Andrew B Dec 15, 1855 - Nov 16, 1902

Apr 3, 1911   Leader
The body of George Gray, the English upholsterer, who took
        laudanum while confined in the police station last
        Wednesday night and died several days later in the St.
        Joseph's Hospital, is still at the undertaking
        establishment of Wiehl & Son, and will probably be
        buried by the city in the Catholic Cemetery.

Greathouse Herman H Dec 23, 1897 - July 7, 1935
Greely John J Jr. Oct 25, 1910 - May 17, 1978 Eunice C June
        3, 1915 - Sept 5, 2001

Green Patrick Joseph June 9, 1934 - Feb 6, 1990 Mary Ann
    Aug 10, 1937 - Oct 30, 2007
Green Warren B Mar 27, 1922 - Oct 25, 1967
Green Warren B Mar 27, 1922 - Oct 25, 1967 Helen W Page
    Dec 17, 1925 - Sept 10, 1987
Greenwald Arthur Sept 29, 1915 - Sept 1, 2003 WWII
Gregory Emile Fall 1871 - 1964
Gregory James C 1840 - 1907
Gregory James F 1899 - 1914
Gribbin Dec 10, 1770 - 185?
Gribbin 1823 - 1840
Gribbin Elizabeth mother of Noah and James Mulholland
Gribbin John Mar 17, 1785 - Aug 13, 1843
Gribbin Peter
Gribbin William Aug 12, 1828 - Aug 12, 1840
Griffin George Dallas DeGraffen Ried 1910 - 1982
Griffin J Fred 1894 - 1963 Agnes J 1891 - 1962
Griffin John A 1900 - 1985 Helen Smith 1905 - 1965
Griffin Rodney O'Leary Jan 2, 1966 - Apr 15, 1968
Griffin Strother Joseph Dec 21, 1933 - Feb 1, 1984
Griffin Strother 1908 - 1978 Mary Minogue 1913
Griffith Connie Reister July 15, 1910 - July 30, 1985

Dec 5, 1903 Leader
Mrs. Josephine Griffith died today at her home in McKinney,
    Ky., of stomach trouble. The body arrived at 3 o'clock
    this afternoon over the Southern railroad and interment
    immediately followed in Catholic Cemetery.

Gritton Julia E July 14, 1912 - Jan 7, 1998
Gritton Orville B 1910 - 1959 At Rest
Gronan M E 1850 - 1905
Gronfield Bernard 1887 - 1955 Elizabeth M 1878 - 1952
Grose T Grannis 1890 - 1953 Anna Clancy 1890 - 1975
Grosser John 1824 - 1887

Grossland Josephine E May 4, 1903 - Feb 16, 1955 At Rest
Grossland Wayne H Oct 2, 1894 - Mar 27, 1951 WWI
Grost F Grannis Sept 28, 1890 - Mar 12, 1953
Gruber James P Dec 25, 1899 - Oct 21, 1976
Gruber Mildred C Dec 5, 1908 - July 28, 1992
Guarnieri Rose M May 31, 1913 - Sept 26, 2005
Guinn Helen Rooney Mar 15, 1950 - Dec 31, 2004 Persian
     Gulf
Gunn Katherine died 193?
Guthrie - Ray - Turner
Gysels Hippolytus Aug 13, 1839 - Aug 13, 1914
Haase Isabelle Oct 13, 2003 Owen F Barbara S
Haefling Bernard J Dec 25, 1908 - Apr 12, 1979 Mildred M
     May 9, 1916 - Aug 8, 1973
Haefling Daniel M Jan 26, 1886 - June 4, 1967 Maud D Apr
     20, 1888 - Aug 20, 1923
Haffey Ralph June 6, 1922 Geraldine Dec 28, 1928
Hagan Andrew 1898 - 1966 Mary 1901 - 1979
Hagan Charles Lucien Apr 19, 1905 - Nov 1, 1994
Hagan H Hart May 10, 1923 - Feb 26, 1997 Norma C Feb 19,
     1924 - July 7, 1997 Barrnett Ann Jan 22, 1953 - Feb
     11, 1953
Hagan Mary Louise Apr 1, 1903 - Mar 5, 1971 Joseph
     Thomas June 18, 1903 - Aug 10, 1985 Faye Teresa
     Dec 16, 1933
Hagan Mary Marcella Feb 12, 1906 - July 17, 2000
Hagan Mary Stewart 1895 - 1976
Hagedorn William S 1847 - 1909 Mary E 1851 - 1952
Haggan Charles M 1903 - 1938
Haggan Charles J 1863 - 1930
Haggan Lucy Walton 1865 - 1905
Haggan Sarah 1856 - 1945
Haggan Sarah 1866 Charles 1858
Haggard Alice Brannon Sept 10, 1905 - June 29, 1961
Hahn Albert George July 24, 1876 - Jan 4, 1942 Maries

Reagan Aug 22, 1877 - Jan 21, 1933
Halcomb Curtis V Nov 9, 1907 - July 12, 1972 Helen E Nov
    19, ? - Oct 14, ?
Hale
Hale Christopher L Jan 29-30, 1954
Hale Mary (Mollie) Mar 1, 1875 - April 6, 1965

Nov 23, 1910 Leader
Mrs. Mary A. Hale died at her home, Tuesday night, aged 75
years. She is survived by seven children. The funeral
services will be held at St. Paul's Church with requiem
mass Thursday morning. The interment will follow in
the family lot in the Catholic Cemetery.

Hale Patrick J 1866 - 1948 Josephine 1873 - 1951 Son Charles
    Aug 9 - Sept 4, 1903
Hale Robert Joseph Jan 1, 1878 - Nov 15, 1931 Nanie Kearns
    Apr 28, 1878 - Feb 21, 1960
Hall Arthur C Mar 13, 1920 - Aug 25, 1998 Alyce Sutton Jan
    6, 1926 - June 2, 1987
Hall Arthur C Mar 13, 1920 - Aug 25, 1998 WWII
Hall George H 1884 - 1969
Hall George W Mar 23, 1909 - Oct 16, 1969 Gertrude Jacob
    Dec 3, ? - Dec 3, 1991
Hall Jordon Alexandra May 15 - June 13, 1998 Daughter of
    Mark and Janet
Hall Mary McKenna 1891 - 1965
Hall Ronald W and Sarah Aug 22, 1966 Twin sons of Ronald
    W & Sarah
Hallman Mary Ann Sept 8, 1964 Infant Daughter of Norman
    R & Nancy
Hamilton Charles T Oct 27, 1918 - July 30, 1981 Louise B
    Mar 20, 1920 - Aug 26, 2001
Hammond Mary Malone Nunn 1889 - 1961
Hampson Catherine Sept 27, 1907 - May 11, 1988 Mary Sept

4, 1902 - Nov 17, 1919 Ellen Kearney Nov 23, 1866 -
July 8, 1942
Hampson Patrick J Sept 10, 1866 - Mar 24, 1932 Mary K Feb
6, 1870 - Jan 10, 1910
Hanaey Pat June 6, 1892 - July 7, 1950
Haney Charles J 1888 - 1963
Haney Daniel 1856 - 1931 Alice K 1886 - 1916 Susie 1896 -
1923 Mary C 1862 - 1933 Margaret 1900 - 1927
Frances R 1903 - 1927
Haney Ellen Smith 1860 - 1936 Annie 1887 - 1904 Michael
1853 - 1898 Ellen 1889 - 1989 Ellen and Michael
married Nov 25, 1883
May 14, 1904 Leader
The funeral services of Miss Annie C. Haney will be held at
St. Paul's Church, Sunday afternoon. The interment
will be in the family lot in the Catholic Cemetery.

Haney Flora B 1892 - 1946
Haney Frank J 1897 - 1959 Emmaline 1907 - 1977
Haney James A 1863 - 1938
Haney James M Sr. Nov 29, 1921 - Oct 5, 1995 Patricia June
20, 1939
Haney John Nov 1878 - ?
Haney John 1850 - 1915 Mary A Tranor 1847 - 1904
Haney John July 25, 1887
Haney John Burnett Sept 12, 1876 - Oct 7, 1941
Haney Margaret Minogue 1908 - 1988
Haney Mary E 1871 - 1930
Haney Michael B 1894 - 1961
Haney Michael B Jr. June 3, 1928 - Nov 15, 1994 Joan
Sullivan June 20, 1933 - June 3, 2000 married July 19,
1958
Haney Norma D 1924 Mary F 1920 - 1997 Charles W 1915 -
1964
Hanke Mary Virginia Rompf Jan 16, 1939 - Feb 5, 1979 wife

of Dan W Hanke
Hanley Kate 1836 - 1892
Hanley William 1920 - 1961 Elizabeth Hunter 1920 - 2000
Hanly Dennis J 1859 - 1929
Hanly Edith Sheldon Oct 6, 1863 - Apr 8, 1930
Hanly Elizabeth A 1859 - 1936
Hanly Gertrude E died Dec 4, 1979
Hanly John H 1935
Hanly John Hays Mar 23, 1788 - Nov 8, 1862
Hanly John Hilary Aug 12, 1854 - June 30, 1932
Hanly Katherine S Nov 7, 1902 - May 15, 1982
Hanly Margaret June 22, 1790 - Feb 8, 1867 wife of John H
      Hanly
Hanly Mary C 1856 - 1938
Hanly Mary H 1939
Mrs. Mary Holmes Hanly, born June 21, 1878, died April 6,
      1939
Death Certificate:
Parents: Edwin Holmes & Elizabeth Bowman
Husband: John H. Hanly
Informant: Gertrude E. Hanly

Hanly Mary Joseph 1894 - 1979
Hanly Thomas P 1862 - 1936
Hanly Thomas R Feb 6, 1826 - Jan 19, 1901
Hanly Thomas R 1897 - 1958
Hanna Mousa Apr 6, 1902 - Apr 22, 1983 Elizabeth Apr 8,
      1920 - July 9, 2009
Hannibal
Hannon Annie 1889 - 1909
Hannon James 1835 - 1909
Hannon Joanna Shea 1854 - 1919 wife of James
Hannon John D 1880 - 1935 Jessie T 1891 - 1913
Hannon Joseph B 1898 - 1929
Hannon Mary 1886 - 1907

Hannon Pete 1884 - 1967 Lexington Police Force 42 Years
Hanrahan Patrick Jan 18, 1875 aged 40 years
Hanscom Mary O 1883 - 19 Harry F 1891 - 1962
Hansen Donald F Jan 16, 1922 - Nov 2, 2003 Kathryn W Oct
	2, 1921 - Sept 1, 2004
Harb Albert 1879 - 1951 Annie Debie 1888 - 1937
Hargrove Calvin D Mar 22, 1930 - Mar 29, 1991
Harkey John
Harkins Charlotte 1942
Harkins Harriet 1831 - 1912
Harkins Harrison 1880
Harkins James M L 1933
Harkins Jerry 1915
Harkins L Newton Y 1929
Harkins Margaret and baby 1904 wife of Newton Y
Harkins Patrick 1816 - 1892
Harkins William 1903
Harman Mary Elizabeth 1908 - 1965
Harnett Lure Aug 15, 1892 - Dec 6, 1976
Harney Ruth Treiber 1902 - 1973
Harold Thomas Nov 20, 1906 - Mar 15, 1946
Harp Infant son of Gene and Ann Feb 18, 1966
Harper Walter J 1888 - 1972 Nellie S 1886 - 1960
Harper Walter P May10, 1922 - May 26, 1997 Betty S Feb 22,
	1930 - Nov 2, 1996
Harrigan Ellen Sept 8, 1862 - Feb 2, 1926
Harrigan Florence Rumsey 1894 - 1974 wife of Joe E
Harrigan Joe E 1890 - 1945
Harrington Daniel Nov 21, 1857 - June 1896 Katherine
	Harrington O'Neill Nov 4, 1870 - Jan 5, 1942
Harrington Elizabeth 1850 - 1917 Jeremiah 1836 - 1910
Harrington Jane Sept 14, 1886 aged 55 Timothy Oct 27, 1888
	aged 58
Harrington John born Apr 14, 1825

Jan 18, 1909 Leader
John Thomas Harrigan, the infant child of Mr. and Mrs.
    Joseph Harrigan, died Sunday morning. The funeral
    took place at the residence, Monday morning. Burial in
    the Catholic Cemetery.

Harrington Michael 1887 - 1936 Elizabeth 185 - 1933
Harrington Timothy Apr 1862 - July 30, 1880 Edward G Nov
    18, 1860 - June 4, 1889 Pat F Ma? 10, 1859 - Dec 8,
    1891
Harrington Matthew Apr 1866 - Mar 15, 1882 Mary J July 2,
    1864 - Jan 29, 1884 Emma J May 5, 1870 - Mar 17,
    1888
Harris Charles died Mar 12, 1898
Harris Eda Menard Aug 7, 1865 - Apr 17, 1957
Harris Ella May Apr 6, 1896 - Sept 12, 1981
Harrison Elijah P 1872 - 1956 Cecile L 1874 - 1946
Hart Patricia S Apr 24, 1951 - May 2, 2009 Our dear Trish, a
    smile forever

Apr 30, 1920   Leader
Mrs. Mary Jane Harting, 79 years old, widow of William
    Harting, and one of Lexington's best known and most
    beloved women, died at her home, Broadway and
    Second Street, Thursday night at 6 o' clock. Interment
    will follow in the family lot in the Catholic Cemetery.

Hartford Anna Mae Apr 7, 1962
Hartford Jesse 1942
Harvener Rita Kunz Apr 10, 1928 - May 18, 1985
Hashen George J 1863 - 1923
Hastings William E Oct 16, 1889 - May 31, 1970 Catherine E
    Unser Feb 24, 1890 - Mar 8, 1979
Haus Joseph F Dec 19, 1919 - Sept 5, 2002 Anna E Beyer Mar
    22, 1921 - May 11, 1989

Hayden William F Oct 26, 1922 Elizabeth W Mar 13, 1922
Hayes Ellen aged 27 years Josie aged 19 years
Hayes John 1830 - 1898 his wife Ellen 1836 - 1910
Hayes Mary 1847 - 1932
Hayes Mary 1855 - 1920
Hayes Philip Joseph Apr 25, 1868 - Mar 7, 1937 son of Mary
        Mayne & Thomas
Hayes Rose McKenna Bush 1886 - 1959
Hayhurst Betty R June 30, 1923 - Sept 17, 1991
Head Loyd R 1884 - 1947 Frances G 1897 - 1950
Heafey Anna died Nov 24, 1939
Heafey Bessie Died Oct 7, 1913
Heafey John died Mar 10, 1901
Heafey John died Jan 16, 1934
Heafey John T died Nov 12, 1934
Heafey Margaret died May 12, 1981
Heafey Mary died Nov 10, 1897
Heafey Sallie Dockery died July 14, 1938
Heafey Thomas died Aug 22, 1888
Healy Rev E
Healy Rev Edward J Aug 15, 1840 - Apr 13, 1907
Hearn Dennis O died Dec 15, 1851 Michael Trainor died May
        13, 1801
Hegarty Frank A 1878 - 1934

June 2, 1903 Morning Herald
Miss Nellie Hagarty - Services were held at St. Paul's Church
        this morning at nine o'clock and the interment will
        follow in the family lot in the Catholic Cemetery.

June 3, 1903 Leader
The funeral services of Miss Nellie Hegarty took place this
        morning at St. Paul's Church. Rev. Father James
        Hegarty, of the Dominican Order, a brother of the
        deceased, sang the High Mass, followed by services at

the grave in the Catholic Cemetery.

Heinl Albert Michael 1866 - 1908 Augusta Klair 1866 - 1913
Oct 22, 1908 Leader
The funeral services of Mr. Albert M. Heinl will be held at St.
    Paul's Church Friday morning and the interment will
    follow in the family lot in the Catholic Cemetery.

Oct 23, 1908 Lexington Herald
Funeral services for M Heinl will be held at St. Paul's Church
    this morning at 9 o'clock and the interment will follow
    in the family lot in the Catholic Cemetery.

Heinrich Charles Emmett Dec 8, 1918 - Feb 8, 1942
Hellaro Catherine F Flaherty July 20, 1803 - Aug 23, 1922
Hendricks Lilye Diamond July 2, 1881 - July 25, 1966
Hendricks A Shelton 1906 - 1989 Gertrude W 1907 - 1994
Hendricks Jason Wayne Aug 15, 1983 - May 13, 1983
Hendricks Stanley M May 8, 1900 - July 31, 1983 Elizabeth R
    July 19, 1900 - May 16, 1990 Stanley M Jr. Sept 14,
    1927 - July 21, 1991
Hendricks Thomas A Aug 10, 1873 - July 26, 1956
Hennessy Annie 1865 - Dec 13, 1881
Hennessy Charles Oct 187? - May 28, 1862
Hennessy Ellen P July 26, 1841 - Nov 5, 1904
Hennessy Mary E 1862 - 1907
Hennessy Michael P 1869 - 1910
Feb 2, 1910 Leader
Mr. Michael P. Hennessy died at the home of Mr. Frank J.
    Wolf, on Friday morning of tuberculosis. The funeral
    services will be held at St. Peter's Church Saturday
    morning and the interment will follow in the family lot
    in the Catholic Cemetery.

Hennessy Nellie 1875 - 1956

Henry died July 5, 1850 aged 36 years
Henry Caroline Leaycraft Jan 17, 1889 - June 15, 1964

June 30, 1906 Leader
The funeral services of Mr. Charles Henry will be held at St.
     Paul's Church Sunday afternoon. The internment will
     be in the family lot in the Catholic Cemetery.

Henry Charles A 1872 - 1942
Henry Charles A Jr. Sept 29, 1903 - Sept 12, 1978
Henry Charles J 1881 - 1944
Henry Colleen Hamilton Oct 17, 1910 - Apr 10, 1980

July 31, 1906 Leader
The funeral services of the infant child of Mr. and Mrs. D. F.
     Henry will take place at the family residence on
     Wednesday afternoon. Burial in the Catholic
     Cemetery.

Henry Edwin B 1942 - 1969
Henry Eleanor B 1873 - 1953
Henry Elizabeth 1879 - 1951
Henry James 1878 - 1910
Henry James B Feb 12, 1884 - Mar 7, 1969
Henry James J 1860 - 1922
Henry James P 1878 - 1952 Frances Boyle 1878 - 1959
Henry James P 1901 - 1928
Henry John M 1885 - 1974
Henry Johnie 1895 - 1918
Henry Joseph 1878 - 1904
Henry Joseph J Jan 8, 1892 - July 4, 1953 WWI
Henry Kate July 11, 1863 - Oct 13, 1942
Henry Leo Patrick Apr 1940
Henry Marie C 1910 - 1947
Henry Mary died Aug 12, 1885

Henry Mary E 1851 - 1922

Henry Michael J 1881 - 1963 Myla S 1902

Henry Patrick 1847 - 1919 Bridget 1850 - 1905

Henry Rose 1890 - 1919

Hensley Martha A 1929 - 2006

Heppner Paul H 1851 - 1883

Herlihy Daniel July 12, 1830 - Aug 8, 1881

Herrick Charles Julius Oct 8, 1903 - Dec 5, 1997 Loretto
      Rives Dec 20, 1905 - July 6, 1997

Herrick Mary A 1868 - 1907

Herrigan Joseph died Jan 7, 1910

Her?n Patrick Feb 23, 1847 - Mar 22, 1922

Hettel Henry Andrew

Hettel Henry Andrew Feb 4, 1896 - June 13, 1969 Myrtle
      Drury Nov 4, 1897 - Feb 8, 1973

Heuerman Eugene O Oct 8, 1911 - Feb 20, 1978 Anne E Mar
      31, 1909 - Apr 13, 1979

Heuerman Amber Marianne Apr 19, 1984 - Apr 22, 2005

Heuerman Michael K July 8, 1947 - Jan 25, 1998 Margot N
      June 22, 1943 - Aug 9, 2003

Hiatt B T Apr 2, 1926

Hiatt Rose Henry Apr 22, 1931

Hickey Andrew F 1944

Hickey Dennis J 1865 - 1915 and wife Alice Murphy 1881 -
      1957

Hickey Father 1837 - 1906

Hickey George W Apr 8, 1878 - Feb 13, 1952

Hickey J P 1869 - 1906

Mar 1, 1906 Leader

John P. Hickey, 36, died February 4, at Georgetown, KY, of
      heart disease. Burial in Lexington Catholic Cemetery.

Hickey J R 1871 - 1907

Hickey James 1911

Hickey John 1863 - 1917

Hickey Margaret Collins 1939
Hickey Michael J Nov 9, 1864 - Nov 23, 1932
Hickey Minnie 1910
Hickey Mother 1839 - 1912
Hickey P H 1873 - 1907
Hickey William D Apr 30, 1936 - Jan 3, 1974
Hickey William E 1884 - 1963 Anna T 1897 - 1966
Hickey William T Apr 12, 1876 - Jan 30, 1938
Hicks Clarence 1892 - 1958
Hicks Lucile B 1898 - 1958
Hicks Paul 1925 - 1929
Higdon Ronald O June 20, 1939 - Mar 25, 1955
Higgins Joy V 1932 Frances G 1926 - 1976
Higgins Ridgle C Sept 24, 1919 - Aug 2, 1999 Doris McCray
     Oct 15, 1925
Hill Alvin Morris 1900 Mary C Glass (Mae) 1893 - 1979
Hill Clement Samuel Oct 27, 1922 - Jan 15, 2008 WWII
Hill Clement Samuel Oct 27, 1922 - Jan 15, 2008 Marita
     Goodin July 24, 1923
Hillenmeyer Anna June 18, 1976 wife of Louis E
Hillenmeyer Carrie July 27, 1844 - Feb 17, 1934 H F Aug
     1878 - Feb 24, 1975 ordained July 19, 1902
Hillenmeyer Donald L Sept 30, 1922 - May 3, 1974
Hillenmeyer Eileen Sullivan July 29, 1821wife of Robert H
Hillenmeyer Ernest R 1880 - 1963 Mathilde Scott 1884 - 1971
Hillenmeyer H F Aug 28, 1849 - Mar 3, 1923 Mary Nov 17,
     1856 - Feb 27, 1933
Mar 4, 1923 Herald
Hector F. Hillenmeyer at age of 74 dies at home near
     Sandersville.

Hillenmeyer Henry R Dec 24, 1920 - Nov 30, 1945
Hillenmeyer Louis Aug 7, 1915 - Feb 22, 1982
Hillenmeyer Louis E Nov 22, 1885 - May 31, 1965
Hillenmeyer Marie Reiling June 6, 1891 - Aug 22, 1955

Hillenmeyer Martha A Mar 26, 1987 wife of Louis E
Hillenmeyer Mary C Mar 12, 1812 - Apr 20, 1881 F X R Oct
   1, 1814 - Dec 15, 1893
Dec 17, 1893   Leader
Mr. Francis Xavier Hillenmeyer, the horticulturist, died last
   night at the residence of his son, Hector F.
   Hillenmeyer, near Sandersville.

Hillenmeyer Raymond J 1881 - 1972
Hillenmeyer Robert H July 10, 1921 - Dec 31, 1999
Hillenmeyer Walter W Aug 27, 1890 - July 15, 1935
Hillnemeyer Mary Conannon 1897 - 1965 wife of Raymond J
Hines John E 1854 - 1919
Hines Owen 1808 - 1898
Hines Paul J 1901 - 1975 Sara D 1902 - 1972 John P 1925
Hines Ray Thomas 1927 - 1977 Merilyn Nichter 1929 - 2001
Hite Eleanor Gunn 1915 - 1948 wife of James L
Hite James L 1909 - 2005
Hite James Louis May 20, 1944 - Feb 17, 1968
Hobaugh John Monroe Feb 2, 1944 - Nov 13, 2001
Hoflich John A 1888 - 1918 Elizabeth Welch 1884 - 11956
Hogan Susan Jan 24, 1896 - Jan 1, 1897
Hogarty Catherine Ahern 1853 - 1931
Hogarty Alexander died Mar 17, 1917 aged 70
Hogarty Martin died Dec 31, 1880 aged 64 Mary Frasher died
   Aug 7, 1896 aged 80
Hogarty Martin J died Dec 13, 1877 Aged 28
Hogarty Michael A died Apr 24, 1904 aged 46
Holbrook Henry Grant 1900 - 1976 Mary Collins 1898 - 1980
Holland Harold H
Holland Harold Herbert Sept 15, 1911 - Mar 1972 Anna Flynn
   Mar 22, 1911 - Dec 5, 1996
Holland John C Sept 15, 1917 - Jan 17, 1996 Mary E Sept 25,
   1914
Holland John C WWII

Hollenkamp Albert 1862 - 1941
Hollenkamp Father 1833 - 1881
Hollenkamp Genevieve 1895 - 1934
Hollenkamp Joseph 1891 - 1918
Hollenkamp Kate 1869 - 1897
Hollenkamp Laura 1866 - 1925
Hollenkamp Mother 1839 - 1917
Holmes Anna Gertrude died Sept 18, 1943 Lina Tarleton died
        June 25, 1952
Holmes Belle died Aug 12, 1895
Holmes Ella Mae Mar 18, 1880 - Feb 25, 1944
Holmes, Kate died age 3 April 13, 1880
Holmes Edward died Jan 28, 1901
Jan 27, 1901   Leader
Edward A. Holmes, Jr., aged 32, and son of Mr. and Mrs. E.
        A. Holmes, died at the home of his parents.

Holmes Edward died Aug 12, 1914
Edward A. Holmes death certificate:
Parents: Rob. Holmes & Matilda Jenkins
Occupation: Picture frame business
Cause of death: Maligment Tumor
Born: May 10, 1846 Died: Aug 11, 1914
Informant: John Hanley

Holmes Eliza died Oct 28, 1901
Oct 28, 1901 Leader
Mrs. Linie Holmes T. Holmes, aged 53, wife of E.A. Holmes,
        died this morning at her residence on S. Broadway
        after an illness of ten months.

Holmes Lillie Mae 1907 - 1933
Holmes Matilda July 27, 1907
July 26, 1907 Leader
Mrs. Matilda Holmes died Friday morning at the residence of

her son, E. A. Holmes. She was in her 86th year and died from the infirmities of old age.

Holmes Robert C 1905 - 1923 Joseph M 1911 - 1923 Brothers
Hopper Grace E Feb 20, 1912 - Feb 29, 1968
Horan Elizabeth July 20, 1826 - Aug 1888
Horan Oct 1868 - Oct 31, 1882
Horan Jeremiah died Aug 5, 1872
Horan Elizabeth 1855 - 1933
Horan Ellen Jan 6, 1846 - Aug 20, 1923
Horan Philip 1888 - 1930
Horgan Denis 1876 - 1898
Horgan Mary Agnes 1878 - 1879
Horgan Patrick 1841 - 1922 Mary1849 - 1927
Horine B O 1860 - 1911 Elizabeth 1858 - 1943 J F Nelson
    1849 - 1894
Horine Elizabeth 1897 - 1975

Dec 26, 1910 Leader
The funeral services of Mrs. Elizabeth Horine took place at St.
    Paul's Catholic Church Monday morning. The burial
    followed in the Catholic Cemetery.

Horine Ella C Murphy 1867 - 1951 wife of Henry T Horine
Horine Frank E 1867 - 1938
Horine George J Apr 26, 1900 - June 11, 1979 Ruth Mainous
    Feb 15, 1909 - Jan 8, 1999
Horine George Patrick Apr 6, 1945 - Aug 4, 2004
Horine Henry T Apr 6, 1867 - Dec 18, 1935
Horine John 1822 - 1905 Bessie Gannon 1831 - 1910
Horine John died Oct 1886 aged 74 yrs
Horine John G June 7, 1897 - Oct 19, 1978
Horine Joseph T 1889 - 1918 died on U S S Hancock
Horine Mary A 1893 - 1973
Horine William E 1891 - 1910

Horine William M 1858 - 1926
Horn Josephine Clifford 1898 - 1942 wife of W Earl
Horn W Earl 1888 - 1944
Horrell Floyd Edwin May 26, 1926 - Jun 27, 1994 WWII
   Korea
Horrell Mary Frances McCarthy 1907 - 1941
Hoskins Mary E July 3, 1892 - Nov 22, 1985
Hoskins Robert J July 20, 1961
Hostetter John William May 1, 1934 - July 1, 2008 Ann S
   Webb July 12, 1939
Houlihan H Joseph Aug 24, 1920
Houlihan Edmund died Feb 8, 1895 aged 65 yrs his wife Bee
   died May 10 1909 aged 76
Feb 8, 1895   Leader
Edmond Houlihan died suddenly at his home this morning. He
   was 66 and was born in Tipperary, Ireland.

Houlihan Edward 1855 illegible
Houlihan Edward T July 11, 1885 - May 22, 1937
Houlihan Elizabeth Callaway May 28, 1922
Houlihan Ethel Carr 1893 - 1987
Houlihan George E Dec 25, 1929 - Feb 16, 1985
Houlihan Harry S Nov 6, 1892 - Apr 14, 1948 Dora R Sept 25,
   1896 - Oct 11, 1987
Houlihan John J 1888 - 1915
Houlihan John J Jr. Nov 19, 1912 - Sept 15, 1978
Houlihan Lucille died Jan 10, 1946
Houlihan Mary died 1914 Catherine died 1921 William
   Shanahan
Houlihan Mary C Aug 23, 1931 - May 3, 2009
Houlihan Mathew 1790 - Jan 8, 1872 Daniel died Aug 4, 1869
   John died Dec 1, 1869 Timothy died July 1872
Houlihan Maysie Hillenmeyer Sept 27, 1883 - Apr 10, 1969
   Wife of Edward L Houlihan
Hovekamp Nancy Ausherman Jan 12, 1951

Howard Ann Allender 1929 - 2005 wife of John Heafey
    Howard
Howard Edward H 1898 - 1954
Howard George W 1860 - 1937
Howard Julian J 1894 - 1953
Howard Molly Simms 1926 - 1994 wife of Julian J Howard Jr.
Howard Norine Heafey 1894 - 1959 wife of Julian J. Howard
Huckle Carrol Bertram died Jan 23, 1964
Huckle Ella D Mahoney died Feb 20, 1971

May 12, 1908 Lexington Herald
The funeral services of Thomas Huckle will be held at St.
    Paul's Catholic Church this morning at 10:30 o'clock.
    The burial will follow in the Catholic Cemetery.

Hudson Alfred Estes Mar 1, 1901 - Aug 196? WWI
Huebener Edward H June 7, 1894 - Aug 29, 1968 WWI
Huff Oscar H 1924 - 1969 Marjorie W 1925
Huges James J Mar 19, 1856 - Apr 14, 1888
Hughes A Layman Feb 3, 1905 - Apr 19, 1986
Hughes Alex M 1880 - 1949
Hughes B Frank Feb 22, 1883 - Sept 12, 1973
Hughes Charles H died Sept 25, 1947
Hughes Elizabeth C Mar 12, 1893 - Oct 2, 1984
Hughes Elizabeth Conley 1883 - 1953 wife of Alex M Hughes
Hughes Elizabeth W Aug 18, 1902 - Aug 22, 1990
Hughes Helen H Jan 20, 1916 - Apr 29, 1982
Hughes James Carl Nov 30, 1935 - Dec 16, 1970
Hughes Pauline A Apr 22, 1910 - May 15, 1943

Apr 30, 1906 Leader
Peter Hughes, 33, died April 23 at St. Joseph's Hospital of
    consumption. Burial in Catholic Cemetery.

Hughes Robert H Oct 29, 1862 - June 21, 1935

Hukill Mary 1857 - 1911 wife of Eugene Hukill
Hukill Thomas A 1884 - 1908
Hungate Marvin Lee Feb 4, 1907 - Oct 13, 199? Hurley Mary
Oct 3, 1910 - Feb 20, 1988
Hungate Michael David 1946 - 1952 son of M L & Mary H
Hungate Teresa Ann Apr 28, 1968 - June 4, 1993 daughter of
John & Catherine
Hunnessy Rose 1860 - 1930
Hunt John H Apr 2, 1935 Ann L Oct 10, 1930
Hunt Margaret July 21, 1900
July 22, 1900 Morning Herald
Miss Margaret Hunt - The funeral Services were held at St.
Paul's Church Monday morning at 9 o'clock. The
interment will be in the Catholic Cemetery.

Hunter Katherine 1890 - 1984
Huston John Wills Sr. Aug 26, 1914 - May 4, 2003 Loraine R
July 27, 1915
Hutchinson Genevieve 1932 - 1996 Julian T Sr. ? - ? Geneva
Ray 1903 - 1989
Hutchinson Mary Gale 1932 - 1981 Charles Edward 1901 -
1965 Margaret Foley 1907 - 1997
Hutchison
Hutchison Albert Sayre June 3, 1920 - June 18, 1981
Hutchison Anna Belle Hamilton Mar 5, 1911 - Dec 20, 1991
Hutchison Charles Richard Oct 30, 1934 - Apr 26, 1935
Hutchison Elizabeth Jan 17, 1906 - Oct 30, 1990 Bridget Dec
29, 1865 - May 20, 1935 Anna Aug 19, 1907 - Sept 20,
1992
Hutchison George Perry Dec 21, 1903 - Nov 21, 1973 Sarah
Golden May 24, 1912 - Jan 15, 1998
Hutchison Joseph E 1924 - 1965
Hutchison Sarah C Sayre Dec 2, 1880 - Feb 28, 1959
Hyde William 1882
Ibershoff Robert E June 24, 1917 - Nov 15, 1968 Eunice M

Mar 28, 1926 - Mar 15, 2007 married Feb 17, 1947
Infant of C E R and R W R 1892
Irwin Lawrence M July 12-18, 1969 Alfred John 1910 - 1969
Irwin Mary Rita Q 1918 - 2004 John 1939 - 1984
Isabelle Unknown
Isola John M 1853 - 1929
Isola Joseph 1822 - 1886
Isola Loretta 1825 - 1913
Isola Louise 1870 - 1910
Jacina Mary M July 29, 1891 - Aug 26, 1972
Jackson James Ora June 4, 1932 - May 6, 2003 Patricia Kelley
      Dec 12, 1931
Jackson Richard Land Jr. July 4, 1926 - June 14, 2009
      Madeline Rhodus Dec 1, 1927 married Oct 20, 1946
Jackson Richard Land Jr. July 4, 1926 - June 14, 2009 WWII
Jacobs Anna Crawley May 6, 1890 - Feb 29, 1984
Jacobs William 1870 - 1938 Mary C 1875 - 1949
Jacobs William W 1904 - 1986 Jessamine F 1913 - 1959
Jacoby Allison Ray Sept 30, 1978 Our Guardian Angel
Jacoby Margaret Louise Oct 18, 1948 daughter of A W & H N
James 1885 - 1893 Anna M 1887 - 1889 Shea area
Jefferson J R (Jack) 1914 - 1992 Marisue 1924 - 1962
Jefferson Margaret D Oct 14, 1921 - July 21, 1989
Jenkins Hester V 1888 - 1966
Jensen Arthur F 1913 - 1974

Jan 21, 1896 Morning Herald
Little Maggie Jesup laid to rest
The Funeral of the child took place from St. Paul's Catholic
      Church at 3 o'clock yesterday afternoon, and the
      mangled little body was laid to rest in the Catholic
      Cemetery

Jeter Christopher Corey Aug 8, 1960 - Aug 21, 2001
Jeter Ella Mae May 7, 1907 - Sept 14, 1977 Jessie Beaumont

June 15, 1884 - Aug 9, 1975

Jeter Ellen Bernadette July 18, 1946 - July 22, 2008

Jeter James L Oct 7, 1941 - Aug 24, 1998

Jeter Jenny Lind Mar 30, 1944

Jeter John Bernard Sr. Mar 12, 1928 - Apr 24, 2007

Jeter John Duncan Oct 14, 1888 - Mar 13, 1954

Jeter John B Mar 12, 1928 - Apr 24, 2007 Dottie Nov15, 1936

Jeter Joseph Anthony 1936 - 1990

Jeter Lawrence 1952 - Betty 1952 - 2006 Lawrence T II 1972
     - 1976

Jeter Leonard Francis Apr 3, 1843 - June 20, 1904 Agnes
     Walsh July 22, 1854 - July 27, 1934

June 21, 1904 Morning Herald

The funeral services of L F Jeter who died yesterday morning
     at 11 o'clock after a lingering illness, will take place at
     St. Paul's Catholic Church this afternoon at 2 o'clock.
     Interment in Catholic Cemetery.

Jeter Leonard M Dec 5, 1934 - Jan 23, 1985

Jeter Mary Russell Michelle Oct 5, 1933

Jeter Mathew R Aug 26, 1887 - May 23, 1913 Grace C Feb
     17, 1887 - Aug 27, 1976

Jeter Philip Ray June 28, 1940 - Apr 24, 2001

Jeter Theodore J Jan 18, 1922 - Dec 19, 1986 WWII

Jeter William A Jr. Aug 15, 1929 - Nov 10, 1960

Jeter William Anthony Jr. Aug 15, 1929 - Nov 10, 1960
     Patricia Jeter DuBois Oct 20, 1930 - Apr 11, 1978

Jeter William Anthony Sr. Mar 21, 1896 - July 4, 975 Thelma
     Harnett Aug 8, 1907 - Mar 28, 1983

Jeter William T Jan 8, 1914 - Jan 10, 1949 WWII

Jobe

John Unknown

John 1869 - 1937 Magee area

John H Lusse area

John Sanlon Aug 1864 - Mar 26, 1901

Johnson Ann Looney Oct 21, 1926 - May 11, 1978
Johnson Bert Edward Feb 18, 1912 - Aug 10, 1993 Catherine
    Cecila May 23, 1910 - Aug 16, 1994 In Gods Care
Johnson Charles A (Moose) Jan 13, 1931 - Mar 6, 1990
Johnson Germaine Villeminot Sept 25, 1904 - May 13, 1965
Johnson Murphy Hutton
Johnson Robert Edward July 19, 1932 - Jan 28, 2002
Johnson William J Feb 20, 1896 - Feb 4, 1969 WWI
Jones Earl 1905 - 19 Margaret 1904 - 1945
Jones John G May 17, 1909 - Aug 10, 1971 Bridget S Nov 22,
    1912 - Nov 22, 1982
Jones Louise Amato June 3, 1928 - Oct 12, 2007
Jones Madeleine B June 28, 1923 - Aug 10, 1974
Jones Margaret W 1876 - 1964
Jones Marvin Francis May 4, 1925 - Mar 12, 2003 Lillian
    May, May 2, 1926
Jones Nowlin N Nov 23, 1924 - July 12, 2002 WWII
Jones Patricia Marie Feb 26, 1962 - Mar 5, 1983
Jones Susan Aug 5, 1953 - Dec 21, 1989
Jorbes Mary Louise Greenbaum May 3, 1918 - Nov 22, 1976
Jordan John F Sept 14, 1941 Peggy Sept 17, 1943
Jordan John H 1875 - 1939 Cecilia Murray 1875 - 1935
    William C 1907 - 1978 Helen Johnson 1909 - 1994
Jordan John W 1909 - 1970 Thelma F 1913 - 1995
Jordan Thomas Murray 1915 - 1970 Florence Waller 1914 -
    1978
Jordon William Lyle 1906 - 1975 Katherine Stewart 1909 -
    1968
Joseph Amon W Feb 12, 1935 - Nov 11, 1981
Joseph Arnold W Feb 14, 1921 Margaret M June 18, 1919 -
    June 17, 1989
Joseph Edward W Mar 25, 1930 - Sept 5, 1990
Joseph Srahym died 1913
Joseph Victoria 1910 - 1997 Wilfred A 1897 - 1982
Joudeh Farid I Feb 4, 1921 - July 5, 1980

Jouden Jaudalaiel 1912 - 1984
Joyce Frank M Feb 25, 1934

Apr 6, 1906 Leader
James C. Joyce, 75, died April 3 of pneumonia. Burial in
    Catholic Cemetery

Joyce Michael J 1861 - 1943 Nellie H 1875 - 1959

July 24, 1908 Lexington Herald
Body of Rota Kafoury is laid to rest in Catholic Cemetery in
    this City.

Kaiser Annie died at St. Joseph Hospital 1894
Kaiser George 1884
Kalaus
Kalaus 1888 - 1945
Kalaus Candioto
Kalaus Gertrude 1868 - 1943
Kalaus Joseph 1868 - ?
Kalaus Joseph 1893 - 1943
Kane
Kane Feb 23, 1886 - aged 28 yrs
Kane Eddie 1881 - 1912
Kane James R May 6, 1913 - Mar 6, 1996 Graham Frederick
    L Dec 27, 1921
Kane John and Anne Family
Kane John F May 28, 1856 - Feb 19, 1887
Kane Mary Sept 25, 1833 - Nov 17, 1884 wife of Thomas
May 17, 1900 Morning Herald
Thomas Kane - accidentally killed at Frankfort by James
        Robertson. Funeral Services were held at St. Paul's
        Catholic Church Wednesday morning and he was
        buried at the Catholic Cemetery.

Karon Jan 1919 - 2008 World famous Violinist and Violin
	Maker
Kashem 1883 - 192?
Kayse Raymond Sept 12, 1901 - Jan 1971 Margaret S Jan
	1905 - Sept 1981 Anita S Oct 16, 1928
Kearns Henry 1834 - 1902
Kearney Andrew T 1905 - 1960 Lora D 1908 - 1979
Kearney Andy 1889 - 1968 Laura Seaman 1893 - 1971 Rest In
	Peace
Kearney Ann M 1927 - 1977
Kearney Barbara West Jan 6, 1911 - July 10, 1980
Kearney Eliza Apr 12, 1832 - Oct 1, 1908 wife of John, Henry
	June 5, 1866 - Mar 4, 1889

Jan 21, 1909 Lexington Herald
Services for Frank Kearney will be held tomorrow at 9 o'clock
	at St. Paul's Church. Interment will be in the Catholic
	Cemetery.

Jan 21, 1909 Leader
A long procession of sorrowing friends followed the body of
	Frank Kearney, the popular prescription clerk, who
	died, Wednesday, to its last resting place Friday in the
	Catholic Cemetery.

Kearney James R Dec 4, 1906 - Mar 12, 1994 Marietta H Apr
	15, 1909 - Nov 21, 1999
Kearney James 1839 - 1912 Anna 1845 - 1890 Thomas 1865 -
	1912 Mary 1898 - 1919
Kearney John 1824 - 1904 Ann Hart 1822 - 1908
Kearney John died Dec 3, 1884 aged 51 years
Kearney John E 1893 - 1954 Marie Carlin 1894 - 1966
Kearney John H 1865 - 1943 Annie E 1868 - 1949
Kearney Lena Keller 1885 - 1970
Kearney Mary July 1878 aged 15 J Rodger July 28, 1858 - Jan

22, 1928

Kearney Michael W 1898 - 1947 Margaret O'Neil 1891 -
1979

Kearney Susan Nov 13, 1878 aged 35 years wife of Patrick
Kearney

Kearney Tillie 1868 - 1952

Kearney William Thomas 1875 - 1932

Kearney William Thomas 1926 - 1991

Kearns

Kearns Charlotte 1834 - 1914

Kearns Charlotte E 1861 - 1909

Kearns David 1866 - 1918

Kearns Henry 1834 - 1902

Apr 18, 1902   Leader

The funeral of Henry Kearns took place this afternoon at his
residence on North Limestone Street. Burial in the
Catholic Cemetery in this city. He died Wednesday
evening at St. Joseph's Hospital of pneumonia. He
leaves a wife and four children. He was at one time
one of the wealthiest men in the city.

Kearns JAS P 1867 - 1927

Kearns Katie C 1858 - 1906

Dec 27, 1906   Leader

The funeral of Miss Katie C. Kearns who died at the home of
her brother, James P. Kearns, on Tuesday was held
Thursday morning at St. Paul's Church, the interment
being in the family lot in the Catholic Cemetery.

Kearns Margaret E 1897 - 1944 Margaret T 1865 - 1933 Mary
K Haefling 1895 - 1947

Kearny Sept 12, 1861 - 1932

Oct 3, 1908 Lexington Herald

Mrs. Eliza Kearney, who died Thursday at her home on the

Ironworks pike, was buried Saturday morning in the family lot in the Catholic Cemetery.

Keating James 1829 - 1912
Keating Mary 1821 - 1906 wife of James
Keating Mary E Nov 15, 1865 - Nov 24, 1954
Keating Paul J July 1885 - Oct 15, 1905
Keefe Ruth M Nov 17, 1917 - Nov 18, 1957
Keefe William 1866 - 1943 Elizabeth 1869 - 195?
Keenan
Keenan Jennie S 1862 - 1928
Keenan Joseph M 1845 - 1911
Keene Anna Mae July 15, 1925 - Jan 17, 1971 James H Oct
    17, 1919 - June 20, 1978
Keene Foley Ella Keene Sept 9, 1889 - Dec 19, 1977
    Marguerite Keene Aug 9, 1922 - Mar 28, 1997
    Margaret Foley Apr 27, 1886 - Feb 20, 1979
Kehrt Esther Gormley Apr 11, 1906 - Aug 2, 1979 Joseph
    Marshall Jan 25, 1908 - Dec 20, 1987
Kehrt George Thomas II Oct 5-7, 1965
Keith Thomas A Jan 4, 1891 - Feb 24, 1949
Keith William P Jan 16, 1885 - Nov 9, 1950 Joseph J Mar 8,
    1888 - July 9, 1961
Keller
Keller May 12, 1903 - Apr 16, 1927
Keller Edward Aug 20, 1927 - Sept 13, 1968
Keller Edward C 1861 - 1902
Dec 12, 1902   Leader
The body of Edward C. Keller arrived in Lexington on a
    special train consisting of a baggage car and four
    coaches, over the L. & N. road from Paris this
    afternoon, and was buried in the Catholic Cemetery
    shortly after its arrival.

Keller Florence Doyle 1921 - 2009 wife of John B

Keller Fred Marion July 14, 1918 - Dec 7, 1991 Ruth Connor
Mar 21, 1920
Keller George Jan 30, 1860 - June 22, 1945 Barbara July 19,
1859 - Jan 23, 1945
Keller George A 1882 - 1979 Rose M Fister 1884 - 1949
Keller George M Feb 4, 1898 - Feb 11, 1981 Cora Phelps Jan
12, 1901 - Apr 23, 1985
Keller Gertrude Dec 21, 1889 - Apr 1, 1963
Keller Helen Marie May 12, 1912 - Nov 7, 1960 J. Raymond
Jan 15, 1907 - Oct 31, 1999
Keller James K Sept 29, 1904 - May 31, 1989 Janet L Sept 21,
1906 - Dec 7, 1967
Keller James P Mar 3, 1875 - Mar 20, 1958 Josephine C Mar
8, 1877 - Oct 2, 1970
Keller John 19?? - Sept 1920
Keller John A 1838 - 1907
Keller John A July 4, 1925 - Sept 6, 1978
Keller John Joseph 1892 - 1963 Mary Shea 1895 - 1977
Keller John B 1920 - 1988
Keller Julian J 1914 - 1991 Ruby R 1921 - 1981
Keller Kimberly Ann Oct 20 - Nov 6, 1977 Daughter of
Michael and Ann
Keller Louise Mar 5, 1927 - Aug 21, 1993
Keller Margaret Julie 1916 - 1930
Keller Mary Eleanor Oct 6, 1908 - Jan 5, 1985
Keller Mary J 1879 - 1964
Keller Mary Scott Aug 17, 1881 - Dec 27, 1966
Keller Mrs. Edw C 1865 - 1931
Keller Nell Banahan 1890 - 1983
Keller Rev Louis Scott June 5, 1906 - Nov 6, 1934 Ordained
in Rome Dec 8, 1932
Keller Rev Theodore Feb 28, 1924 Ordained Oct 20, 1946
Keller Thekla Roth 1848 - 1927
Keller Theodore Aug 13, 1890 - Oct 30, 1974
Keller William Jan 20, 1891 - Oct 15, 1946 Mary Haney Apr

1, 1890 - Jan 26, 1935
Keller William Leo 1892 - 1940
Kelley Agnes Pierce Mar 27, 1893 - June 28, 1963
Kelley Catherine Smith 1891 - 1958
Kelley Elizabeth Smith 1917 - 1976
Kelley Frank J Aug 15, 1907 - Mar 2, 1995 Adelaide Bosau
    Nov 16, 1909 - Feb 27, 2002
Kelley James W Jr. 1891 - 1939
Kelley John Anthony June 20, 1890 - Sept 29, 1977
Kelley Mary A Dec 24, 1866 - Feb 25, 1947
Kelley Michael Sept 29, 1851 - Dec 18, 1919
Kelley Richard W 1900 - 1932
Kelley Rose Punch Oct 9, 1908 - Mar 11, 1944
Kelly Clement F Sr. Feb 18, 1889 - Aug 14, 1963 Flora N Aug
    18, 1895 - Mar 19, 1978
Kelly Harry 1888 - 1969 Susan 1890 - 1972

June 29, 1914 Leader
The 3-year-old son of Mr. and Mrs. J. M. Kelly, who died at
    the Good Samaritan hospital yesterday afternoon, was
    buried this morning in the family lot in the Catholic
    Cemetery.

Kelly John B 1860 - 1893
Kelly John B Oct 25, 1860 - May 16, 1893

Nov 28, 1913   Leader
Mr. John P. Kelly, of Covington, Ky., died in that city on
    Wednesday evening. The body will arrive in this city
    Saturday morning and be taken immediately to the
    Catholic Cemetery for interment.

Kelly Joseph 1901 son of John M & M
Kelly Lucy L Murphy Jan 30, 1942 wife of J Frank Kelly

Feb 21, 1905 Leader
Mrs. Margaret Kelly died at St. Joseph's Hospital Monday
afternoon. Mrs. Kelly was the step-mother of Mrs.
James McKenna, Jr., of this city. The funeral services
were held at St. Paul's Church Tuesday morning and
the internment was in the Catholic Cemetery.

Kelly Mary Apr 21, 1921 aged 72 years
Kelly Mary Galvin 1860 - 1909
Kelly Richard T Feb 11, 1914 - Aug 1967
Kennard Cliff D 1886 - 1957
Kennard Florence Miller 1890 - 1954 wife of Cliff D
Kennedy Bernard Apr 20, 1908 - Apr 2, 1965
Kennedy Ellen Heafey died Sept 28, 1921
Kennedy Lawrence E Oct 22, 1884 - Nov 9, 1916
Kennedy Louise B Apr 16, 1910 - Apr 13, 1968 Mullanne O B
July 11, 1903 - Nov 10, 1971
Kenney Andrew Sept 20, 1863 - Jan 5, 1937
Kenney Edward died Sept 23, 1881 aged 73 yrs. Bridget died
May 16, 1899 aged 79 yrs
Kenney Gertrude Marie 1889 - 1973
Kenney Michael Aug 10, 1848 - Sept 20, 1876
Kenny James Apr 29, 1880 - Feb 25, 196?
Kenny John 1886 - 1961
Kenton Simon 1960 - 1961 son of Gordon & Eleanore
Kerigan Edward Died July 10, 1881
Kerney Mary died Jan 16, 1872 wife of Pheolox Kerney
Kerrigan John 1860 - May 10, 1881
Kertickles Peter J 1913 - 1962 Gertrude M 1910 - 2001
Kesheimer Barbara 1839 - 1921
Kesheimer Juliana 1871 - 1900
Kesheimer Junaita F 1895 - 1983
Kesheimer Myrtle V 1891 - 1950
Kesheimer Peter F 1868 - 1930

Kesler Virginia Dec 7, 1965
Kessler Clarence A July 27, 1906 - Sept 18, 1983 Margaret K
    Sept 25, 1908 - Apr 15, 2000
Ketron William M Dec 13, 1888 - Sept 25, 1945 Virginia Cox
    July 31, 1901 - Jan 6, 1986
Ketterer George Joseph Jan 22, 1930 - Apr 23, 2006 Judith
    Leigh Dec 15, 1935 - May 29, 2003
Kilcoyne John F Sept 1904 - Sept 3, 194? WWII
Kilcoyne Patrick W 1865 - 1949 Rose C 1873 - 1918
Kilcoyne William Aug 22, 1892 - July 28, 1957 WWI
Kimmins Edward F Aug 8, 1904 - May 18, 1970 Charlotte M
    Mar 20, 1904 -Apr 23, 1990
King Alice Young 1885 - 1937
King Anna M 1895 - 1981
King Ben H Feb 1, 1888 - June 15, 1937
King F S Apr 23, 1887 - Nov 7, 1962
King Gus his wife Hattie May 1, 189? Oct 20, 19??
King Stanley M Jan 28, 1900 - Mar 17, 1968 Louise W Jan 9,
    1900 - Apr 6, 1987
Kinkead Mary L Gormely
Kinnaird Anna Pearl Chasteen 1922 - 1988 George Holtby
    1922 -
Kinnaird Eileen W 1915 - 2001
Kinnaird Frances H 1882 - 1958
Kinnaird William L 1916 - 1972
Kinnard Mary Banahan 1859 - 1933
Kirby
Kirby Gertrude Mary Feb 28, 1985
Kirby John Alonzo July 8, 1878 - Oct 12, 1918
Kirby Kate Slavin died Sept 22, 1939
Kirby Lillian Mary Jan 13, 1898 - Oct 9, 1918
Kirby Lloyd June 22, 1852 - Oct 26, 1926
Kirby Minerva Marguerite Aug 4, 1964
Kirgasner John Oct 8, 1844 - Jan 2, 1925 Anna Mar1842 -
    Nov 1924

Kirk McCullough Mary 1906

Kirk Taylor Whitney July 9, 2006

Klair Barbara Feb 27, 1839 - July 13, 1899

Klair Henry M Sept 22, 1876 - July 4, 1911

Klair John H Mar 25, 1869 - July 29, 1904

Klair William Frederick Dec 14, 1874 - Oct 29, 1937 Mary
    Slavin Feb 1, 1873 - June 29, 1945

Klarenaar Wm Apr 8, 1894 aged 59 years

Kleier Clarence R Feb 22, 1898 - Nov 1, 1958 Martha Oakley
    Apr 26, 1902 - Dec 3, 1977

Kleintank Minnie E Aug 5, 1872 - Feb 7, 1900 and our baby
    died Jan 10, 1900 wife of Harry F. Kleintank

Kloecker Carl F Mar 19, 1899 - July 1984

Kloecker Catherine Heidkamp Feb 13, 1869 - May 9, 1964
    wife of John Kloecker

Kloecker Esther Munger Apr 29, 1895 - Dec 4, 1980 wife of
    John H Kloecker

Kloecker John 1888 - 1981

Kloecker John H Nov 9, 1896 - June 14, 1973 son of John and
    Catherine

Kloecker Martha Elizabeth Minihan Mar 4, 1907 - Apr 18,
    1995

Kluska Nettie 1898 - 1974

Knapp Josephine Tucker Feb 3, 1842 - Nov 26, 1910 wife of
    Charles

Knight James W Apr 4, 1837 - July 14, 1873

Knight John C Mar 14, 1859 - Sept 29, 1883

Koester James 1920

Kokinda Andrew Dec 1919 - ? Katherine Apr 1926

Koonz Abbe Mae Mar 27, 1911 - Nov 6, 1998

Koonz George June 30, 1849 - June 28, 1917

Koonz Hubert J Nov 7, 1914 - Feb 5, 1990

Koontz John S III Aug 4, 1932 - Feb 26, 1983

Koonz Josephine O'Neil Jan 8, 1881 - Jan 5, 1978

Koonz Leonard J Aug 9, 1919 - Jan 14, 1985 US Navy WWII

Koonz Louis J Dec 28, 1876 - Sept 11, 1934
Koonz Louis J Jr. June 7, 1909 - Mar 17, 1966
Koonz Pauline June 8, 1879 - Apr 12, 1954
Koonz Rosa 1853 - Jan 11, 1913
Jan 12, 1913 Leader
The funeral of Mrs. Rosa Koonz will be held at St. Paul's
    Church at 9 o'clock Monday morning, followed by
    interment in the Catholic Cemetery.

Kopser Frederick J May 10, 1912 - June 22, 2002 Anna C Feb
    18, 1915 - July 5, 2005
Koroluck Edward Jan 8, 193? - May 12, 200? Lillian Dec 1,
    1932 - Oct 11, 2001
Kotmair Doris M Sept 11, ? - Sept 1987
Kowalske Leo B 1880 - 1968 Lucy O 1883 - 19 Walker
    Prudence K 1908 - 1979 William J 1901 - 1974
Kreis William James 1874 - 1943 Gertrude Matlack 1887 -
    1953
Krieger Kathryn M Jan 3, 1972
Krieger Matilda Apr 13, 1935
Krom Kervyn Trumbull WWII
Kurre Mary Ann Jan 29, 1883 - Nov 12, 1953
Labate Marie McC Sayer 1898 - 1969
LaBonte Francis X 1902 - 1977 Winifred S 1906 - 1984
Lacey Catherine died Mar 10, 1897 wife of P C Lacey Mary
    Ellen Lacey Dec 27, 1872 - June 21, 1890
Lacey David Mar 9, 1867 - Nov 8, 1893 Thomas F Sept 13,
    1864 - Sept 7, 1894
Lacey John William 1905 - 1966
Lacey Mary Clark Jan 18, 1938 wife of William
Lacey P C & J
Lacey Patrick Jr. Mat 21, 1865 - Oct 26, 1893 M J

April 11, 1904 Morning Herald
Patrick Lacey, formerly of Lexington, was killed in a collision

at Kansas City. Burial in Catholic Cemetery Tuesday.

Ladd Donald Alan Oct 7, 1945 - June 3, ?
Ladd Eugene Guy Aug 27, 1911 - Sept 24, 1986
Laden Katherine M 1899 - 1989

July 3, 1904 Morning Herald
The funeral for little Nellie Laden who was killed by a street
　　car will be this afternoon at 5 o'clock in the Catholic
　　Cemetery.

Laden Van G 1866 - 1936 Bridget C 1865 - 1918
Lalley E Barnett Jan 22, 1905 - July 26, 1965 Evelyn Johnson
　　Apr 6, 1905 - Dec 12, 1988
Lalley Edward L 1872 - 1948 Elizabeth N 1874 - 1933
Lambecin Rev Aug 1826 - 1895
Lancaster Edward Guedry 1913 - 1965
Lancaster John D 1871 - 1954 Anastasia H 1885 - 1949
Land Katherine Doyle died Mar 4, 1916 wife of George W
Langan Vincent J Mar 5, 1915 - Oct 10, 1968 Ruth W May
　　20, 1920 - 1988
Langan Vincent J Mar 5, 1915 - Oct 10, 1968 WWII
Lapierre Elizabeth Jul 15, 1918 - Oct 15, 1979 Joseph Oct 28,
　　1921
Lapierre Eugene A 1887 - 1948 Winifred H Oct 30, 1884 -
　　Feb 25, 1981
Lapierre Eugene A 1887 - 1948 WWI
Larimore A L Larry June 20, 1909 - Dec 8, 1989 Edna
　　Watkins Feb 8, 1912 - Mar 24, 2006
Larimore Robert L Oct 28, 1939 - Oct 29, 2000 Phyllis M Aug
　　1, 1943 - Nov 1, 2006
Lario Frances Villeminot Jan 5, 1881 - Apr 8, 1969
Larkin Geo V May 23, 1906 - Apr 8, 1959
Larkin J W 1878 - 1956 Mary 1885 - 1976
Larkin Lee 1910 - 1914

Larkin Naldie Sarah Oct 26, 1918 - Apr 24, 2006
Lasher Charles William May 8, 1936 Helen Marie June 25,
    1941 - Aug 14, 1992
Lassen Manuel A Nov 1890 - Aug 5, 1960
Lassen Mary K July 30, 1893 - July 3, 1973

Nov 14, 1911 Leader
The funeral services of Miss Katherine Laudeman were held at
    St. Peter's Catholic Church Tuesday morning. The
    interment was in the family lot in the Catholic
    Cemetery.

Laughlin Bernard J July 15, 1838 - Oct 13, 1911
Laughlin James L 1890 - 1971 Mary Gleason 189? - 1954
Laughlin Katherine 1882 - 1962
Laughlin Mary O'Connor 1877 - 1963
Laughlin Mary Ruth Jan 25, 1843 - Apr 18, 1909
Lavery George 1856 - 1902
Nov 12, 1902 Morning Herald
The funeral service over the remains of Geo Lavery will be
    held at 9 o'clock at St. Paul's Church. The Burial will
    follow in the Catholic Cemetery.

Lavery John May 14, 1855 - May 14, 1899
Lavery Kate 1855 - 1936
Lavery Mary Aug 8, 1860 - Jan 15, 1915
Lavery Nellie Heafey 1893 - 1976
Lavery Patrick 1837 - July 3, 1896
Lavery William J 1890 - 9161
Lavin Annie 1864 - 1949
Lavin Annie B Oct 29, 1942
Lavin Catherine 1837 - 1906
Lavin Catherine 1900
Lavin Charles B 1870 - 1924
Lavin Cormar died May 22, 1877

Lavin Curtis L 1858 - 1928
Lavin Dr W J May 8, 1922
Lavin Elizabeth G 1868 - 1960
Lavin Jane died Nov 24, 1908
Nov 25, 1908 Leader
Miss Jane Lavin died at the home of her niece, Miss Mary
Brannin in Covington Tuesday, aged 92 years. The
body will be brought here Wednesday at noon over the
L & N Railroad for interment in the family lot in the
Catholic Cemetery.

Lavin John 1866 - 1906
Lavin Katherine J Feb 21, 1937
Lavin Margaret died Oct 23, 1908
Oct 25, 1908 Leader
The funeral services of Miss Margaret Lavin will be held at St.
Paul's Church Sunday afternoon. The interment will
follow in the family lot in the Catholic Cemetery.

Mar 8, 1910 Leader
Margaret, the five-days-old daughter of Dr. and Mrs. William
Lavin, died Tuesday morning at the home on the
Richmond pike. The burial will take place in the
family lot in the Catholic Cemetery Tuesday afternoon.

Lavin Mary M 1855 - 1888
Lavin Sara A July 30, 1943
Lavin Thomas 1820 - 1887
Lavin Thomas A May 22, 1950

Aug 6, 1904 Leader
Lew Lawes, one of the most popular and respected young men
of Lexington died late Friday of tuberculosis. The
funeral was held this afternoon at St. Paul's Catholic
Church and the interment will be in the Catholic

Cemetery.

Lawler Margaret Diamond Feb 28, 1885 - Feb 26, 1966
Lawler Margaret Furlong 1898 - 1934
Lawler Vincent Cassin Sr. 1892 - 1946
Learned Robert Carl July 29, 1959 - Aug 3, 1959
Lee Bobby G Dec 16, 1939 Geraldine E Mar 22, 1940 - Jan
    31, 1996 Sharon Ann Feb 1, 1961 - Sept 15, 1964
    Michael Ray Aug 9, 1962 - June 26, 1981
Lee Donnie 1940 Ronnie 1940 - 1941 sons of T L & Edna Lee
Lee Helen Scully July 6, 1900 - Nov 16, 1937
Lee Zach W May 21, 1902 - Sept 15, 1989 Elizabeth Aug 4,
    1904 - Jan 29, 1998
Lehihan Margaret Mahoney Sept 10, 1897 - Mar 9, 1973 wife
    of William A Lenihan
Lehman Elizabeth Curry Aug 2, 1872 - Oct 10, 1970 Wife of
    Joseph A
Lehman Joseph A Aug 8, 1871 - Dec 20, 1941
Leigh Ben A 1877 - 1929
Leitner Anton 1891 - 1953 Josefine 1892 - 1976
Lenahan Edward May 6, 1853 - Dec 11, 1918 Frances E Jan
    29, 1847
Lenihan James W Feb 13, 1923 - Aug 28, 1971
Lenihan Lodema (Peggy) July 25, 1915 - Mar 16, 1984
Lenihan William A May 6, 1895 - Oct 27, 1942
Lentini Frank A Jan 15, 1910 - Nov 24, 1965
Lenz Bernard J 1889 - 1933
Lenz Oma S 189? - 1936
Lester Charles K Dec 22, 1907 - June 6, 1950
Lester Frances Fitzgerald 1908 - 1986
Liebermann Donald L Jr. 1943 - 1998 Anna C 1911 - 1974
Liebermann Lina K 1916 - 1992 Donald L 1916 - 2004
Lightner Mary N Jan 30, 1896 - Nov 19, 1945 Alvin W Aug
    27, 1885 - Dec 20, 1967
Ligibel Josephine July 27, 1898 - Jan 4, 1971

Lilly Clyde 1916 - 1968 Toy W 1916
Lilly Jack E Jan 28, 1925 - July 16, 1992
Lilly Larry Timothy Sept 8, 1952 - Aug 30, 1971 Joseph
    Ronald Jan 17, 1858 - Mar 2, 1982
Lilly Roy E July 26, 1891 - Aug 5, 1960 Lucy J Feb 5, 1891 -
    Jan 25, 1931
Lilly Roy T Jr. Jan 1, 1917 - Aug 23, 1940
Linsey Tyshae Marie Jan 27, 1993
Livingston Harold C May 2, 1912 - Sept 8, 1960 Kathleen M
    Mar 15, 1913 - Jan 6, 1970
Lloyd James J 1977 - 1913
Lloyd Katie Knight Sept 1892 - Nov 19, 1980 Robert L July
    13, 1884 - Mar 22, 1967
Lloyd Mary 1841 - 1932

Apr 26, 1902 Morning Herald
The remains of Willie Lloyd, The sixteen-year-old son of Mrs.
    Maggie Lillis, arrived in this city yesterday and will be
    interred in the Catholic Cemetery this morning.

Lock Katherine died Jan 31, 1865
Locklin Andrew 1862 - 1925
Locklin Andrew 1896 - 1984
Locklin Anna Theresa 1895 - 1967
Locklin Catherine 1888 - 1915
Locklin Charles W 1890 - 1963
Locklin Elizabeth 1893 - 1923
Locklin Kate Cuilfoyle 1864 - 1957
Locklin Mary Agnes 1898 - 1960
Logan Bridget McAllister1838 - 1913 Wife of Michael Logan
Logan Michael 1843 - 1917
Logsdon David S June 1, 1988 - Feb 18, 1990 Susan M Jan
    22, 1937 - May 25, 2009
Long William J 1894 - 1949 Kathryne G 1894 - 1970
Looney William E 1866 - 1923

Lorenz Henry T Dec 27, 1887 - Feb 21, 1913
Louisignau Ray 1916 - 1982 Denice1915 - 1959
Lowery Vernon M Sept 9, 1938 - Aug 13, 2004 Judi M Nov
19, 1942
Luanon Annie Nov 7, 1868 - Jan 16, 1946
Luby Carroll 1901 - 1918
Luby John J 1871 - 1929
Luby John James Dec 17, 1902 - July 31, 1994 Malka
Williams Dec 19, 1908 - Sept 21, 2002
Luby Julia G 1874 - 1940
Luby Michael 1808 - 1888 Catherine Fox 1825 - 1897
Lucier Joseph A July 17, 1940 - June 16, 2006 Frances A July
31, 1941 married Aug 25, 1962
Luigart Dorothy Fitzgerald 1904 - 1978
Luigart Elizabeth
Luigart Flora
Luigart Francis D 1873 - 1920
Luigart Frank
Luigart Fred 1865 - 1916
Luigart Fred W Jr. May 20, 1928 - Oct 28, 1973
Luigart Fred William 1905 - 1980
Luigart George Apr 8, 1862 - Apr 25, 1906
April 27, 1906 Leader
The funeral of Mr. George Luigart, who died at his home, on
Wednesday night of an attack of kidney trouble, was
held at St. Paul's Church Friday morning and the
interment was in the family lot in the Catholic
Cemetery.

April 30, 1906 Leader
George Luigart, 43, died April 25 of heart and kidney dropsy.
Burial in Catholic Cemetery.

Luigart Gust
Luigart Jack A 1924 - 1988

Luigart John
Luigart John A 1899 - 1970
Luigart John F 1850 - ? Elizabeth 1856 - 1937 Josephine L
    McGuff 1880 - 1934
Luigart Joseph A Dec 2, 1894 - Apr 2, 1956
Luigart Joseph Flora Frank Gusy
Luigart Josephine
Luigart Katherine Slavin Apr 16, 1896 - Apr 12, 1983
Luigart Laurence Emmett 1900 - 1966
Luigart Louise
Luigart Margaret
Luigart Mary F 1905 - 1981
Luigart Mollie 1865 - 1936
Luigart William
Luigart William 1875 - 1959 Margaret 1871 - 1953
Lusse Through The Mercy Of God May They Rest In Peace
Lusse Anna Mary nee Busse Jan 29, 1856 - Feb 28, 1937
Lusse Herman Bernard Mar 8, 1884 - Apr 27, 1951
Lusse J B Sept 30, 1849 - Mar 1, 1899
Lusse Jacob John Aug 27, 1888 - Nov 26, 1959
Lusse Johanna L July 20, 1890 - Dec 17, 1960
Lusse Margaret E Nov 16, 1893 - Jan 24, 1919
Luther 1853 - 19 illegible
Lyle Cloy V Oct 23, 1914 - Aug 10, 1995 Anita B Sallee Mar
    21, 1909 - Oct 28, 2005
Lynch Anna K Aug 4, 1875 - June 10, 1910

May 1, 1910 Leader
Miss Anna Lee Lynch died at her home on the Richmond pike
    Saturday afternoon after an illness of several weeks.
    The funeral services will be held at St. Peter's Church
    Monday morning and the interment will follow in the
    small family lot into the Catholic Cemetery.

Lynch Anna O Day 1897 - 1952 wife of Joseph B Lynch

Lynch Austin died Feb 16, 1939 Emma died Oct 22, 1934
Lynch Delia Feb 22, 1884 - Aug 5, 1982
Lynch Elizabeth died Oct 1, 1970
Lynch Elizabeth W Apr 20, 1933 - Aug 21, 1994
Lynch Daniel Family
Lynch James J Dec 1866 - Oct 6, 1944
Lynch Jane Marie May 21, 1921 - Aug 15, 1993
Lynch John Francis Oct 2, 1869 - Jan 14, 1942
Lynch John Joseph Feb 24, 1881 - Apr 28, 1965 Eva Hughes
    June 22, 1892 - Mar 27, 1979
Lynch Joseph B Sr. 1894 - 1958
Lynch Joseph A July 20, 1954 - Nov 8, 1995
Lynch Joseph B Jr. Mar 25, 192? - Oct 21, 1978
Lynch Michel 1862 - 1906
Oct 12, 1906   Leader
The body of Michael Lynch, 46 years of age, who died
    Thursday at his home near Eubanks, Ky., will arrive
    here Saturday morning. Mr. Lynch's death is the result
    of an accident with which he met while in the employ
    of his duties as section boss of the Q. & C. Road.

Lynch Michelle Kathleen June 26, 1963 - May 8, 1984
Lynch Patrick Joseph 1853 - 1928 Ann Donlan 1850 - 1939
Lynch Patrick Mar 17, 1831 - June 15, 1904 Bridget Walsh
    Mar 29, 1842 - Feb 8, 1905
June 16, 1904 Leader
Mr. Patrick Lynch died at his home at Brighton, this county
    Wednesday night, aged 73 years. Mr. Lynch was born
    in Ireland, but had been a resident of Fayette County
    for a great many years.

Feb 8, 1905 Leader
Mrs. Bridget Lynch died very suddenly Wednesday morning
    at her home near Brighton, this county, after an illness
    of only a few days. She was the wife of the late Patrick

Lynch and survived by four sons and two daughters.

Lynch William Doris Sept 18, 1928 - Dec 1970 WWII
Lynch William F Oct 28, 1938 - Jan 28, 1993
Lynch William J Oct 29, 1878 - Nov 20, 1951
Lynch William Michael June 22, 1959 - Aug 25, 1970
Lyons Katherine F Kitz Rasenfoss 1892 - 1987 wife of Albert
    S Lyons
Lyons Margaret 1832 - 1905
Lyons Margaret Wilson Mar 10, 1918 - May 4, 1967
Mabel Label
Mabellini Peter Nov 29, 1876 - Jan 26, 1944
Madden John E 1856 - 1929
Madden John E III 1929 - 1970
Madden Joseph M 1899 - 1932
Madden Joseph M Jr. 1932 - 2008
Madican Kathryn J Sept 25, 1893 - Oct 24, 1964
Madigan Ann 1831 - 1876
Madigan John W 1827 - 1877
Madigan John W 1881 - 1906
Madigan Mary 1855 - 1936 Matte E 1856 - 1929
Madigan Matte 1883 - 1907
Magee Alice 1881 - 1966
Magee Ella 1866 - 1945

Dec 18, 1905 Leader
Henry C. Magee, 69, died December 11 of pneumonia. Burial
    in Catholic Cemetery December 16.

Magee James 1883 - 1939
Magee James Oliver Apr 2, 1917 - Apr 26, 2000 Virginia
    McCarthy Dec 20, 1916 - Aug 10, 2008
Magee Joseph H Apr 9, 1871 - Oct 21, 1957
Magee Joseph Henry Dec 5, 1922 - Apr 12, 2006
Magee Margaret Apr 10, 1848 - Feb 24, 1905

Magee Rose Dodd 1881 - 1935
Magee Samuel C 1870 - 1915
Maggard Lillie A Feb 17, 1921 - Feb 24, 1972
Maguire Edward A July 20, 1916 - May 9, 1975 Mary K Mar
    12, 1918 - Jan 9, 1991
Maguire Edward J
Maguire John and James
Maguire John D died Mar 30, 1949 WWI
Maguire John Drummond Jun 5, 1911 - Sept 3, 1987 WWII
Maguire Kate Nunan 1849 - 1932
Maguire Lavena K Apr 22, 1892 - Dec 19, 1972
Maguire Mary E
Maguire Mary J 1883 - 1960
Maguire Philip F
Maguire Philip F Jr.
Maguire Thomas A Dec 23, 1890 - Jan 8, 1968 Superintendent
    Calvary Cemetery 31 yrs
Maguire Thomas F 1876 - 1948
Maguire Thomas J 1849 - 1933
Maguire Katie 1879 - 1972
Maher Bridget Thomas Nugent Aug 5, 1825 - Feb 11, 1915
Maher Christine L May 23, 1880 - Nov 23, 1975
Maher Mary Stewart Aug 9, 1934 William S May 17, 1935
Maher Timothy 1838 - 1913 Honora Houlihan 1853 - 1896
June 7, 1913   Leader
The funeral services of Mr. Timothy Maher will be in St.
    Paul's Roman Catholic Church Sunday afternoon and
    the interment will be in the Catholic Cemetery
    immediately following the services at the church.

Maher William E Mar 14, 1876 - Dec 29, 1944
Mahoney Besse

Oct 29, 1908 Leader
The funeral services of Charles Mahoney were at St. Paul's

Church Thursday afternoon. Burial followed in the family lot at the Catholic Cemetery.

Mahoney Daniel A 1875 - 1955
Mahoney Dennis Mary Shanahan Mary Patrick Mary Dore James
Mahoney Ella D Hukle died Feb 20, 1971
Mahoney Fannie B 1882 - 1956
Mahoney Infant of J T and M E
Mahoney J T Sept 1, 1866 - Jan 12, 1932
Mahoney J T Jr. Mar 27, 1908 - Aug 13, 1983
Mahoney James Grant Sr. Oct 26, 1921 - Apr 24, 1971 Ruth Stevewright June 9, 1924 - Sept 3, 2007
Mahoney Jerry S 1916 - 1931
Mahoney John Oct 15, 1860 - May 16, 1881
Mahoney Kathleen C died Oct 1927
Mahoney Margaret Flynn Oct 31, 1867 - Nov 3, 1941 wife of JT Mahoney
Mahoney Mary 1859 - 1946
Mahoney Mary B 1871 - 1943
Mahoney Michael
Mahoney Nell May 20, 1864 - June 5, 1951
Mahoney Patrick 1842 - 1910 Anna 1844 - 1926
Mahoney Thomas Tierney Feb 8, 1895 - Dec 15, 1948
Malias Louise McCarthy May 23, 1911 -Aug 16, 2001
Mallenny Jeannie Aug 8, 1859 - Mar 19, 1880
Maloney Richard & Mildred
Maloney Ella C Lenihan May 7, 1864 - May 18, 1953 wife of Patrick L
Maloney Gertrude June 22, 1885 - Dec 2, 1971
Maloney Henry E Jan 5, 1896 - Feb 10, 1977
Maloney John Sept 15, 1898
Maloney John A June 3, 1898 - March 19 WWI & WWII
Maloney Katherine Aug 25, 1893 - Sept 6, 1963
Maloney Lena Oct 25, 1889 - Aug 31, 1958

Maloney Nellie May 2, 1891 - Aug 13, 1956
Maloney Patrick July 22, 1902
Maloney Ruth S July 10, 1898 - Jan 11, 1980
Maloney William Bennett 1900 - ? WWII
Maloney William P Aug 7, 1923 - Jan 6, 1971
Manfredo Susan Nov 2-3, 1962 daughter of Francis &
    Carmela
Mangione Angeline July 29, 1900 - Mar 26, 1989
Mangione Anthony Feb 4, 1864 - June 30, 1935
Mangione Antonina Dec 23, 1871 - Apr 7, 1950
Mangione Joseph A Sept 28, 1910 - Sept 24, 1982
Mangione Mary C Barkman Apr 4, 1913 - Apr 14, 1936
Mangione Matthew A June 13, 1897 - Oct 10, 1985 Carmelina
    B Apr 20, 1902 - Feb 26, 1988
Mangione Natalie May 30, 1898 - Jan 2, 1993 Genevieve Aug
    6, 1914 - July 3, 2003
Mangione Phillip 1873 - 1952 Cosima 1879 - 1941 Joseph
    1909 - 1932
Mann Frank H 1886 - 1957 Ethel C 1894 - 1979
Manz William A Jr. July 9, 1959 - Oct 14, 1963
Marcellin Marion J Jan 26, 1896 - Feb 8, 1944
Marcellino Fannie Levin Aug 4, 1902 - May 1997
Marcum Floyd Thomas Jr. Mar 6, 1961 - May 27, 1963
Margaret Unknown
Margaret 1873 - 1941 Magee area
Marquis Lawrence O Mar 5, 1901 - Sept 18, 1958
Marquis Wyleen O Dec 2, 1900 - Oct 4, 1998
Marsh Thomas and Marsh Infant Sept 4, 1968
Marshall Ann Brittingham Dec 30, 1910 - Apr 11, 1990
Marshall Freddie L died June 6, 1888 infant son of Fred &
    Emma C. aged 22 months
Marshall James William Apr 1, 1910 - July 14, 2001
Martha Azizeh Mansour Dec 16, 1921 - July 14, 1993
Martha Ibrahim K June 5, 1933 - Dec 9, 1995 Naimeh I Dec
    13, 1924 married Dec 2, 1951

Martin Edmond Lewis July 29, 1918 - May 24, 1987 Mary
        Louise Weisenberger Jan 11, 1920 - June 4, 2004
Martin Michael Apr 23, 1954 - June 3, 1999
Martina Henry O Dec 15, 1904 - Nov 1, 1976 Ines S Feb 18,
        1908 - Feb 1, 1964
Mary Unknown
Mary Unknown
Mary Edward C Jr. Aug 29, 1886 - Feb 13, 1918
Mary Edward C Sr. Oct 28, 1854 - Jan 28, 1910
Mary Loretta Sept 1905 - July 1906
Mary Mary Collins April 12, 1855 - June 4, 1903
Mary Nellie Apr 1891 - Sept 27, 1971
Mary Phill J Sept 29, 1888 - Oct 27, 1939
Mascolino Angelina July 16, 1892 - Feb 11, 1971 Salvatore
        Apr 29, 1887 - Mar 8, 1936
Mascolino Thomasina Mar 7, 1912 - Aug 2, 2000
Mason Regina Egalite May 12, 1929 - Mar 5, 2008
Massadd Rev J 1881 - 1918 first Pastor of Jenkins Ky.
Masse Norman R 1935 - 1977 Frances R 1947

Feb 9, 1906   Leader
Mari Matey, 2, died February 5 of pneumonia. Burial in
        Catholic Cemetery.

Matlack Charles A 1884 - 1960
Matlack Charles Jr. 1916 - 1919
Matlack David T 1852 - 1930
Matlack James William July 4, 1928 - Jan 5, 2007 Doris
        McGruder Jan 23, 1931
Matlack James William July 4, 1928 - Jan 5, 2007 Korea
Matlack Margaret Lynn 1854 - 1913
June 2, 1913   Leader
The body of Mrs. D. T. Matlick was laid to rest Sunday
        afternoon with impressive services, which were held at
        the St. Paul's Catholic Church. The body was afterward

interred in the Catholic Cemetery.

Matlack Mary B 1888 - 1969
Matlick William L 1878 - 1928 Margaret F 1881 - 1928
Matry Mary 1855 - 1936
Matthews John R 1939 - 1981
Mattingly Ruth West Jan 28, 1901 - Sept 20, 1988 Alfred S Sr.
    Feb 11, 1898 - Nov 9, 1974
Mattingly James E Aug 2, 1879 - Apr 9, 1941
Mattingly L E 1868 - 1943
Mattingly Mary A Dec 13, 1884 - Dec 15, 1970
Mattone Frank 1916 - 1979 Lucille 1918
Mattone Frank 1916 - 1979 WWII
Mauck Kathleen July 7, 1900 - Dec 21, 1974 Arnold Benson
    Jan 28, 1895 - Jan 2, 1970
Maxwell Elmer Stephens Dec 4, 1888 - Jan 9, 1959 Mary
    Burchiel May 20, 1895 - Oct 9, 1981
Maxwell Paul G 1911 - 2000
Maxwell Ruth Rovane Madden 1904 - 1973
May Martin D Oct 17, 1942 - May 13, 2000
May Naomi Alice Smith 1902 - 1961
Mayer Ella Henry 1898 - 1982
Maynes Jas died Sept 2, 1907 his wife died July 189?
Mazza Susanna
McAllister James
McAllister Patrick
McAllister Patrick May 1843 - Mar 12, 1882
McArdle James Phillip 1841 - 1934
McArdle James William 1880 - 1952
McArdle Lydia Ward Owens 1853 - 1940 wife of James
    Phillip
McAvoy Elizabeth Ryan 1961 - 1917 wife of Thomas
McAvoy Mary Eliz Flynn 1900 - 1935 wife of Wm A
McAvoy William A Oct 5, 1893 - May 4, 1981 WWI
McBride Mary Nicole Dec 23, 1982 daughter of Marsha Hale

& David Brent McBride

McBride Robert Joseph 1896 - 1975 Rose Keller 1900 - 1971

McCabe Frank R 1891 - 1930 Dora H 1904 - 1995

McCabe Jennie Ballard July 28, 1867 - Dec 1, ?

McCabe Mary Joe McCarney Mar 18, 1908 - Apr 3, 1953 wife of John J McCabe

McCabe Russell May 3, 1930 - May 31, 1999 Frank R May 3, 1930 - June 20, 1998

McCafferty Mary Aug 1, 1814 - Aug 8, 1882

McCain John David Sept 23, 1953 - Feb 27, 1992

McCain Mary G June 23, 1916 - Sept 13, 1995

McCann James B 1885 - 1922

McCann Lt Thomas P Sept 11, 1917 - Dec 14, 1944 Killed In Action

McCann Minnie P May 30, 1879 - June 22, 1948

McCann Teresa died Sept 10, 1898

McCann Thomas Sept 15, 1842 - Oct 14, 1905 his wife Bridget Apr 25, 1849 - Jan 4, 1933

McCann Thomas B Apr 2, 1870 - July 1, 1941

McCann William A Apr 8, 1885 - July 29, 1950

McCarney A D 1848 - 1895

McCarney J Edward 1875 - 1910 Mary Jane Welch 1873 - 1955

McCarney Richard T 1903 - 1967

McCarney William S Aug 12, 1881 - Mar 30, 1957 Phoebe Scott Nov 20, 1889 - Feb 4, 1952

McCarthy Annie Aug 29, 1859 - Mar 15, 1904 wife of John

McCarthy Annie Garland 1866 - 1941

McCarthy Charles 1851 - 1919 Bridget McNamee and Daniel

McCarthy Charles B 1890 - 1948

McCarthy Charles Bernard Nov 7, 1918 - Mar 20, 1920 son of C E & M F

McCarthy Charles Edward Mar 3, 1886 - Jan 28, 1965

McCarthy Chas D 1831 - 1915

McCarthy Cornelia Reagan Nov 5, 1909 - Oct 23, 1996

McCarthy Daniel Pembroke 1891 - 1912
McCarthy Daniel Joseph 1847 - 1932 Mary Cleophus 1850 - 1932
McCarthy Elizabeth 1875 - 1967
McCarthy - Esenbock
McCarthy Florence Dec 25, 1825 - Sept 26, 1904
McCarthy Frank 1886 - 1890 Daniel W 1887 - 1890 Charles 1888 - 1890
McCarthy Frank L 1893 - 1978
McCarthy Helen Kane 1890 - 1945
McCarthy J William Sept 2, 1882 - Sept 5, 1975 Elizabeth July 23, 1886 - July 4, 1975 Nell Sept 27, 1909 - July 21, 1991
McCarthy John May 3, 1856 - Mar 7, 1904
McCarthy John E 1891 - 1952
McCarthy John Thomas 1872 - 1931
McCarthy Joseph 1883 - 1906
McCarthy Justin R died Jan 12, 1975
McCarthy Margaret 1864 - 1946
McCarthy Marie F died May 17, 1954
McCarthy Mary Sept 6, 1856 - 1894
McCarthy Mary Agnes died July 2, 1958
McCarthy Mary Foley May 4, 1893 - Dec 23, 1971
McCarthy Mary Frances Fotsch Jan 6, 1889 - May 3, 1963 wife of Charles E McCarthy
McCarthy Mary R 1891 - 1938
McCarthy Michael 1861 - 1936 Martha 1862 - 1902
McCarthy Patrick 1859 - 1908
McCarthy R C 1850 - 1934 his wife Ellen 1856 - 1926
McCarthy Rosa R 1877 - 1969
McCarthy Sara T 1844 - 1895
McCarthy William Desmond 1883 - 1945
McCartt James Ross June 16, 1921 - Apr 10, 1985 Mary Rose Sept 28, 1921 - Apr 10, 1985
McCarty Anne Norton 1911 - 2001

McCarty Annie Heafey 1868 - 1936 wife of James B

McCarty C Nellie

McCarty D E July 1868 - Dec 1896 Lizzie Feb 1856 - Apr 1904

McCarty James B 1866 - 1931

McCarty James C 1900 - 1968

McCarty James Thomas 1870 - 1950 Mary I Sheehan 1863 - 1947

McCarty John

May 23, 1908 Lexington Herald

Services for L. McCarthy, who departed this life on Wednesday morning, will take place this morning from St. Paul's Catholic Church at 10 o'clock, The interment will be in the Catholic Cemetery.

McCarty Lon 1864 - 1929

McCarty Maude South 1870 - 1931

McCarty Michael 1814 - 1884 Eliza Farrell 1837 - 1888 Nellie McM Campbell 1868 - 1953 Thomas 1859 - 1928 John 1862 - 1889 Michael 1871 - 1931 Daniel 1871 - 1936 May They Rest In Peace

McCarty Thomas A (Father) died Jan 23, 1962 Ordained Jun 1927

McCarty Thomas South 1908 - 1980

McCarty Wm Sept 1822 - Jan 1898 Abbie May 1831 - Nov 1894

McCauliffe Dennis 1873 - 1896

McCauliffe Mary Catherine 1871 - 1965

McCauliffe Rose Anna 1874 - 1933

McCauliffe Timothy 1827 - 1892

McCauliffe Winfred 1881 - 1969

McCauliffe Winifred Cannon 1839 - 1913

McClintock Catherine 1890 - 1963

McClintock Robert W Feb 17, 1919 - May 5, 1945 WWII

McCloskey James 1863 - 1912 Roessler Fred 1875 - 1905

Mary McCloskey Roessler 1864 - 1950
McClure Deborah Jolyn Sept 12, 1960 - 1995
McClure John F Mar 26, 1939 - June 1, 1985
McCool Dorothy Minihan Nov 27, 1915 - Mar 30, 1993
McCool Lonnie Franklin Jan 2, 1913 - Sept 2, 2002
McCool Martha Clare May 3, 1955
McCormick Annie 1865 - 1948
McCormick Charles 1872 - 1913
McCormick Jas J 1834 - 1897
McCormick John Richard Dec 24, 1879 - Feb 17, 1943 Helen
    Josephine Service Mar 19 1894
McCormick John L 1891 - 1950
McCormick John M
McCormick Julia D 1863 - 1932
McCormick Mary wife of Jas. J
McCormick Thomas J 1861 - 1934
McCormick William 1848 - 1918 Mary 1845 - 1923
McCormick William 1870 - 1934
McCormick Jas J Jr.
McCourt Annie 1832 - Sept 28, 1897
McCourt Elizabeth 1839 - May 8, 1899
McCourt Patrick H 1869 - 1960

Aug 30, 1901 Morning Herald
The remains of W A McCourt aged thirty, who died in
    Winchester, were buried in the Lexington Catholic
    Cemetery yesterday.

McCoy John 1862 - 1898
McCoy Alexander
McCoy Ann
McCoy James
McCoy Jane
McCoy John
McCoy Mary

McCoy Nancy McNeil wife of Neil
McCoy Neil
McCray Albert S July 12, 1891 - June 25, 1944
McCray Bonita Steiff July 19, 1901 - Jan 4, 1986
McCrystal Bernard 1852 - 1927
McCrystal Charles B 1884 - 1927
McCrystal James died Dec 25, 1851
McCrystal John died Jan 2, 1911 Mary died Aug 3, 1937
McCrystal Margaret E 1854 - 1929
McCrystal Thomas J 1888 - 1963 Ann Fischer 1894 - 1965
McCullough Beatrice 1895 - 1976
McCullough Charles 1833 - 1985 Mary 1838
McCullough Elizabeth W 1866 - 1941
McCullough Frank P 1868 - 1924
McCullough Jerry 1930 - 1933
McCullough John Pius 1864 - 1934

Jan 21, 1902 Leader
The funeral services of Miss Mamie McCullough will be held
    in Georgetown Thursday morning and interment in the
    Catholic Cemetery near Bryan Station.

McCullough Margaret 1895 - 1936
McCullough Sophia 1868 - 1947
McCullough Thomas 1932 - 1934
McCullough Wallace L 1902 - 1970
McDevitt Patrick 1836 - 1894 Ellen C 1846 - 1900 Mary Ann
    1871 - 1904 John R Ella A Thomas B
June 24, 1904 Leader
Miss Mollie E. McDevitt died at the home of her mother, Mrs.
    Ellen McDevitt, Thursday afternoon after a lingering
    illness. The interment will be in the family lot in the
    Catholic Cemetery.

Nov 18, 1909 Leader

Mrs. Ella McDevitt died at St. Joseph's Hospital Wednesday afternoon after an illness of two weeks. Mrs. McDevitt was 65 years of age. Burial in the Catholic Cemetery.

McDevitt Wm H 1871 - 1928

Aug 7, 1913 Leader
The body of Mrs. Ella McDonald arrived in Lexington from Cincinnati Thursday morning, and was laid to rest shortly afterwards in the Catholic Cemetery.

McDonald James Yeaman Dec 5, 1933 - May 25, 1997
McDowell Jessica W 1871 - 1946
McElhone Andrew Joseph Aug 12, 1890 - 1948 Margaret
       Saunier June 13, 1897 - May 25, 1988
McElhone Felix July 2, 1854 - Dec 1925
McElhone Feliz J Feb 25, 1891 - Nov 30, 1952
McElhone J W 1911 Louise M 1909 - 1975
McElhone James A 1886 - 1961 Agnes Worland 1884 - 1964
McElhone James B Jan 6, 1925 Jesus I Trust In You
McElhone Josephine Nov 24, 1913 - Feb 11, 1914 Joseph Sept
       27, 1916 - Jan 16, 1919 Frank Aug 1, 1921 - June 17,
       1922
McElhone Margaret Dec 4, 1897 - June 12, 1948
McElhone Mary McNamee Aug 28, 1853 - Nov 27, 1899 wife
       of Felix
McElhone Sara C Sept 8, 1892 - Jan 1968
McElhone Valinda Alice Aug 31, 1881 - July 22, 1957 Patrick
       Joseph Mar 16, 1882 - Dec 9, 1954 In Gods Care
McElhone William I 1928 - 1972 Wanda 1926 - 1981
McElory Thomas J 1868 - 1935
McElroy Agnes J 1905 - 1993
McElroy John C 1855 - 1915
McElroy John H 1890 - 1960
McElroy Leo P 1901 - 1961

McElroy Mary M 1896 - 1976

McElroy Patrick J 1886 - 1977

McElroy Terence F 1858 - 1914 Bridget C 1861 - 1926

McElroy Thomas 1922 - 1925

McElroy Thomas P 1887 - 1942

McEvoy Alice Marie Apr 18, 1906 - Jan 24, 1992 William M
    Apr 6, 1898 - Dec 1, 1957

McEvoy Thomas F 1862 - 1931 Mary Jane 1862 - 1944

McFadden John G 1844 - 1926

McFadden John G 1910 - 1972 Mary K 1910 - 2002

Sept 19, 1902 Leader

John McFadden, aged 40, son of the late Mrs. Mary
    McFadden and brother of the late Constable A.J.
    McFadden of this city, died last night at the home of
    his sister, Mrs. Nellie Coffelter in Richmond, Ky., after
    a long illness. The interment will be in the Catholic
    Cemetery in this city.

McFadden Kenneth Wayne July 20, 1955 - Jan 25, 1997

McFadden Maria Hollins 1851 - 1920

McFadden Mary K Sept 23, 1872 - Sept 26, 1963

McFadden Robert Dec 12, 1912 - July 5, 1997 Helen B Nov
    19, 1912 - June 15, 1970 Wm L "Billy" Mar 28, 1918
    Doris J McFadden O'Nan Sept 26, 1936 - Dec 22,
    2005

McFadden Sally Jane Aug 23, 1973

McGarry Kevin Vincent May 18, 1929

McGarry Parr Witt

McGarvey 1822 - July 11, 1877

McGarvey Aug 14, 1882 - July 17, 1889

McGarvey Nov 7, 1887 - June 26, 1888

McGarvey June 25, 1889 - Oct 24, 1890

McGarvey Oct 23, 1890 - July 13, 1891

McGarvey Feb 23, 1896 82 years

McGarvey wife of Frank Aug 14, 1855 - Nov 17, 1905
Nov 19, 1905 Leader
Mrs. Catherine McGarvey, 50, died November17; burial
    November 20 in Catholic Cemetery. Cause of death:
    heart disease.

McGarvey Isabella 1827 - Apr 28, 1889
McGarvey John 1883 - 1958 Rose 1887 - 1962
McGarvey John died Apr 25, 1895 his wife Mary died Feb 23,
    1896
McGarvey Katherine Harney 1910 - 1938 James Leo 1885 -
    1934 Lelia Glass 1888 - 1972 Anna Lucille 1913 -
    1972
McGarvey Mary Frances 1878 - 1954

May 2, 1908 Leader
Peter McGarvey, aged 50 years, died at his residence near
    Millville, of cancer of the throat. The interment will be
    in the Lexington Catholic Cemetery.

McGeorge Frank Nov 16, 1911 - Jan 16, 1936
McGeough James J July 27, 1869 - Aug 16, 1988
McGinnis Mary Dec 23, 1887
McGinnis Michael died Jan ? 80 years
McGinnis Sarah O'Neill Jan 25, 1913 - Mar 2, 2001
McGinnis W Louis Feb 12, 1910 - Aug 23, 2003
McGinnis Wallace June 1, 1880 - Mar 31, 1967 Ann Scully
    Feb 23, 1883 - Sept 15, 1948 Joseph Justin Mar 1921 -
    Nov 12, 1948
McGinnis William Louis Jr. Nov 16, 1943 - Oct 18, 1986

Jan 31, 1896 Morning Herald
McGinty - The funeral services of the late John McGinty will
    be held at St. Paul's Catholic Church at 9 o'clock this
    morning. Burial at the Catholic Cemetery.

McGlade Michael 1856 - 1906
McGlone Charlie Apr 18, 1872

Jan 20, 1906
The funeral services of Mr. Charles McGlone, who died at St.
Joseph's Hospital Friday afternoon, will take place
from the home of his brother-in-law, Mr. James
Douglass, Sunday afternoon. The interment will be in
the family lot in the Catholic Cemetery.

Jan 22, 1906 Leader
Charles McGlone, 50, died at St. Joseph's Hospital, January
19, of tuberculosis. Burial in Catholic Cemetery.

McGlone James J 1868 - 1922
McGlone John A 1866 - 1936
McGlone Mary 1838 - 1922
McGlone Mattie Feb 24, 1876 - Sept 1945
McGlone Nancy June 26, 1864 - July 4, 1879
McGlore James 1825 - 1887
McGovern Anne Teresa Feb 10, 1941
McGovern Hugh Jan 17, 1823 - Nov 29, 1898
McGovern Hugh E Nov 1, 1954
McGovern Margaret Gertrude May 27, 1948
McGovern Mary Ellen Oct 19, 1948
McGovern Mary Frederickson July 21, 1936
McGovern Nora A Apr 12, 1956
McGovern Patrick A Mar 12, 1941
McGovern Philip Lawrence Sept 14, 1948

June 27, 1911   Leader
The funeral services of Mr. William McGovern, who died
Saturday night in the county, took place Tuesday
morning at St. Peter's Church. Burial followed in the

family lot at the Catholic Cemetery.

McGrady Alice 1857 - 190?
McGrady Hugh 1860 - 1915
McGrady Hugh and Alice
McGrady Joseph 1866 - 1928
McGrady Mary O 1860 - 1958
McGrady Rev Thomas June 6, 1863 - Nov 26, 1907
McGrath Agnes M Norman died 1953 wife of Miles
McGrath Mary died Oct 6, 1881
McGrath Miles A 1866 - 1898
McGrath Norman 1889 - 1915
McGrath P J Oct 13, 1863 - Sept 2, 1895
McGrath Philip died June 6, 1879
McGruder Frances Malone Dec 14, 1898 - Aug 18, 1993
McGruder James Malone July 4, 1932 - Feb 23, 1986
McGruder Merle James 1897 - 1957
McGuire Hugh J Nov 24, 1899 - July 25, 1975 Hazel E Nov
      16, 1903 - Mar 4, 1978
McGurk Anna Mullholland 1882 - 1954

July 12, 1909 Leader
Arthur S. McGurk died at the home of his father, Mr. Daniel
      McGurk, Monday morning, aged 16 years. Interment
      will follow in the Catholic Cemetery.

July 14, 1909 Leader
Arthur McGurk, 16 years of age, who was taken ill with acute
      indigestion Sunday afternoon and died, was buried
      Tuesday afternoon. Burial in the family lot at the
      Catholic Cemetery.

McGurk Donald 1913 - 2006
McGurk Helen Sutherland 1913 - 1991
McGurk James died July 4, 1899 Margaret Padden died June

3, 1922
McGurk James Joseph 1908 - 1976
McGurk James T 1878 - 1951
McGurk Jane Mar 24, 187? - Sept 4, 1960
McGurk John Sept 22, 1873 - Aug 28, 1907
McGurk John Emerson 1906 - 1972
McGurk John Joseph 1876 - 1939
McGurk Lillie Parker 1891 - 1925
McGurk Margaret Blackerby 1921
McGurk Margaret Welch 1918
McGurk Marjorie Feb 12, 1921 - 1971
McGurk Mary Elizabeth July 25, 1872 - Aug 5, 1916
McGurk Mary Shellen 1842 - 1929
McGurk Roger John Jr. Dec 8, 1952 - Mar 20, 1959
McGurk William Edward 1901 - 1966 Josephine O Keefe
        1915 - 1998
McG - - - - Y Jan 13, 1851 - Jan 29, 1896
McKechnie James C July 17, 1924 - Mar 12, 1986 Helen Apr
        4, 1916 - May 23, 2005
McKee Agnes 1874 - 1888
McKee Agnes Jan 5, 1900 - July 17, 1903 daughter of R J &
        Rose M
McKee Anne A 1878 - 1911
McKee area died Oct 30, 1863 23 years
McKee Family of Richard J
McKee Gladys Feb 1, 1904 - Jan 20, 1975
McKee John 1837 - 1884
McKee Lydia 1872 - 1942
McKee Mary Owens 1839 - 1922 wife of Owen
McKee Owen 1832 - 1903
McKee Philip 1822 - 1855
McKee Richard J Feb 16, 1870 - Jan 22, 1924
McKee Richard J May 29, 1909 - Apr 1, 1959 son of R J &
        Rose M
McKee Rose McKenna Aug 1872 - 1962 wife of Richard S

McKeever John 1833 - 1890
McKeever Anna 1858 - 1909 daughter of J and C McKeever
April 13, 1909 Leader
Miss Anna McKeever, aged 50, died at her home in Frankfort
    Tuesday morning after an illness of several weeks and
    will be buried in the Catholic Cemetery here
    Wednesday afternoon.

McKeever Catherine 1836 - 1915 wife of John McKeever
McKeever James I 1883 - 1952
McKeever John 1864 - 1905 son of J and C McKeever
McKeever John L (Finnie) 1885 - 1932
McKeever John W 1857 - 1914 Bridget Bradley 1859 - 1934
McKeever Margaret 1856 - 188?
McKeever Sallie Slavin 1870 - 1959
McKeever William E 1888 - 19
McKeever William J 1862 - 1917 son of J and C McKeever
McKenna Alex 1857 - 1934
McKenna Catherine 1823 - 1905
McKenna Catherine Erskine 1856 - 1927
McKenna Charlene G Feb 20, 1939
McKenna Charles L Oct 20, 1871 - May 28, 1953
McKenna Charles L Jr. Aug 6, 1904 - July 28, 1978
McKenna Chas W 1877 - 1921
McKenna Chris R WWII
McKenna David G
McKenna David G 1919 - 1975 Willis Ray 1910 - 1961
        Joseph E 1910
McKenna Elizabeth Roche 1905 - 1987
McKenna Harry C Feb 6, 1935
McKenna Helen Dec 18, 1907 - Jan 3, 1999
McKenna James 1862 - 1902 Margaret 1861 - 19
McKenna James died Oct 11, 1920
McKenna James Bernard Jan 7, 1876 - Sept 28, 1941 McArdle
        Lydia Jan 4, 1883 - Sept 1, 1961

McKenna James C 1843 - 1913
McKenna James Stephen 1896 - 1971
McKenna Jane C 1846 - 1918
McKenna John 1868 - 1936
McKenna John died 1911
McKenna John J 1870 - 1912
McKenna Julia Margaret Aug 20, 1902 - July 23, 1983
McKenna Kate A Mar 17, 1861 - Nov 25, 1914
McKenna Lawrence May 21, 1833 - Oct 20, 1898
McKenna Lawrence 1864 - 1915
McKenna Lawrence Jr. 1898 - 1900
McKenna Lawrence R Nov 27, 1900 - July 19, 1946 WWI
McKenna Lizzie C O'Brien 1869 - 1909 wife of Lawrence
    McKenna
McKenna Mamie T 1873 - 1945
McKenna Margaret E Sept 30, 1900 - Dec 24, 1988
McKenna Mary 1855 - 1930
McKenna Mary Fister Nov 5, 1875 - Dec 15, 1966
McKenna Mary Foster 1885 - 1901
McKenna Mary McNichols died Sept 11, 1925 wife of James
    McKenna
McKenna Mrs. Alex 1854 - 1920
McKenna Nora Coyne
McKenna Rose C Sept 12, 1900 - Oct 7, 1992
McKenna Stephen M 1893 - 1921
McKenna Thomas C Jan 6, 1903 - Dec 15, 1981
McKenna Thomas Joseph

Aug 16, 1904 Leader
William, the infant son of Mr. and Mrs. J. P. McKenna, died at
    their home, aged six months. The funeral took place
    from the residence Tuesday afternoon, the interment
    being in the family lot in the Catholic Cemetery

McKenna Wilson M 1906 - 1944

McKinney Jo Ann Amato Mar 30, 1931 - Jan 22, 1975
McKinney Todd Christopher Jan 6, 1964 - Jan 14, 1984
McLaughlin Michase died 1900
McLaughlin Ann F 1870 - 1958
McLaughlin Annie died June 24, 1907
McLaughlin Edward C 1869 - 1935
McLaughlin James Marion July 5, 1933 - Oct 23, 1984 Iris
     Beam Jan 16, 1935 - Oct 6, 1996 Andrew James Mar
     29, 1960 - July 6, 1979
McLaughlin Jim 1878 - 1935
McLaughlin John died 1859
McLaughlin John B 1866 - 1936
McLaughlin Margaret 1843 - 1917
McLaughlin Marguerite 1882 - 1961
McLaughlin Martin 1831 - 1885
McLaughlin Mary G 1875 - 1952
McLaughlin Mary Leonard died 1854
McLaughlin Sarah
McLaughlin Thomas A 1873 - 1933
McLaughling Bridget Jan 1, 1856 - Oct 3, 1884
McLeod Joseph H Oct 22, 1899 - Oct 1971 Relda Jacob Aug
     14, 1899 - Feb 17, 1988
McMahan Patrick May 8, 1818 - Aug 29, 1883
McMahon - Johnson Cletus Joseph Oct 25, 1915 - Dec 30,
     1964 Gertrude Clary Oct 2, 1917 - Apr 5, 2008 Ruth
     Clary Sept 29, 1915 - July 19, 1999 Robert Scott July
     23, 1913 - Sept 1, 1983
McManus Ellen died Aug 17, 1917
McManus James Apr 12, 1865 - Jan 26, 1925
McManus James Edward Aug 7, 1902 - Dec 19, 1921
McManus Kate Glass Oct 19, 1870 - Feb 14, 1935
McManus Patrick died Dec 24, 1890
McMeekin Sarah May 5, 1836 - May 19, 1876 mother to Belle
     Breezing
McMenama Arthur P Jr. Aug 19, 1913 - Sept 18, 1995

McMenama Bernard 1888 - 1960

McMenama Dau Rosemary July 7, 1916 - May 21, 1941
Father Arthur P Oct 9, 1890 - Nov 9, 1959

McMenama Nell Bly 1890 - 1972

McMenama Rose 1882 - 1970

McMenara Bernard Oct 1885

McNally Bridget Mahoney 1871 - 1950

McNally James 1864 - 1943

McNally Jane M 1863 - 1909

McNally John 1859 - 1910

McNally Patrick 1819 - 1906 Mary Kerney 1825 - 1903

July 23, 1906 Leader

Patrick McNally died at his home in Georgetown Sunday
morning. The funeral will be held at St. John's Church
(Georgetown), Tuesday morning, interment in the
family lot in the Catholic Cemetery, Lexington.

McNamara May 15, 1988 - July 4, 19??

Mar 9, 1910 Leader

The funeral services of Mr. Dennis J. McNamara will be held
at St. Peter's Church Thursday morning and the
internment will follow in the family lot in the Catholic
Cemetery.

McNamara John June 20, 1889 husband of Catherine O'Regan

McNamara John died Dec 2, 1883 his wife Mary Died Aug
11, 1917

Sept 20, 1908

The services for Miss Mary McNamara will take place at St.
Paul's Church at 9 o'clock. The burial will follow in
the family lot in the Catholic Cemetery.

Mar 25, 1910 Leader

132

The funeral of Thomas McNamara who died at St. Joseph's hospital Wednesday morning was held Friday morning at the family residence on Loudon Avenue, the burial following in the Catholic Cemetery.

July 22, 1908 Lexington Herald
The burial of James McNamee, who died in Somerset yesterday morning at 5:20 o'clock, will take place in the Lexington Catholic Cemetery this afternoon on the arrival of the 3 o'clock Cincinnati Southern Train.

McNamee John died Jan 27, 1824
McNamee Katherine 1858 - 1923
McNeese William B Apr 12, 1919 - Nov 5, 1986
McNeil Lawrence J 1900 - 1979 Emma B 1916 - 1967
McNenna Susie Sutherland 1887 - 1962 Joseph B 1884 - 1937
McNichols John 1830 - 1880
McNichols Mary A 1858 - 1943
McNulty Francis 1889 - 1910
McNulty Joseph 1892 - 1912
McNulty Margaret A 1881 - 1899
Aug 28, 1899 Morning Herald
Miss McNulty, was about 20 years of age, and was prepared to enter the sisterhood.
The funeral will occur at St. Church at 9 o'clock this morning. Burial in the Catholic Cemetery.

McNulty Mary Ellen 1859 - 1910
McNulty Patrick 1851 - 1910
May 13, 1910 Leader
The funeral services of Mr. Patrick McNulty, who died at his home in Chicago on May 10, were held at St. Paul's Church Friday morning. The interment followed in the family lot in the Catholic Cemetery.

McQuad Genevieve M 1881 - 1935
McQuad Nell 1878 - 1962
McQuaid Edward 1834 - 1891
McQuaid Ellen McFadden 1848 - 1932
McQuaid John R 1876 - 1961
McQuaid Mae Murphy 1892 - 1972
McQuaid Mary F 1875 - 1894
McQuaid William J 1877 - 1956

Apr 10, 1910 Leader
The funeral services of Dennis J. McQueeney, who died
    Friday afternoon at the home of his brother, Owen
    O'Neill, will be held at the St. Peters Catholic Church
    Sunday afternoon. Interment in the Catholic Cemetery.

Sept 22, 1899 Morning Herald
Miss Katie McQueeney Dead
Funeral will be held at St. Paul's Church this morning at 9
    o'clock. Burial in the Catholic Cemetery.

McQuiad Edward R 1882 - 1930
McSherry Barney J 1896 - 1964
McWilliams Albert 1865 - 1915
McWilliams John 1829 - 1909 Manerva 1835 - 1875
Meadows Bernard Looney May 29, 1892 - Apr14, 1893
Measel Maryanne I Jan 6, 1944 - Nov 28, 1994
Meehan Joe 1931 - 2001 Betty A 1939 - 1999
Meehan John W Aug 1, 1918 - Aug 2, 1939
Meehan Timothy John P Teedy Jimmie Foushee Annie Homer
Meford Mark S 1905 - 1979 Margaret 1917 - ?
Meiler Alice Klein Aug 21, 1867 - Mar 23, 1948 wife of
    Anthony
Meiler Anthony J Sept 8, 1833 - July 2, 1901
Meiler Joseph M 1860 - 1916
Mellaney Elizabeth Sept 20, 1817 - May 19, 1882

Melvin John died Feb 24, 1913 James died Nov 15, 1877
    Virginia died May 22, 1880
Menchero Baldomero A Apr 22, 1904 - Dec 13, 1996 Mattie
    Lawrence Mar 7, 1911 - Dec 22, 1993
Mengelle Jeanne 1879 - 1948
Merchant Peter P 1840 - Sept 4, 1904 Catherine Bradley July
    28, 1925
Sept 4, 1904 Leader
The funeral services of Peter F. Merchant were held Tuesday
    morning at St. Paul's Church. The burial was in the
    Catholic Cemetery.

Merrick Sallie Lee June 4, 1906 - Oct 13, 1991
Messmer Edward 1889 - 1947 Gertrude 1891 - 1974 Infant
    Grandson
Metcalfe Elizabeth Walsh 1868 - 1949 wife of John J
Metz Emil 1851 - 1935 Louis Rebolt ? - 1933
Meyer Edward E 1910 - 1974
Meyer Edward M 1882 - 1955
Meyer Mary E Casey 1883 - 1955 wife of Edward M Meyer
Meyer Roberta 1934 daughter of Edward E and Roberta
    Meyer
Meyer Roberta D. Pearson 1913 - 2006 wife of Edward E.
    Meyer
Meyers Edward July 7, 1865 - Nov 17, 1893 son of L & E
Meyers Mary Mar 24, 1879 - Aug 25, 1889 daughter of A R &
    A
Mezzler Chas W Apr 25, 1834 - Dec 8, 1912
Michael Beulah 1908 - 1947
Michoud Linwood J June 17, 1897 - July 12, 1967 WWI
Mielcarek Chester Nicholas Jan 7, 1921 - Sept 26, 2009 Clara
    Raines Apr 25, 1927 - Mar 30, 1970
Milbourn William P 1867 - 1943 Catherine R 1870 - 1952
Milbourn WM T 1902 - 1952
Miles Anne Murphy Aug 7, 1940 - Aug 16, 1994

Miles James T Sept 1910 - Dec 19? Martha H Jan 20, 1914
Miley Elsie Ego Dec 25, 1888 - Oct 1, 1941
Miley Fred P Sept 6, 1885 - Sept 12, 1956
Miley John R May 30, 1929 John T Nov 22, 1900 - Apr 1,
      1967 Bernadina Sweeney Feb 7, 1903 - July 30, 1984
Miley Joseph Oct 31, 1926 - Feb 19, 1996 Dolores July 24,
      1929
Miley Marion E Mar 14, 1914 - Sept 28, 1941
Miller Amelia West 1866 - 1921
Miller Clarence W Feb 9, 1883 - Dec 3, 1978
Miller Clint S July 8, 1863 - July 31, 1921
Miller Edward W Sept 19, 1903 - Feb 18, 1987 Catherine M
      Mar 9, 1906 - Feb 4, 2003
Miller Eugene D 1904 - 1938
Miller J. Richard 1880 - 1944
Miller Josephine Clancy Apr 21, 1888 - Nov 25, 1988
Miller Margaret A Nov 11, 1880 - Feb 19, 1942
Miller Norman P Oct 5, 1884 - Sept 10, 1937
Miller Rassenfoss Mary W 1886 - 1960 wife of J Richard
      Miller
Mills Maria Louise Aug 30 - Sept 4, 1962 daughter of Robert
      & Susan
Miner Ann Wallace 1873 - 1948
Miner Edward J 1872 - 1942
Miner Sarto E 1903 - 1961
Minihan Ellen N Feb 8, 1909 - Apr 15, 1994
Minihan Margaret 1876 - 1954 wife of Timothy Minihan
Minihan Mary Margaret
Minihan Timothy 1862 - 1927
Minihan William A 1896 - 1948 Christine b 1900 - 1961
Minogue Dennis 1869 - 1948
Minogue Mary Carpenter 1880 - 1970
Minor Ann Denney Oct 12, 1914 - Oct 5, 1978
Minor Frank 1866 - 1910
Minor Harriet Tatman 1925 - 1956 wife of Harold

Minor James William Feb 27, 1911 - Nov 11, 1964
Minor John 1857 - 1923
Minor John Savage July 11, 1906 - Apr 22, 1966
Minor Marcella 1876 - 1962
Minor Nora Savage 1862 - 1944
Minor Phil 1868 - 1927 Eleanor 1904 - 1975
Minor Phil 1909 - 1981
Minor Philip 1824 - 1896 Mary 1835 - 1901
Minter Patrick B Mar 17, 1966 - Sept 23, 2007
Mischler Frank July 17, 1856 - Dec 2, 1918 Kate Aug 23,
    1853 - May 2, 1932
Mischler Frank C 1889 - 1964 Mae Bowen 1888 - 1968
Mitchell Alice C Feb 16, 1934 - May 30, 1980
Mitchell Elizabeth A Aug 6, 1960 - Mar 17, 2009
Mitchell Harry L 1868 - 1945 Ella Norris 1873 - 1938
Mitchell James Lusian June 3, 1910 - Jan 23, 1981 Clyda D
    Apr 25, 1913 - Jan 24, 1982
Mitchell James T Jr. Apr 7-8, 1957
Mitchell Mary Meehan 1894 - 1979 Joseph Gay 1888 - 1967
Mitchell Mathew Oct 8-15, 1965
Mitchell Robert 1894 - 1934
Mitchell Robert B Apr 16, 1931 - June 25, 2000 Mary Ann
    Aug 8, 1936 - Sept 15, 1995
Mitchell William Edward Nov 7, 1892 - Oct 20, 1990 Clara
    Wyatt Dec 6, 1900 - Nov 26, 1991
Mobyes Charles A Sept 12, 1882 - Jan 6, 1943
Mobyes Margaret D May 3, 1877 - Nov 24, 1949
Modica Anthony June 13, 1888 - May 22, 1966 John B Sept
    19, 1921, Ordained Sept 22, 1945 Anna Amato Oct 25,
    1889 - May 17, 1973
Modica Joseph A Aug 14, 1911 - Apr 5, 1997 Justina F Jan
    26, 1915 - Dec 27, 1997
Modica Joseph W WWI
Modica Mary Cecelia May 1, 1900 - June 11, 1982
Modica Paul Joseph Oct 24, 1902 - May 31, 1982 Myrta

Parsons Apr 2, 1903 - Dec 4, 1991
Modica Vincent 1871 - 1948 Elizabeth 1874 - 1949
Moler Charles A 1917 - Virginia C 1918 - 1969
Molere John B 1874 - 1959
Mollere Esilda Bouquoi 1874 - 1944 wife of John B
Molloy William Abbott Oct 27, 1878 - Dec 1968
Moloney
Moloney Agnes 1891 - 1944
Moloney Donald P July 21, 1921 - Apr 18, 1972
Moloney Dorothy B Sept 3, 1923 - Mar 13, 1986
Moloney Howard P Oct 18, 1929 - Dec 2, 1972
Moloney Joan Haney June 24, 1929 - Aug 23, 2001
Moloney Joseph E 1891 - 1949
Moloney Katherine 1886 - 1976
Moloney William P 1881 - 1955
Monaghan James Nov 9, 1857 - Jan 16, 1860 Thomas Feb 1,
    1866 - Oct 9, 1871
Monaghan Rosa died Aug 12, 1903 wife of Wm
Monaghan Rose 1860 - 1945
Monaghan William died Jan 11, 1882
Monahan Francis J 1916 - 1996 Katherine E 1919 - 1983

Sept 18, 1910 Leader
Mr. Charles L. Monsch, 66 years of age, died Saturday
    afternoon at the home of James Myers, after a long
    illness. The interment will be in the Catholic Cemetery
    Sunday afternoon.

Montague Anna C June 17, 1902 - Jan 9, 1968
Montague James M July 3, 1952 - Sept 4, 1996
Montague Leo W July 14, 1891 - Oct 13, 1959
Montague Mary C Nov 25, 1920 - Jan 9, 2002
Montague William H Sept 11, 1921 - Sept 6, 1994
Montgomery Julia Hogarty 1886 - 1977
Montgomery William H June 14, 1916 - Dec 7, 1980 Emma G

Jan 19, 1916 - Mar 7, 1991

Mooney Catherine Dec 25, 1826 - Dec 25, 1893

Mooney John June 21, 1820 - Jan 6, 1888

Mooney Laura Byrnes Feb 2, 1874 - Mar 25, 1956

Mooney Margaret E June 16, 1863 - June 9, 1939

Mooney Mary E Mar 19, 1866 - Feb 10, 1927

Mooney Michael A Sept 22, 1895 - Aug 9, 1896 Mary C Jan
    11, 1897 - Oct 31, 1898

Mooney Michael J Sept 28, 1870 - Jan 22, 1905

Jan 24, 1905 Leader

The funeral services over the body of Michael J. Mooney, the
    engineer who was killed Sunday in a collision on the
    L. & N. road at Shawnee, Tenn., was held Tuesday
    morning at St. Paul's Catholic Church, interment being
    in the Catholic Cemetery.

Mooney Patrick J July 26, 1860 - Apr 20, 1911

Apr 22, 1911   Leader

Attended by one of the largest gatherings ever seen at St.
    Peter's Church, including many Protestants as well as
    Catholics, the funeral services of Alderman Patrick J.
    Mooney were held Saturday morning, and an hour
    afterwards all that was mortal of the dead official,
    followed by sorrowing relatives and friends, was laid
    tenderly to rest in the Catholic Cemetery.

Mooney Pearl Boyd Dec 9, 1909 - Feb 9, 1952

Mooney Thomas G May 27, 1906 - Jan 12, 1956

Moore Anne Kenney 1857 - 1950 wife of H W

Moore Austin Nov 30, 1902 - Oct 27, 1949

Moore David H Dec 11, 1901 - Feb 21, 1918

Moore David Patrick July 28, ? Infant son of John& Grayce

Moore Elmer Richard (Father) Sept 20, 1923 - Jan 10, 1998
    ordained 1954

Moore Fontenelle L Jan 21, 1891 - Sept 21, 1967 Georgia

Major Oct 25, 1902 - July 12, 1970
Moore Grayce Albrecht Apr 12, 1926 - Mar 4, 1966 wife of
John J
Moore Leo John Apr 11, 1860 - June 27, 1908
June 29, 1908 Leader
The funeral services of Mr. L. J. Moore will be held Tuesday
morning at St. Paul's Church. The interment will be in
the family lot in the Catholic Cemetery.

Moore Mary Francis Sept 14, 1912 -Feb 28, 2008
Moore Mary Maloney June 22, 1900 - Oct 6, 1981
Moore Matthew 1866 - 1928 Lydia 1861 - 1954
Moore Mayme Sharkey died Oct 27, 1925 wife of J Will
Moore Nehill Mary 1856 - 1934
Moore Rose Donahue May 2, 1887 - Aug 31, 1965
Moore Susan Foley Aug 7, 1877 - Aug 19, 1950
Moore Teresa Cleophas Apr 6, 1901 - Apr 11, 1901 Daughter
of L J & T C
Moore Teresa Molloy May 5, 1866 - Apr 30, 1956
Moore Thomas 1829 - 1900 Margaret 1833 - 1901
Moore Thomas Joseph Dec 20, 1893 - Feb 27, 1958 WWI
Moore Thos F Nov 17, 1870 - Dec 31, 1907
Moore Will C 1948 Mary E 1959
Moore William 1854 - 1922
Moore William Gene June 19, 1937 - Jan 18, 1986
Moore William Patrick Oct 16, 1881 - Nov 27, 1966
Moran Augustus T Dec 10, 1890 - Apr 29, 1940 Margaret
Kennedy Sept 29, 1889 - Dec 4, 1959
Moran Genevive 1896 - Oct 9, 1950
Moran John A June 24, 1917 - Sept 24, 1999
Moran John 1852 - 1929 Rosa 1863 - 1942 Thomas 1892 -
1939 Feeney 1890 - 1940
Moran Wm C 1895 - 1969 Kathleen 1900 - 1968
Morgan Ann 1903 - 1985 Martha Morgan Jopling 1894 - 1976
Morgan Father died 1898

Morgan James Mar 9, 1892 - Dec 14, 1928
Morgan James died 1917
Morgan Jesse Mar 30, 1861 - Sept 22, 1944 Sarah Mayne Aug
    4, 1867 - June 18, 1931
Morgan Jesse L Mar 1899 - June 9, 1963
Morgan John B Oct 24, 1896 - May 26, 1952
Morgan John O 1920 - 2006 Irene 1923 - 1984
Morgan Katherine died 1926
Morgan Katherine O 1884 - 1976 John H 1881 - 1939
Morgan Mary died 1915
Morgan Maurice died 1906
Morgan Mother 1998
Morgan Robert Neal July 17, 1920 - Sept 27, 1998 Grace L
    Nov 28 - Sept 17, 200?
Morris Isabel T 1903 - 1970
Morris Ray B 1912 - 1994
Morrison Elizabeth Ready Oct 13, 1927 - Feb 6, 1994
Morrison Merle died 1876
Morrissey Bridget died 1807
Morrissey Edna Jones 1910 - 1982
Morrissey John W 1907 - 1971
Morrissey John William Mar 19, 1943 - Jan 2, 2006
Morrissey John William Jr. Mar 19, 1943 - Jan 2, 2006 US
    Navy
Morrissey Johnnie Mar 9, 1907 - June 9, 1997
Morrissey Laura C Mar 28, 1876 - Mar 30, 1948
Morrissey Maggie died Oct 10, 1884 aged 22 years

July 17, 1905 Leader
The funeral of Norinne Morissey, the infant daughter of Mr.
    and Mrs. William Morissey, will take place this
    afternoon. She will be buried in the Catholic Cemetery.

Morrissey T J 1872 - 1922
Morrissey William 1873 - 1931 Mary A Maher 1871 - 1928

Morrisseys J B 1863 - 1923

Morton Elizabeth Barkman Dec 16, 1927 - Oct 2, 1982

Mosier Albert II 1893 - 1952 Elmer B 1928 - 1950

Mother Right Sect

Mount Benj T 1900 - 1966 Helen 1903 - 1984

Mousa Francis June 13, 1882 - Mar 5, 1945

Moynahan Esther 1904 - ?

Moynahan George B May 17, 1895 - Nov30, 1932

Moynahan Jerry 1870 - 1923 Catherine Ramsey Ryan 1873 -
    1940

Moynahan ?

Moynahan Thomas K 1895 - 1962 Nellie 1892 - 19

MSGR John F Murphy Feb 25, 1923 - Aug 1, 2001 Ordained
    June 7, 1947

Mucci Henry D Apr 15, 1886 - Apr 11, 1943

Mucci John Henry July 17, 1907 - July 11, 1942

Mucci Katherine T Mar 2, 1885 - Apr 7, 1962

Mucci Verna Freeland Aug 6, 1894 - Mar 6, 1952

Mudd Francis P July 13, 1921 Marie G Nov 24, 1921 - May 7,
    1998

Mudd Jos Gerald 1911 - 1993 Mary Helen 1913 - 2001

Mudd Lyo Edward Apr 19, 1923 - May 6, 1995 Helen
    Hamilton Nov 1927

Mueller John Arthur Oct 17, 1913 - July 25, 1979 Rosemarie
    Stark Nov 4, 1914

Mueller Robert John May 1928 - June 1981 Patricia
    Llitenberger May 29, 2001

Mulcahy D T May 8, 1910 - Dec 1, 1988 Ann L Jan 22, 1917 -
    July 21, 2009

Muldrow Rainey J Mar 22, 1947 - July 16, 1974

Mulholland Children of Noah and Nell

Mulholland D E Nov 25, 1890 - Oct 25, 1960

Mulholland James June 12, 1849 - Mar 24, 1916

Mulholland James Joseph 1876 - 1946 Margaret E Fitzgerald
    1884 - 1979

Mulholland Katherine Pieri Sept 19, 1888 - Apr 5, 1940
Mulholland Mary E Mar 4, 1861 - May 5, 1921
Mulholland Nell Conner Jan 30, 1890 - June 4, 1974
Mulholland Noah Sept 13, 1876 -Oct 6, 1946
Mulholland Noah W 1918 - 1995 Cora lee Hamilton 1924 -
    2001
Mulholland Rosemary Sept 15, 1949 infant daughter of Joseph
    and Rosemary Mullholland
Mull Harry Nov 28, 1885 - Oct 23, 1933 Alice Conway July
    14, 1887
Mullane Robert D 1846 - 1911
Mullane Sarah C 1862 - 1926
Mullen Anna Dec 20, 1838 - Aug 16, 1935
Mullen Thomas Sept 5, 1823 - Feb 21, 1891
Mulligan Denis Morgan July 17, 1882 - Dec 28, 1942
Mulligan Dennis 1818 - 1900
Mulligan Henrietta Duke Aug 15, 1887 - Mar 19, 1893
Mulligan James Hilary 1844 - 1915
Mulligan John died July 31, 1849
Mulligan Kathleen Dec 14, 1889 - May 15, 1971
Mulligan Louis Huston Nov 24, 1869 - Feb 13, 1954
Mulligan McCoy Ellen Alice 1818 - 1904 wife of Dennis
May 5, 1904   Leader
The funeral services of Mrs. Ellen Alice McCoy Mulligan
        were held at St. Paul's Church Thursday morning. Rev.
        Father Barry officiated and the burial followed in the
        Catholic Cemetery.

Mulligan Sadie Daily July 6, 1880 - Dec 3, 1955 wife of Louis
    Huston Milligan
Mulligan Samuel Dold Apr 4, 1884 - Aug 3, 1885 son of
    James & Genevieve M
Mulligan Virginia Sharp 1898 - 1974
Mulligan Willoughby Williams May 24, 1899 - Mar 9, 1966
Mulloy Elizabeth

Mulloy Louis Tweedie Apr 17, 1925 - July 21, 1991
Mulloy Roger L Jan 12, 1895 - Aug 25, 1959 Elizabeth Jacobs
 Dec 2, 1897 - Jan 30, 1975 Albert J T weedie July 29,
 1844 - Sept 17, 1934 Mary McCauliffe June 28, 1852 -
 Nov 5, 1987
Murphy Agnes Scott Mar 5, 1871 - Oct 19, 1962 wife of
 Lawrence P
Murphy Anna died Nov 14, 1921
Murphy Catherine 1865 - 1952
Murphy Claude W 1875 - 1922
Murphy Daniel died Sept 11, 1893 aged 58 yrs
Murphy Daniel C 1926 - 1999 M Jean 1925 - 2005
Murphy Daniel Charles Jr. Oct 8, 1926 - Nov 3, 1999

Jan 14, 1909 Leader
Mrs. Ellen Murphy, widow of Patrick Murphy, died at
 Covington, Ky., Wednesday. Mrs. Murphy was
 formerly a resident of this city and the mother of the
 late Capt. Thomas F. Murphy prominent in State
 military circles a number of years ago. The body will
 be brought here Friday morning and the interment will
 follow in the family lot in the Catholic Cemetery.

Murphy Emily B 1915 - 1988
Murphy Gertrude Nov 12, 1906 - Sept 27, 1972
Murphy Hannah C 1857 - 1939
Murphy James Daniel 1904 - 1954
Murphy John Feb 4, 1827 - Feb 3, 1892
Murphy John died Feb 3, 1892 Mary died Apr 24, 1909
Murphy John B Feb 3, 1921 - Mar 27, 1988 WWII
Murphy John F 1890 - 1961 Elizabeth G 1893 - 1986
Murphy Joseph E 1902 - 1984
Murphy Judy K Tretter June 1, 1941 - Nov 17, 1983
Murphy Kathryn P 1903 - 1997 Mary L 1905 - 1986
Murphy Laura died June 7, 1885

Murphy Lawrence P May 26, 1865 - Apr 28, 1952
Murphy Margaret A 1897 - 1950
Murphy Mary Kennedy Mar 20, 1926 - Mar 16, 1983
Murphy Mary Jan 1, 1840 - Apr 24, 1909
Murphy Michael F 1858 - 1907
Nov 10, 1907 Lexington Herald-leader
The body of Michael Murphy was today interred in the
    Catholic Cemetery.

Murphy Owen B 1911 - 1984
Murphy Owen Benedict Mar 18, 1877 - Mar 30, 1947 Mary
    McGarry
Murphy Patrick 1891 - 1978
Murphy Scottie 1899 - Aug 16, 19

Mar 19, 1905 Leader
The body of T. F. Murphy, aged 56, who died at his home in
    Covington Friday morning of meningitis, will arrive in
    Lexington Monday morning at 11:45 o'clock over the
    L & N road. The body will be taken to the Catholic
    Cemetery immediately for the burial.

Murray Bea Devlin died Sept 17, 1914
Murray Bernard June 20, 1985 - July 1, 1955 Sarah E
    Costello May 17, 1889 - Sept 24, 1931
Murray Edward F. (Father) Feb 1916 - Apr 13, 1996 Son of
    Francis X and Elizabeth Lloyd Murray Ordained June
    3, 1950 WWII
Murray Edward James Aug 21, 1885 - Nov 25, 1966 Aimee
    Harris Apr 20, 1891 - Sept 12, 1952
Murray Edward Joseph died Apr 23, 1952
Murray Ellie died Oct 30, 1929
Murray James E May 28, 1920 - July 5, 1998 Mary K Jan 4,
    1926
Murray James L 1888 - 1929

Murray James S July 2, 1948 - July 25, 1999
Murray John H died July 29, 1935
Murray John Stephen 1888 - 1969
Murray Katherine died Mar 13, 1939
Murray Maggie 1851 - 1908
Murray Margaret Bernice Sept 9, 1934 - Nov 4, 1964
Murray Margaret Frances Nov 5, 1942
Murray Mary A 1841 - 1894
Murray Mary Costello July 6, 1897 - May 2, 1984
Murray Norma Fitch 1905 - 1987
Murray Patrick Nov 1902 Margaret Jan 26, 1929
Murray Patrick died June 18, 1916
Murray Thomas P 1872 - 1937 Mary H 1874 - 1963
Murry Glenna M 1896 - 1923
Muth Elizabeth Matlack Apr 21, 1923 - Dec 23, 1990
Muth Henrietta 1888 - 1956
Muth John Luigart Feb 3, 1922 - Apr 16, 1990
Muth John Victor June 4, 1890 - Nov 24, 1970
Muth Louis J 1896 - 1984 Sarah Clarke 1885 - 1970
Muth Mary Luigart Aug 13, 1895 - May 7, 1966
Muth Pierre 1863 - 1938 Mary 1868 - 1944
Muth - Frye Frank May 15, 1912 - Mar 15, 1988 Mary May 8,
        1918 - Nov 18, 1988 David Feb 21, 1937 Paula Dec
        16, 1943
Mutran Shaheen Tony 1891 - 1967 Anna Francis 1888 - 1974
Myers Katherine A Aug 12, 1913 - Feb 16, 1978
Nageotte Margaret Lynch Dec 1, 1891 - Apr 7, 1979
Nancy 1877 - 1963 Magee area
Nash Buford 1895 - 1963
Nash Frank died 1986 Nell died 195?
Nash Gladys S July 29, 1915 - Mar 23, 2001
Nash Lillian S 1896 - 1983
Nash Thomas B July 31, 1918 - Dec 8, 1998
Nash William Harlan Sept 20, 1907 - Oct 26, 1963 William
        Timothy born and died Nov 20, 1957

Navarra Frank May 18, 1879 - May 27, 1955
Navarra Mary R 1882 - 18
Navarra Rosina 1883 - 1923
Navarra Salvatore 1873 - 1945
Naven John June 22, 1822 - May 5, 1885 Elizabeth R July 17,
1837 - July 27, 1905
Naylor John C Dec 30, 1922 - Jan 25, 1972

Sept 20, 1908 Lexington Leader
The funeral of Patrick F. Naven will be held at St. Paul's
Church Monday morning, Rev. Father Barry
officiating. The interment will follow in the Catholic
Cemetery

Neagle Carty F 1861 - 1926
Neal Agnes Welch 1883 - 1940
Neal Katie 1880 - 1949
Neal Pratt Y 1865 - 1927
Neal Theresa Agnes 1897 - 1984
Neill Dryden 1915 - 1985 Mary Blake 1918 - Mary Anne
1941 - 1993 Agnes Blake 1894 - 1954
Nevitte Catherine Nov 24, 1844 - Nov 1, 1925
Nevite
Nevitt Anna L Oct 27, 1874 - Nov 25, 1959
Nevitt C A MD Apr 27, 1873 - Oct 27, 1942
Nevitt Cecelia Vogt Oct 6, 1890 - Oct 22, 1953
Nevitt Elizabeth Apr 24, 1880 - Feb 24, 1952
Nevitt Pearl Wimp 1877 - 1913 wife of C A
Feb 13, 1913 Leader
The funeral services of Mrs. Ora Pearl Nevitt, wife of Dr.
Charles A. Nevitt, who died Saturday afternoon at St.
Joseph's Hospital, were held Monday morning at St.
Paul's Catholic Church, followed by burial in the
Catholic Cemetery.

Nevitt Richard O Aug 30, 1876 - Nov 12, 1954

Newman Lawrence E 1871 - 1933

Newman Mary McQueenny 1867 - 1933 wife of Lawrence E

Newton Andrew Nov 2, 1915 - May 14, 1989 Evelyn July 22,
1921 - Nov 21, 2007

Nguyen Bryan Triphat Sept 24, 1997 - Mar 29, 1998

Nicholas Margaret A 1886 - 1913

Nicholas Margaret E 1906 - 1913

Nicholls Charles R July 28, 1926 - Nov 19, 1998

Nicholls Septa Furlong 1905 - 1987

Nicklen Dan Alice Moffat Jan 19, 1879 - Feb 27, 1964

Nierva Zenaida S Jan 25, 1945 - Mar 22, 2001

Nolan John F died Mar 24, 1951

Nolan Robert D died Jan 22, 1934

Noplis Winston Jr. Mar 30, 1934 - June 13, 1979

Nord Edward J 1919 - 1973 Katherine K 1926

Norman John Sr. died 1905 Ellen died 1882 Blanche died
1889 Edward died 1904 Margaret died 1908 Susan
died 1885 John Jr. died 1902 William died 1918 Maria
died 1946

Nov 18, 1905 Leader

The funeral of John A. Norman, formerly of Lexington, who
died in Louisville at the age of 67, was held in that city
and the body brought here Saturday over the C. & O.,
burial taking place from the train in the Catholic
Cemetery.

Norris Ann M 1881 - 1941

Norton Edward T 1863 - 1955

Norton Edward Thomas Sr. Aug 22, 1902 -Sept 5, 1972 Rita
Dodd May 30, 1921

Mar 12, 1898 Morning Herald

Tragic Death Attacked by a Hemorrage, J S Norton dies on the
Street

The Funeral will take place Sunday afternoon at 4 o'clock at
St. Paul's Catholic Church, and the interment will be
made in the Catholic Cemetery.

Norton John Keller 1904 - 1932
Norton Katherine Nov 5, 1867 - Sept 17, 1935 Michael Aug 4,
1865 - Jan 25, 1935
Norton Martin 1826 - 1870 Annie Norton Hays 1838 - 1915

May 16, 1905 Leader
Mary Norton, the infant daughter of Mr. and Mrs. Edward
Norton, who was born last Friday, died Sunday and
was buried Monday in the Catholic Cemetery.

Norton Rev Joseph M 1909 - 1982 ordained May 26, 1934
Norton Thekla Keller 1877 - 1963
Norton William J 1862 - 1930 his wife Agnes Hearn 1862 -
1924
Notaro Dorothy G Nov 28, 1905 - Aug 24, 1980 Dominic Mar
10, 1904 - Oct 1984
Novella Joseph 1915 - 1979
Nugent Elizabeth 1882 - 1960
Nugent James 1815 - 1900
Nugent James 1875 - 1959
Nugent John B 1877 - 1956
Nugent Mary E 1870 - 1942
Nugent Mother 1840 - 1916
Nugent Thomas Dec 21, 1825 - Oct 19, 1898
Nugent Will 1882 - 1951
Nuller Katherine Diamond Jan 8, 1893 - Sept 19, 1921 wife of
James A
Nunan
Nunan Elizabeth DeBoor 1945
Nunan John F 1866 - 1922
Nunan Mary Aug 12, 1894 Catherine Dec 6, 1914 Hannah

Nov 11, 1933 Alice L Aug 24, 1914 Thomas L Sept
11, 1916 Mary Alice Nov 2, 1941 Nicholas Dec 6,
1945
Nunan Matthew Enright Oct 21, 1920 - Aug 30, 1939
Nunan Sara Madigan 1896 - 1963 Dennis Joseph 1896 - 1970
O'Brien
O'Brien Andrew died 1858 aged 50 yrs wife of Drew
O'Brien Bridget Higgins 1855 - 1920
O'Brien Bridget M Feb 2, 1851 - Oct 11, 1899

Mar 5, 1906 Leader
Infant of J. J. O'Brien died March 3 stillborn. Burial in
Catholic Cemetery.

O'Brien John Richard Sept 21, 1910 - Aug 26, 19?3 WWII
O'Brien John S died Feb 16, 1940 Kate C died Apr 18, 1920
O'Brien John Patrick Aug 10, 1981 - Aug 4, 1972 Anna
Theresa May 30, 1931 - Jan 19, 1991
O'Brien Kate Fox 1847 - 1923
O'Brien Mary F Mar 13, 1899 - Sept 3, 1986
O'Brien Patrick 1841 - 1875
O'Brien Richard died Aug 4, 1875

Feb 17, 1909 Lexington Leader
Many sorrowing relatives and friends followed the body of
Smith O'Brien to its last resting place in the family lot
in the local Catholic Cemetery Wednesday morning.
The funeral services which were simple but
impressive, were held at St. Paul's Catholic Church.

O'Brien Ward James 1902 - ? WII
O'Cara Sarah Died Jan 24, 1887 in her 74th year wife of Hugh
O'Cara Sarah

Aug 11, 1905 Morning Herald

The interment Mr. O'Connell who was killed by officers in Chicago Sunday will take place in the Catholic Cemetery. He was the son of Mrs. Margaret O'Connell and formerly lived here.

O'Connell Anna C 1861 - 1946
O'Connell Bonnie Dec 20, 1900
O'Connell Cornelius 1837 - 1909 Mary 1852 - 1912
O Connell John 1874 - 1907
O'Connell John J 1858 - 1925
O'Connell Margaret E died Dec 11, 1975
O'Connell Margaret Hickey 1873 - 1960 wife of Michael
O Connell Mary J died Jun 11, 1986

Mar 29, 1912   Leader
The funeral services of Mrs. Mary O'Connell, 60 years old, who died Wednesday night at her home, will be held Saturday morning at St. Paul's Catholic Church. Burial will take place in the Catholic Cemetery.

O'Connell Michael 1859 - 1927
O'Connell Nellie Feb 8, 1905
Feb 8, 1905   Leader
The funeral services of Miss Nellie Teresa O'Connell will be held at St. Paul's Church Thursday morning and the internment will be in the Catholic Cemetery.

O'Connell Peari Guyn Sept 22, 1878 - Jan 18, 1964 Mary Springate Aug 29, 1902 - Dec 9, 1978
O'Conner Thomas died Aug 18, 1884
O'Connor Ann Bradley 1857 - 1919 wife of John
O'Connor James C 1889 - 1936
O Connor Jeremiah Jan 20, 1842 - Oct 17, 1867

Apr 13, 1914 Leader

Mr. John O'Connor, 69 years old, died at St. Joseph's hospital
Sunday morning. Funeral services will be held at St.
Paul's Church Tuesday morning, after which burial
will take place in the Catholic Cemetery.

O'Connor John 1849 - 1926
O'Connor John Aug 26, 1905 Mary Jan 27, 1913 - Mary Hall
O'Connor John P 1892 - 1913
O'Connor Mark B 1900 - 1958
O'Connor Mary A died Feb 24, 1973 his infant baby Dec 19,
1862 - July 2, 1873 wife of P O'Connor

May 13, 1901 Morning Herald
Patrick O'Connor - died at St. Joseph's Hospital Sunday
Morning. The funeral will be held in St. Paul's
Catholic Church this afternoon at 2 o'clock. Interment
in the Catholic Cemetery.

O Connor Paul J 1881 - 1933
O'Daniel
O'Daniel Terri Bridget Aug 26, 1961 - Dec 3, 1981
O'Day Margaret 1832 - 1899
O'Day Alma Anderson May 24, 1901 - Nov 3, 1985
O'Day Ellen 1862 - 1923
O'Day John 1867 - 1914
O'Day Margaret Mar 7, 1832 - Jan 5, 1899 wife of Thos
O'Day
O'Day Margaret 1869 - 1922
O'Day Mary Bell Jones Dec 2, 1861 - Sept 19, 1938
O'Day Michael 1824 - Apr 25, 1898 Catherine 1825 - June 12,
1884
O'Day Michael May 24, 1859 - Apr 29, 1881
O'Day Michael Nov 1, 1864 - Dec 14, 1885
O'Day Patrick June 5, 1860 - Nov 4, 1898
O'Day Thomas Mar 27, 1859 - Apr 22, 1942

O'Day Thomas died Aug 25, 1883 in the 61 year of his age
O'Day Thomas J 1864 - 1928 Mary Maher 1865 - 1929
O'Donnell
O'Donnell Nicholas 1871 - 1931
O'Donnell Nicholas L 1871 - 1931
O'Driscoll Hannah "Nancy" Sept 15, 1895 - July 20, 1931
O'Geary Ella Blake Dec 26, 1874 - Dec 8, 1949
O'Geary J Donald 1898 - 1955
O'Geary John Michael Oct 23, 1861 - May 5, 1926
O'Keefe John P Apr 1819 - May 1888 Bridget Nov 1823 - Jan
    1902

Dec 20, 1906 Leader
The funeral services of Mrs. Katherine O' Keefe, wife of Jerry
    O'Keefe, will be held at St. Paul's Church Friday
    morning instead of Saturday as published. The
    interment will be in the family lot in the Catholic
    Cemetery.

O'Kelly John P 1880 - 1949 Anne F 1878 - 1930
O'Kelly Connie Wallace July 8, 1914 - Nov 10, 2007
O'Kelly John H 1912 - 1962
O'Leary Elizabeth 1852 - 1892
O'Milla Rev Father James A Nov 1, 1891 - June 11, 1936
    ordained May 26, 1923
O'Neal Beatrice 1875 - 1927
O'Neil Abbie 1850 - 1929
O'Neil Chas B died Aug 21, 1918
O'Neil Daniel died Nov 24, 1898
O'Neil Eliza died 1946
O'Neil Eugene died 1931
O'Neil John 1843 - 1927
O'Neil Mary May 10, 1825 - Feb 2, 1872 wife of James
O'Neil Owen died 1939

Dec 29, 1905 Leader
Infant of P. P. O'Neil, died December 28, still born. Burial in
 Catholic Cemetery, December 28.

O'Neil Peter 1898 Annie 1872 - 1902
O'Neil Rev John J May 27, 1861 - Aug 22, 1909 ordained
 Priest Nov 1, 1886
O'Neill Martin P Oct 19, 1888 - July 8, 1952
O Neill Annie 1870 - 1944 Bridget 1877 - 1946
O'Neill Catherine G 1874 - 1955
O'Neill Ellen 1858 - 1890
O'Neill Father
O'Neill Frank
O'Neill Frank W 1911 - 1984
O'Neill James M 1907 - 1938
O'Neill James Sarah and James
O'Neill John 1843 - 1927
O'Neill M Louise Crowley 1912 - 1967
O'Neill Mamie 1871 - 1953
O'Neill Margaret 1905 - 1996
O'Neill Margaret 1824 - 1881
O'Neill Marion Morrissey Nov 19, 1905 - Aug 25, 1986
O'Neill Martin 1858 - 1910
O'Neill Mary
O'Neill Mary 1845 - 1918
O'Neill Mary 1855 - 1916
O'Neill Mary 1885 - 1889
O'Neill Mother
O'Neill Nancy 1848 - 1929
O'Neill Patrick F 1907 - 1966
O'Neill Patrick 1847 - 1882
O'Neill Patrick 1867 - 1942
O'Neill Patrick died Mar 19, 1932
O'Neill Paul 1861 - 1911 Bridget Haney 1881 - 19
O'Neill Paul 1865 - 1938

O'Neill Paul Joseph June 24, 1900 - June 10, 1991
O'Neill Peter P 1864 - 1937
O'Neill Peter Sr.   1805 - 1891
O'Neill Richard Garland (Father) Oct 31, 1907 - Jul 21, 1973
O'Neill Rosemary 1897 - 1949
O'Neill Susan
O'Campo Ricardo Aguilar July 2, 1937 - Sept 11, 2007
O'Canty Edward Patrick Feb 5, 1916 Doris Smith Apr 2, 1917
    - May 23, 2002
O'Connell Margaret died June 20, 1912
Odenbaugh H Clay 1873 - Sept 5, 1934
Offield Dorothy Saunier died 1994 wife of Irvan T
Offield Irvan Thomas died 1960
O'Hara Elizabeth died Aug 15, 1909 Daughter of Elizabeth
    Oct 16, 1869
O'Hara John B died July 8, 1915
O'Hara Kate died Sept 18, 1939
O'Keene Jerry Apr 16, 1854 Catherine Oct 16, 1854 - Dec 13,
    1906
O'Mahony Emma l 1855 - 1909
O'Mahony John 1800 - 1887
O'Mahony Katie C 1848 - 1882
O'Mahony Richard J 1844 - 1916
O'Mahony Sarah 1876

June 15, 1907 Lexington Herald-Leader
The funeral service for Bartholomew O'Reagan will be held at
    St. Paul's Catholic Church Monday morning at 9
    o'clock. Interment in family lot in the Catholic
    Cemetery.

Omer Eleanor Bradley (Nellie) July 9, 1912 - Feb 7, 1989
Omer Joseph Farrar Apr 10, 1906 - July 22, 1972
Oram Edward 1983 Under Tree Cover
Oram Louise Keller 1892 - 1990

Osborne Nell Jan 15, 1889 - Aug 25, 1943
Oster Leopold U 1912 - 1973
Owans Mary Aug 9, 1873 wife of Pete Owans
Owen Lloyd Edward Feb 25, 1918 - Feb 17, 1986
Owen Lloyd Edward II 1942 - 1963
Owens Billy Roberts Oct 1, 1928 - Dec 29, 1988
Owens Daniel Co. E 2 Ky Inf 53 SP AM WAR
Owens Dorothy Chastern
Owens E W July 19, 1923 Mary E Feb 10, 1928
Owens James W Aug 4, 1848 - July 9, 1893
Owens Lawrence Co. ? ? Ky Inf 53 SP AM WAR
Owens Richard Oct 4, 1813 - Jan 7, 1876
Owens Sarah F 1850 - 1930
Owens Elizabeth C Willard J Edward Sr. Kate C Edward Jr.
     Katherine W Augustus J
Owens Eliza Aug 15, 1816 - Nov 13, 1878
Owings Edward II 1850 - 1916
Owings Edward III 1896 - 1899
Papania Antonina Sept 16, 1841 - Dec 3, 1914
Papania Cosima J 1879 - 1919 wife of Joseph Papania
Papania Joseph III Aug 14, 1929 - Jan 11, 1998
Papania Joseph Sr. 1872 - 1959
Papania Mark Kenneth Apr 17, 1943 - Dec 7, 1993
Papania Maude A 1885 - 1958
Papania Michael V in sweet paradise
Papania Michael V Jan 5, 1951 - Feb 5, 1999
Papania Nancy Jean Bright Nov 17, 1929 - Sept 9, 2005
Papania Onofrio June 3, 1868 - Dec 21, 1948 Rosina Oct 1,
     1872 - Apr 18, 1944
Papania Salvatore Sept 24, 1899 - June 4, 1967 Rena Adams
     Jan 6, 1900 - Jan 19, 1983
Papania Sam Jr. Oct 10, 1922 - July 7, 2004 Dorothy M Mar
     2, 1921
Pardegn Carlo Mar 13, 1911 age 37
Parker John S Feb 26, 1894 - Jan 2, 1963

Parker John W 1858 - 1936 Catherine O 1865 - 1943
Parker Mary Luella Dec 11, 1888 - Mar 20, 1959
Parker Ralph Rettig Jr. Jan 14, 1930 - Mar 30, 1947
Parker Virgie Mar 7, 1908
Parks Viola Elizabeth Pieri Sept 14, 1881 - Jan 5, 1965 wife of
    William Edward
Parks William Edward Sept 9, 1883 - Dec 16, 1953 Viola
    Elizabeth Pieri Sept 14, 1881 - Jan 5, 1965
Parks William Edward Sept 9, 1883 - Dec 16, 1953
Parson 1838 - 1921
Parsons Jas H 1862 - 1925 Mary B 1864 - 1923 Willie Mae
    1886 - 1920
Parsons Mary E Curry Mar 14, 1893 - Mar 29, 1925 Wife of
    Charles
Paul Frederic 1904 - 1927
Pavesigh Paul 1849 - 1920
Pawlowsky Louis P Aug 5, 1911 Stone Sarah Dec 7, 1911 -
    Mar 15, 1959 Stone Margaret O Jan 25, 1888 - Jan 17,
    1971 O'Neil Charles S Oct 10, 1889 - July 15, 1959
Payne Anna Clara Carrico died Sept 13, 1929 Betty Jean Feb
    25, 1933
Payne Booby Joe Apr 3, 1941 Greta Sue July 18, 1939
Peak Anna B 1881 - 1962
Peak Warren 1884 - 1915
Peck Nell Goodwin Dec 25, 1897 - Jan 22, 1969
Pelster James Louis Sept 20, 1958 - May 10, 1981 Joan
    Connor Nov 17, 1931 - Sept 7, 1980
Pemberton Horace Mills Sept 29, 1910 - Mar 15, 1988
    Eleanor Keith May 29, 1916 - Sept 26, 1987
Penney Geraldine P Williams 1926 - 1999 Mary Scully 1902 -
    1967
Pepiot Adam C Dec 7, 1891 - July 26, 1966 Rachel A Sept 23,
    1913 - Dec 28, 1975
Perkins Frank Sr. May 11, 1912 - Apr 13, 1968
Perkins John 1870 - 1918 Betty died 1925 M Carolyn

Allender 1921 - 1922
Perkins Mary E Feb 27, 1876 - Sept 6, 1956

Sept 12, 1910 Leader
After a short illness Mary Evelyn, the fourteen months old
daughter of Mr. and Mrs. John J. Perkins, died at the
residence of her parents Sunday. The burial occurred at
the Catholic Cemetery.

Perkins Wilhelmina June 1, 1906 - Apr 1, 1992
Perraut Sarah A 1878 - 1936
Perrin Elizabeth
Perrin Rosa
Perrin William
Peterson Anna N Jan 27, 1905 Alphonse J Sept 25, 1903 -
June 28, 1975
Petit Earl Frances 1912 - 1992 Alba J Collins 1916 - 1988
Petit George L Jr. Feb 28, 1915 - Feb 20, 1990 Lucille R Aug
6, 1916 - Apr 9, 1988
Petit George L Sr. 1876 - 1956 Mary Cannavan 1878 - 1954
Petit Herbert H Aug 16, 1911 - Sept 28, 1982 May Hanley
Nov 2, 1884 - Nov 5, 1945
Petit Herbert L Jr. Oct 2,1928 Lucille K Dec 14, 1931 J
Kearney Mar 14, 1972 -Mar 8, 2005
Petit Herbert Lisle 1898 - 1965 Viola Findley 1905 - 1990
Petit Lorene Marie 1901 - 1915
Petrie Mary Fitzgerald Aug 16, 1898 - Oct 2, 1945
Petsch Mulligan Mary J Nov 11, 1924 - Mar 19, 1962
Phelps William H Jr. Mar 17, 1925 - Nov 29, 2002 Lois F Feb
14, 1927
Phillips Marjorie Garland Sept 5, 1918 - Apr 2, 1999
Phillips Mary 1815 - 1884
Phillips N Randall Dec 13, 1914 - June 21, 1972
Phillips Sallie M 1877 - 1959 George W 1875 - 1946
Pierce John Samuel Jan 5, 1847 - Apr 13, 1926 Mary

Elizabeth Aug 28, 1859 - June 22, 1927

Pieri Antonio 1870 - 1912

Pieri Dollie J Watkins July 14, 1857 - Dec 2, 1940 wife of Louis

Pieri Louis Oct 15, 1853 in Lucca Italy - Aug 23, 1927

Pieri Thomas J 1890 - 1938 Margaret B 1903 - 1984

Piper John Joseph Sept 13, 1948 - Mar 5, 1969

Ponder Herbert Francis July 30, 1942 - Dec 2, 1973

Powell

Powell Annie Jeter Mar 1, 1882 - June 18, 1960

Powell Caroline Henry July 13, 1914 - Aug 30, 1991

Powell Earl Joseph Mar 7, 1911 - July 14, 1964

Powell James Thomas Dec 9, 1872 - July 3, 1928

Powell John Duncan Apr 14, 1915 - July 24, 1970 Stella Hughes Nov 18, 1915

Powell Leonard Marion Mar 12, 1912 Gladys Tudor Aug 19, 1909 - Mar 21, 1968

Powell William M 1923 - 1978 WWII

Power James Harold Nov 7, 1953 Lisa Kay June 21, 1955 - Jan 13, 2009 married Sept 11, 1976

Powers Mary Donovan 1835 - 1885 wife of John

Prather

Prather Charles G Aug 2, 1933

Prather Floyd Sr. 1896 - 1977 Kathleen B 1898 - 1967

Prather Helen Gum May 21, 1933 wife of Charles G

Prather L S Aug 5, 1898 - Mar 6, 1990

Prather Leona Gilman July 21, 1899 - Dec 20, 1975 wife of L S

Prebble Susan Caden died 1966

Prewitt Rita Riley Apr 19, 1946 - Feb 23, 1993

Price - Hall, Dwight L Price Mar 31, 1931 Peggy Hall Price Aug 31, 1934 Bruce Hall Price July 29, 1959 - Oct 10, 1960 Roy B Hall July 29, 1959 - Oct 10, 1960 Aline Ice Hall Oct 20, 1904 - Mar 19, 1947

Price Austin Bennett Aug 31, 1871 - Feb 22, 1958 Anna

Elizabeth Gill June 12, 1887 - Mar 16, 1964
Price Mary Kane 1869 - 1934
Proctor Thomas 1954 - 1977
Pryor Joe July 9, 1808 - Mar 13, 1913
Pulliam Helen Grose 1920 - 1980
Pyman Lee A 1885 - 1962
Pyman Maude Ellis 1889 - 1969 wife of Lee A
Queeney Ann M died Nov 9, 1926
Quileen Robert R Oct 6, 1963 - Dec 9, 1983
Quinn Claude F 1901 - 19 Charlotta 1900 - 1960
Quinn Frank Feb 25, 1900 - Mar 9, 1918
Quinn James A Jan 20, 1871 - Dec 28, 1943
Quinn John F June 21, 1864 - Jan 13, 1937
Quinn Joseph J Aug 11, 1898 - May 6, 1968
Quinn Margaret July 4, 1866 - Aug 21, 1954
Quinn Marguerite Lee Oct 14, 1898 - Sept 27, 1964 wife of
        Joseph J
Quinn Mary Sept 25, 1866 - Jan 6, 1947
Quinn Nora Frances July 26, 1876 - Mar 12, 1963
Quinn Sallie Murphy Apr 26, 1875 - Jan 2, 1969
Quinn Thomas died Aug 15, 1871 his wife Mary 1835 - 1897
Jan 29, 1897 Morning Herald
Mary C. Quinn, who died at St. Joseph's Hospital Monday
        Evening, will be held at St. Paul's Catholic Church
        Saturday morning at 10 o'clock. Interment in the
        Catholic Cemetery.

Quinn Thomas F died May 29, 1944
Quinn Thomas M died May 19, 1958
Quisenberry Mary Ann O'Neill May 11, 1948 - Jan 6, 1973
Raley Robert D 1918 - 1967 Dorothy 1925 Arch M 1894 -
        1959 Antonette M 1895 - 1977
Ramsey John H (Father) July 27, 1910 - Feb 15, 1995
        ordained June 6, 1936
Ramsey Edward Ross May 3, 1926 - Dec 5, 1981 Willy Jo W

Jan 15, 1926 - Jan 21, 1976

Ramsey Kelly C Oct 11, 1889 - Apr 8, 1966 Margaret S Mar
24, 1900 - Dec 10, 1964

Rand R J Jr. Dec 10, 1948 - Feb 23, 1949

Randolph Glover L Mar 13, 1906 - Feb 22, 1970

Randolph Margaret Drummy Sept 15, 1906 - Mar 23, 1989

Rankin Molly Shannon Dec 28, 1930 - July 1, 1985

Rankins Corine Tucker 1920 - 1975

Rassenfoss

Rassenfoss Edward F 1887 - 1968

Rassenfoss George A 1894 - 1984

Rassenfoss George A 1863 - 1930

Rassenfoss Martha J 1914 - 2005

Rassenfoss Mary Alice 1921 - 1993

Rassenfoss Mrs. Geo. A 1863 - 1932

Rassenfoss Robin F Hoop 1895 - 1987 Wife of Edward F

Rassenfoss Ruth G 1897 - 1987

Rath Henry Jonathan Feb 8, 1858 - Mar 23, 1904

Rath Mary 1841 - 1930

Rawe F Anthony 1893 - 1942 Edith A 1893 - 1944

Ray John W 1936

Ray Joseph E 1896 - 1966 Marge C 1909 - 1992

Ray Leonard "Babe" Aug 20, 1927 - May 8, 2008 Ann L Dec
29, 1928

Ray Margaret E Nov 9, 1903 - July 22, 1979

Raymond Chauncey 1853 - 1918

Raymond Flora Fugazzi 1884 - 1919

Ready 1883 - 1910

Ready Edward

Ready Honorable Judge from 1936 - 1961 Thomas J 1873 -
1965

Ready James died Dec 14, 1912 age 33

Ready John June 20, 1837 - July 15, 1893 Elizabeth Oct 19,
1845 - Aug 25, 1881

Ready John C died May 1, 1910 age 34

May 1, 1910 Leader

The funeral services of Mr. John T. Ready will be held at St. Paul's Church Monday morning. The interment will be in the family lot in the Catholic Cemetery.

Ready Mary
Ready Patrick
Ready Vallie A 1893 - 1977
Reagan Annie J July 5, 1923 Bridget Kenny 1852 - 1925
Reagan Cornelious died Nov 9, 1881in his 75 year
Reagan Cornelius 1882 - 1909 son of Mary Powers and Daniel Reagan

Jan 20, 1909 Leader

The funeral of Cornelius Reagan will be held this afternoon at St. Paul's Church. Interment will be in the Catholic Cemetery.

Reagan Cornelius J Feb 22, 1856 - Sep 3, 1926 Nellie Anglin Jan 4, 1881 - Oct 2, 1940
Reagan Daniel 1847 - 1905
Reagan Gerald A Dec 11, 1901 - Aug 30, 1933
Reagan John J 1880 - 1906 son of Mary Powers and Daniel Reagan

April 4, 1906 Leader

John J. Regan, 26, died March 31 of heart disease. Burial in Catholic Cemetery.

Reagan John W June 17, 1851 - June 7, 1876
Reagan Mary Powers 1857 - 1952 wife of Daniel
Reagan Robert 1900 - 1909 son of Corn and Nettie

Jan 15, 1909 Leader

The funeral services of Robert Urban Reagan, the little son of Mr. and Mrs. C. J. Reagan, will be held at St. Paul's Church Saturday morning. The interment will follow in the family lot in the Catholic Cemetery.

Reagan Timothy 1859 - 1889
Rebmann Robert F 1910 - 1979 Marguerite J 1911 - 1984
Rebsamen Lloyd G July 10, 1920 Mela V July 18, 1927 - Nov
23, 1974
Recketenwald Wm J 1885 - 1944
Recktenwald Eleanor Schick Dec 14, 1896 - Jan 29, 1971
Recktenwald Elizabeth Link Sept 21, 1927 - Sept 9, 2008
Recktenwald Gerald W
Recktenwald Helen Rose Aug 31, 1921 - July 25, 2007
Recktenwald Kenneth L Sept 11, 1923 - Feb 8, 1957
Records Walter T May 6, 1892 - Mar 31, 1947 WWI
Records Walter T 1892 - 1947 Mary Woods 1889 - 1973
Redden Annie N 1872 - 1949
Redden Elizabeth A 1808 - 1919
Redden F D 1873 - 1953
Reddick Anna M 1871 - 1953
Reddick Patrick H 1879 - 1930
Reeves Anna Mae Wood 1903 - 1928 wife of Edward C
Reeves Elijah S 1866 - 1928
Reeves Letitia J 1872 - 1954
Regan Annie J died June 5, 1923 Bridget Kenney 1852 - 1925
Regan Daniel Jr. 1884 - 1949 son of Mary Powers and Daniel
Reagan
Regan Lillian Ellen Aug 11, 1915 - Nov 3, 2007
Regan wife of Welch Leonard Sept 23, - Feb 1915 our baby
Richard B Welch Dec 1903
Rehm Jean Schuster wife of Walter G
Rehm Walter G Feb 27, 1889 - July 28, 1962
Rehm Walter G Jr. June 25, 1917 - Feb 9, 1943
Rehn Norman H Oct 29, 1892 - Feb 6, 1969 Gertrude Dugan
Apr 22 1892 - Feb 9, 1985
Reidel John A 1868 - 1946 his wife Elizabeth Dalton 1870 -
1933
Reiling Henry B Dec 29, 1892 - Aug 31, 1942

Reinhardt Anna Benedix Mar 8, 1898 - June 20, 1979
    Nagdalena Ziegenthaler Oct 10, 1923
Reinig William L Sr. 1906 - 1987 Margaret E 1908 - 19??
Reiser Eileen Monaghan 1910 - 1992
Reiser Harry E 1905 - 1972
Reister
Reister Alice Daugherty Mar 15, 1914 - Jan 20, 1991
Reister Brenda Nickell Dec 16, 1948 - Dec 9, 1987
Reister Willie Stewart June 12, 1883 - Apr 12, 1955 wife of
    Joseph H Reister
Renfor Susan Lynn Jan 6, 1953 - June 18, 1954
Renfroe Michelle E Aug 17, 1955 - Oct 7, 1955
Reordan
Reordan Edward P 1855 - 1886
Reordan Ellen F 1829 - 1904
Reordan John B 1858 - 1907
April 7, 1907 Lexington Herald-Leader
The funeral services of John Breckinridge Reordan will take
    place at St. Paul's Catholic Church this afternoon at
    3:45 o'clock.

Reordan Katie B 1866 - 1881
Reordan Patrick H 1823 - 1884
Resiter Joseph S July 29, 1912 - Mar 26, 1960
Restrepo Martha Monto A June 19, 1897 - Mar 28, 1974
Revering David Sept 30, 1966
Reynolds Benson Mar 26, 1926 - Jul 7, 1979 WWI
Reynolds George Jan 3, 1865 - Dec 18, 1946 Nora Ready June
    25, 1869 - Feb 15, 1958 Mary R Freeman Dec 7, 1895
    - Dec 9, 1981
Reynolds Jay T June 6, 1953 - Mar 22, 1983
Reynolds Margaret M May 28, 1861 - June 3, 1939
Reynolds Mary E Nov 30, 1854 - July 18, 1894
Reynolds William C Jr. Dec 21, 1947 - Nov 11, 2007 Mary S
    June 11, 1947

Reynolds William C Sr. Apr 5, 1925 - May 27, 2002
Rhorer Anna 1875 - 1960
Rhorer Columbia 1877 - 1940
Rhorer Edward A 1873 - 1900
Rhorer Elizabeth 1860 - 1938
Rhorer Emma 1870 - 1966
Rhorer Emma Harp 1867 - 1948
Rhorer Father 1839 - 1929
Rhorer J P 1868 - 1939
Rhorer John Thos 1862 - 1944
Rhorer M Frances 1864 - 1955
Rhorer Mother 1844 - 1877
Rhorer W H 1860 - 1938
RHR Rubbetin Friede? 1889 - 1954
Rice Paul R Jan 30, 1924 - Dec 29, 1980 Mary Ann K Dec 20,
    1924 - May 20, 2008
Rice Paul Raymond Jan 30, 1924 - Dec 29, 1980 US Army
Rice Robert Lee Feb 1867 - 1955 Frances Sept 23, 1877 - June
    20, 1945
Richard Andrew Jan 17, 1902 - Dec 21, 1981
Richard Anna Bell Aug 6, 1913 - Mar 11, 1989
Richard Katherine Aug 12, 1909 - Apr 21, 2004
Richard Louise Nov 22, 1922 - June 27, 2007
Richard Mike Aug 28, 1872 - May 24, 1952 Mary Heins June
    22, 1877 - Apr 3, 1958
Richards Henry P Mar 17, 1911 - Nov 6, 1938

Jan 1, 1904 Leader
The funeral of Charles Frederick Richardson, the bright 4-
    year-old son of Mr. and Mrs. Charles Richardson, who
    died last night, will take place tomorrow morning from
    the family residence. Burial in Catholic Cemetery.

Richardson Eloise Nov 2, 1933 - July 17, 1979
Richardson Henry 1873 - 1950 Elizabeth 1877 - 1957

Richardson John 1841 - 1923 Sarah 1832 - 1902
Richardson Catherine Sept 16, 1875 - Sept 3, 1924

Mar 27, 1902 Morning Herald
The funeral services of Miss Maggie A Riche will be held
    beside the grave in the Catholic Cemetery this
    afternoon about 2 o'clock.

Richey John Francis Dec 4, 1910 - June 7, 2004 Helen Yates
    Apr 20, 1909 - Mar 8, 2001
Ricketts Clinton Sept 9, 1888 - May 2, 1955 Rosa Feb 24,
    1889 - July 15, 1979
Riester Joseph H Nov 26, 1879 - Dec 20, 1950
Riffle John M 1855 - 1935
Riffle Little Henry 1893 - 1893
Riffle Mary Grady 1857 - 1957
Riley
Riley Baby June 7, 1961 infant daughter of Tom and Phyllis
Riley Bridget 1823 - 1893
Riley Bridget Healy died Aug 30, 1923
Riley Elizabeth 1821 - 1905
Riley Frances 1860 - 1916
Riley Frances A died Sept 9, 1943
Riley James 1828 - 1886
Riley John 1830 - 1895
Riley John died June 30, 1909
Riley John died Oct 17, 1933
Riley John J 1860 - 1923
Riley Julia Drummy died 1956 wife of Thomas
Riley Laurence July 7, 1904 - Apr 2, 1991 Ann O'Neill Oct
    25, 1904 - Jan 19, 1979
Riley Mae K May 5, 1901 - July 2, 1983 Thomas E Nov 25,
    1902 - Feb 14, 1962
Riley Margaret E died Dec 5, 1969
Riley Martin died June 19, 1902

Riley Mary May 1835 - Nov 1835
Riley Maude Blandin 1870 - 1950 wife of John J
Riley Thomas 1894 - 1926
Riley William 1856 - 1878
Riley William E died Feb 7, 1942
Ringe Donald A 1923 Lucy B 1922 - 1984
Rives Anne E Shannon Nov 7, 1875 - Nov 28, 1961 wife of
    Robert C
Rives J Louis 1911 - 1966 Elizabeth 1981
Rives Laura Marie Jan 20, 1980 - Jan 2 1981 daughter of
    Louis and Sandy
Rives Robert C Jr. May 17, 1900 - Feb 12, 1991
Rives Robert G Feb 20, 1873 - Nov 22, 1945
Rives Virginia S Gayle Mar 11, 1907 - May 18, 1977 wife of
    Robert C Jr.
Robert Mary A W Oct 19, 1918 -Oct 30, 2002
Roberts Frank Staiar 1905 - 1968 Elizabeth Butler 1909 -
    1953
Robertson Paul L Feb 8, 1931 Ann S Mar 6, 1928 - Sept 21,
    2008
Robinson Mary Stout Sept 8, 1951 - Oct 17, 1988
Rocco Kathleen Wilson May 24, 1904 - May 28, 1973
Roche
Roche 1858 - 1927
Roche 1863 - 1932
Roche Albert b 1862 - 1916 Mollie Welch 1864 - 1962 Mary
    L 1899 - 1960
Roche David Anthony Sept 26, 1901 - Jan 22, 1991 Sarah
    Douds May 30, 1907 - June 22, 1996

July 14, 1908 Leader
The funeral services of Edward Roche were held at St. Paul's
    Church Tuesday morning and interment followed in
    the family lot in the Catholic Cemetery.

Roche James 1829 - 1864
Roche James M 1858 - 1942 Historian

May 2, 1911 Leader
At the advanced age of 82 years, Mrs. Johanna Roche died
    Monday at her. Burial will follow in the family lot in
    the Catholic Cemetery.

Roche John 1903 - 1984
Roche Joseph James 1888 - 1945
Roche Josephine Mildred 1892 - 1894
Roche Mary 1839 - 1921
Roche Mary Josephine 1884 - 1910
Roche Minnie A 1860 - 1911
Roche Rose Marie Aug 6, 1928
Roche Walter L 1890 - 1952 Anna M 1899 - 1987
Rodriguez Andrea Maria 1960 - 1963
Rodriguez Juan G Dec 23, 1920 Lorraine D July 4, 1920
Roe Jane Gormley 1927 - 1957 wife of Gardner
Rogers Anna 1899
Rogers Annie 1869 - 1956
Rogers Elizabeth C Oct 8, 1887 - Oct 24, 1967
Rogers Frank 1871 - 1933
Rogers Henry died Apr 18, 1930
Rogers John 1827 - 1877
Rogers John B Oct 26, 1861 - Dec 30, 1902
Rogers Patrick 1829 - 1901
Rogers 1919
Rose Alexander B Nov 26, 1876 - Apr 24, 1932 and wife
    Lillie Osborne Mar 24, 1891 - Feb 15, 1952
Rose Billie Mae Dec 2, 1915 - July 1, 1998
Rose Ruth Banta on earth Aug 4, 1919 - in Heaven Apr 12,
    2006
Rose Thomas M Feb 13, 1908 - Sept 11, 1993
Rose - Heinz Edna S 1905 - 2005 Raymond L 1904 - 1982

Marshall 1939 Wilbur 1935
Ross Charles
Ross James Patrick 1880 - 19 Mary Donlon 1883 - 1946
Ross Margaret A 1897 - 1987
Ross Marion Drake 1884 - 1957
Ross Marion M Apr 16, 1885 - Dec 27, 1978
Rothan J Martin Oct 3, 1881 - Apr 14, 1962 Anna C June 24,
1884 - Nov 25, 1956
Rothan Martin J Jr. 1909 - 1978
Rottman Edward H 1907 - 1959 Frances W 1910 - 1997
Rowland John 1852 - 1937
Ruddle Harold E Jan 20, 1911 - Aug 5, 1998 Agnes E Sept 9,
1915 - Feb 13, 2000
Rudebeaux Ralph 1867 - 1929 Cecile R 1870 - 1934
Ruggles Ester C Oct 31, 1928 Bettie P Sept 11, 1929 Timothy
C Aug 22, 1964
Ruh Alfred 1863 - 1933
Ruh Alfred 1897 - 1969 Catherine 1902 - 1983
Ruh Elmer J 1896 - 1938
Ruh Lucretia L 1900 - 1987
Ruh Maria 1828 - 1923
Ruh Martin 1824 - 1884
Ruh Rosa Stifel 1865 - 1943
Ruh Ruth L 1892 - 1928
Ruh Thomas Martin 1936 - 2001
Ruh Walter A 1892 - 1951
Runk Allan June 26, 1920 - Sept 16, 2005 Marianne W Oct 5,
1920 - Apr 8, 1984
Runyon Sue Frances July 1, 1936 Our Baby
Rush Paul Moore Mar 1, 1902 - Agnes Clancy Apr 6, 1900 -
May 31, 1957
Russell Ella 1874 - 1922
Russell Frances B Nov 7, 1910 - Oct 15, 1958
Russell Matthew Dec 15, 1865 - 1906
Rutherford Helen 1921 - 1927

Rutherford Lewis 1898 - 1977 Margaret C 1897 - 1995 Miner
Edward J 1905 - 1980 Agnes C 1909 - 2005
Rutledge Joseph R May 7, 1932 - June 2, 1996 Joan Tracey
Feb 28, 1936 - Sept 26, 2005
Rutledge Joseph R May 7, 1932 - June 2, 1996 Korea
Ryan Ann died Sept 23, 1876 wife of Patrick meet me in
Heaven
Ryan Ann Sheran 1845 - 1876
Ryan James died Aug 7, 1874 aged 84
Ryan James F 1871 - 1936
Ryan John R 1869 - 1890
Ryan Kate Burke 1857 - 1890
Ryan Margaret 1883 - 1969

Aug 20, 1905 Leader
The funeral services of Miss Margaret Ryan will be held at St.
Paul's Church Monday morning instead of in the
afternoon as erroneously stated. The burial will be in
the Catholic Cemetery.

Ryan Mary G 1866 - 1952
Ryan Patrick 1844 - 1923
Ryan Unknown
Ryan Unknown July 14, 1891 - Nov ??
Rye Leigh Fowler 1886 - 1961
Rynyan Sue Francis July 1, 1936
Sabatini Maria Grazia Sept 20, 1888 - Jan 29, 1971
Sackleh James A Mar 15, 1902 - Oct 2, 1957
Sackleh Rose George Feb 28, 1913 - July 7, 1970 wife of
James
Sackllah Fareed E July 18, 1927 - Apr 15, 200? Rose F Dec 5,
1929 - Aug 20, 1999
Sacklllah Essa July 10, 1893 - Apr 3, 1948
Sakly Gnem A Aug 15, 1901 - July 9, 1981
Salazar Dr Miguel A Carbonell Nov 11, 1897 - Mar 21, 1965

Sale Elizabeth Saulpaugh Mar 26, 1921 - June 3, 1998 Walter
  Minor Dec 24, 1917 - Oct 22, 1999
Sallee Andrew Brady Jr. 1907 - 1941
Sallee Andrew Brady Sr. 1884 - 1949
Sallee Anna Ginocchio 1881 - 1974
Sallee Elvira P 1911 - 1912
Sallee Hubert B 1888 - 1928 Marguerite E 1891 - 1970
Sallee Hubert Bernard Apr 22, 1922 - Mar 11, 2003 Maxine
  Marie Dec 1, 1925 - Nov 24, 1979
Sallee John D 1872 - 1934 Julia Lyons 1877 - 1957
Sallee Mary Mercedes 1915 - 1940
Sallee Teresa Laura 1921 - 1946
Saloshin Jake N Jan 31, 1894 - Nov 11, 1983
Saloshin Margaret B 1892 - 1971
Sanchez Odile B Jan 14, 1871 - July 26, 1938
Sartin Catherine H 1873 - 1951
Sartin Charles H 1879 - 1914
Sartin J W 1878 - 1930
Sartin Mary Henry 1878 - 1953
Saruso Antonio 1867 - 1908
Satterwhite Henrie Ta Unser 1895 - 1926
Saulpaugh Alvah P Jan 22, 1889 - Oct 20, 1973 Anna T Dec
  25, 1893 - Apr 19, 1978
Saulsbury Jefferson Davis June 5, 1901 - Nov 17, 1973
  Evelyn Morrissey Sept 8, 1902 - Apr 7, 1979
Saunier
Saunier Helen G died 1960
Saunier John Chevalier 1893 - 1965
Saunier Joseph Anthony 1892 - 1974
Saunier Louis Colson 1898 - 1980
Saunier Margaret Watkins 1861 - 1936
Saunier Mary Aug 18, 1949 Stanley M III Mar 18, 1954 - Dec
  2001
Saunier Stanley Milward Sr. Nov 10, 1895 - June 20, 1971
  Mary L Brown Jan 17, 1898 - July 30, 1975

Saunier Stephen C 1856 - 1926
Saunier Stephen Thaddus 1891 - 1949
Savage

Dec 9, 1899 Morning Herald
John Savage - Interment taking place in the Catholic
    Cemetery.

Savage Margaret died Apr 26, 1928
Savage Mary Died Dec 3, 1923
Savage Mollie 1864 - 1949
Savage Patrick Died June 1, 1924
Savage Roxie 1886 - 1935 Mary Margaret 1887 - 1888
Savage William 1872 - 1949
Savard Francis X Aug 10, 1843 - Nov 17, 1921
Savard Katherine McGurk Sept 1861 - June 1923 wife of
    Francis X
Saxton Lillian Rumsey 1892 - 1954
Sayer Conway 1893 - 1941
Sayre William J 1903 - 1937
Scaffer Joseph N 1885 - 1950
Scanlin Anna Bruin 1878 - 1940
Scanlon Frank Joseph Jan 21, 1894 - Oct 28, 1965 Frances
    Desha Aug 4, 1895 - Mar 6, 1990
Scanlon Frank Joseph Jr. May 1, 1923 - Nov 11, 1998
Scanlon Henry Kate H July 11, 1863 - Sept 3, 1942 wife of
    John
Scanlon John Aug 4, 1864 - Mar 26, 1901
Scanlon John Desha Aug 13, 1927 - Sept 26, 1975 Mona
    Sullivan July 1, 1925
Scanlon Mike 1887 - 1958 Margaret H 1888 - 1951
Scanlon William L Apr 20, 1913 - June 1951
Schafer
Schafer Annie Isola 1864 - 1959
Schafer Esther T Sept 10, 1904 - Aug 1, 1946

Schafer Harry W July 26, 1864 - Aug 19, 1937
Schafer Harry W Jr. May 7, 1902 - Jan 31, 1959
Scaffer Joseph N 1885 - 1950
Schafer Mary K Aug 5, 1870 - Dec 27, 1946
Scheffel Lila P 1943
Schmitz Adam M May 5, 1924 - Mar 3, 2008 Jean Cash June
    18, 1925 - Dec 8, 1986
Schneider Arthur Anthony Oct 27, 1896 - Mar 26, 1961 Nellie
    O'Hare Apr 9, 1898 - Feb 14, 1985
Schneider Arthur Patricia Sept 8, ? - ? Foley Aug ? - Apr ?
Schneider Franklin died July 23, 1898 husband of Julianna,
    father of 5 children
Schneider Henry J Mar 18, 1932 - Jan 23, 1962
Schoenbachler Valerie died Dec 25, 1965 Mary died Feb 27,
    1953
Schrader John H 1908 - 19? Mary E 1918 - 1976

Feb 19, 1906 Leader
Henry Schlutze, 60, died February 16 at St. Joseph's Hospital
    of pneumonia. Burial in Catholic Cemetery.

Schultz Mary Kaeder Dec 23, 1942 - June 1, 1971
Schweickart Henry C 1856 – 19?3
Schweickart Margaret C 1889 - 1999
Schweickart Theresa 1861 - 1925
Schwendeman Eithnea O'Donnell 1902 - 1978 Joseph
    Raymond 1897 - 1984 married Oct 12, 1912
Schwertfeger Mary Elizabeth Petit 1947 - 2007
Sciantarell Guido Lawrence Sept 1914 - Feb 16, 1987 WWII
Sciassis Angelo Apr 12, 1889 - Apr 4, 1911
Scollard Ella June 20, 1843 - May 24, 1927
Scollard Michael died Oct 18, 1895 aged 68
Scott
Scott Anna A 1868 - 1960
Scott Anne Long 1833 - 1915

Scott Ellen E 1850 - 1923
Scott Gertrude T 1876 - 1950
Scott John 1856 - 1926
Scott Louis A 1846 - 1916
Scott Matilda 1826 - 1892
Scott Patricia L 1945 Thelma 1916 - 1980
Scott Patrick 1823 - 1886
Scott Thomas 1892 - 1894
Scott William 1862 - 1882
Scully Angeline M 1902 - 1963 Robert T 1900 - 1980
Scully Annette Apr 18, 1927 - Oct 21, 2003
Scully Catherine Oct 23, 1881 - Dec 19, 1946
Scully Edward July 30, 1858 - Nov 10, 1918
Scully Edward B 1882 - 1968 Sarah F 1883 - 1949
Scully Ellen died Sept 18, 1867 John died Jan 15, 1870
        Michael died Aug 15, 1876
Scully Harry B 1894 - 1961
Scully J W Apr 4, 1923 - June 6, 1930
Scully James F 1872 - 1934
Scully James 1845 - 1913
Scully James died Mar 5, 1913
Scully James H Dec 27, 1879 - Dec 13, 1937 his wife Mary
        McBrayer June 12, 1884 - Feb 22, 1980
Scully James J Nov 14, 1896 - Dec 9, 1943 Edna B Dec 11,
        1898 - July 1987
Scully John 1865 - 1919
Scully John J 1896
Scully Joseph Lawrence 1906 - 1959 our baby Mary Elizabeth
        July 26, 1950 Madeleine Guyaard 1918
Scully Katherine 1846 - 1889
Scully Kearney John 1926 - 1966
Scully Lucille Hadden 1902 - 1934
Scully Margaret B died 1865
Scully Margaret E 1897 - 1979
Scully Martin Joseph 1893 - 1965 Tillie Kearney 1896 - 1966

Scully Martin Joseph Jr. Nov 5, 1928 - June 1, 2004 Alice
    Ann Feb 6, 1932
Scully Martin S 1861 - 1937 Nellie S 1866 - 1907
Scully Mary E Moore 1874 - 1923 wife of James F
Scully Mary H 1856 - 1927
Scully Mary H 1970 - 1947
Scully Michael H July 31, 1902 - July 22, 1969 Nettie Smith
    May 18, 1900 - Mar 24, 1965

Feb 25, 1906 Leader
Michael J. Scully, 43, died February 21 of hemorrhage. Burial
    in Catholic Cemetery.

Scully Robert T II July 24, 1938 - Dec 11, 1944
Scully Thomas A 1884 - 1944
Scully Thomas J Jan 1, 1892 - Jan 10, 1975
Scully Tunis F 1902 - 1969
Scully Wilhelmina 1898 - 1968
Scully William P May 14, 1870 - May 6, 1941
Scully William P Sept 3, 1913 - Feb 26, 1962 Helen E May 7,
    1918 - Feb 7, 1982
Seale Frank Earl Feb 25, 1911 - Aug 6, 1985
Seale Viola Elizabeth Parks Oct 23, 1910 - Jan 15, 1976 Frank
    Earl Feb 25, 1911 - Aug 6, 1985
Seale Viola Elizabeth Parks Oct 23, 1910 - Jan 15, 1976 wife
    of Frank Earl
Searcy Muriel Notaro 1929 - 1958 wife of James Searcy Jr.
Seiver Lucy Ellen 1943 - 1966
Selby Brack Edward Apr 16, 1964 - Dec 5, 1997
Seller John Lyn Apr 2, 1888 - Aor 196? Nora Clancy June 3,
    1892 - Dec 18, 196?
Semma Joseph 1857 - 1945 Rose S Semma 1867 - 1955
Sergeant Helen M 1889 - 1978
Seufert Frederick B Apr 3, 1831 - Aug 26, 1917 Anna M Aug
    7, 1876 - May 6, 1915 Florence H 1882 - June 10,

1934

Shade Thomas A Nov 19, 1968
Shaffer Joseph N 1885 - 1890
Shahon Mary A Nov 9, 1845 - Oct 11, 1884
Shanahan Bridget 1853 - 1924 Lawrence 1840 - 1902
Shanahan Hangra S died Apr 7, 1853 aged 60 Thomas died
    Feb 2, 1885
Shanahan William L Nov 19, 1893 - June 24, 1954 WWI
Shannon Alma C Aug 19, 1822 - Dec 30, 1866 wife of
    Edward
Shannon Amy Woods July 12, 1895 - Sept 8, 1973 wife of
    Thomas A
Shannon Bernadette Sept 12, 1879 - Aug 23, 1959
Shannon Bridget Cassidy Sept 1839 - May 5, 1930
Shannon C Barry Nov 4, 1891 - Sept 28, 1946
Shannon Catherine T Apr 11, 1871 - Aug 5, 1943 wife of John
    B
Shannon Edward born Aug 30, 1863 aged 18 months
Shannon Ellen Aug 1840 - Mar 15, 1888
Shannon Ellen Haley 1895 John P 1944 Michael 1903 Mary
    1966 Michael J 1965
Shannon Gormley, Mary G 1865 - 1939 Patrick R 1863 - 1925
    Bridget 1836 - 1895 Philip 1810 - 1895
Shannon Infant 1943
Shannon J Harry Aug 9, 1881 - May 15, 1918
Shannon James June 1821 - Nov 22, 1891
Shannon James 1868
Shannon James T Aug 28, 1869 - Aug 13, 1879
Shannon James May 28, 1869 - Sept 22, 1934
Shannon John Apr 10, 1843 - Mar 3, 1917
Shannon John B Sept 1870 - Nov 14, 1951
Shannon John M Mar 28, 1873 - Feb 6, 1943
Shannon John Thomas Oct 3, 1934 - Sept 6, 1999
Shannon John W 1866 - 1901
Shannon Julia M 1891 - 1983 Edward V 1891 - 1974

Shannon Martin Feb 15, 1855 - Feb 18, 1902
Shannon Mary A Dec 25, 1864 - Feb 23, 1919
Shannon Mary Ann 1849 - 1934
Shannon Mary Ferry Smith 1906 - 1984
Shannon Mary William Aug 14, 1885 - June 10, 1918
Shannon Michael 1873 - 1918
Shannon Patrick 1812 - 1892 his wife Mary Jane James 1820 -
    1902 their daughter Annie 1851 - 1907
Mar 26, 1902   Leader
Mrs. Mary Jane Shannon died at her home, seven and a half
    miles from this city, on the Russell Cave Pike,
    Wednesday morning, aged 81 years. The interment
    will be in the Catholic Cemetery.

Nov 26, 1907 Leader
The funeral services of Miss Anna A. Shannon will be held at
    St. Paul's Church Wednesday morning, and the
    interment will follow in the family lot in the Catholic
    Cemetery

Shannon Robert H Oct 16, 1888 - July 25, 1953 WWI
Shannon Thomas 1870
Shannon Thomas A MD Jan 15, 1874 - Mar 8, 1969
Shannon Thomas H Feb 21, 1871 - Oct 9, 1906

Oct 17, 1913 Leader
The funeral of Mrs. Anne Sharkey will be held at St. Paul's
    Catholic Church Saturday morning. Interment will
    follow in the family lot in the Catholic Cemetery.

Sharkey John J Dec 23, 1868 - Oct 1, 1941
Sharkey John J Aug 1, 1905 - June 30, 1938
Sharkey Mary Dugan May 12, 1869 - June 22, 1941
Sharkey Mary Gormley 1900 - 1980
Sharkey Mattie Annie James Hugh Ellen Rosa

Sharkey Owen 1839 - 1915 Mary 1840 - 1906

Sharkey Owen and Maggie

Sharkey erected by Owen and Mary in memory of their
children

Sharkey Owen R Sept 1900 - June 19??

Sharp Leonard 1898 - 1954

Shay Johannah 1883 - 1888

Shay John D 1854 - 1917

Shay Mary B 1859 - 1926

Shay Timothy died Jan 5, 1887 aged 28

Shea Johanna May 3, 1856 - Mar 1, 1877

Shea Agnes Welsh 1875 - 1939

Shea Ann Shinners

Shea Cornelious May 1835 - Jan 16, 187?

Shea Ellie 1868 - 1888

Shea Frank A 1895 - 1944

Shea James H 1871 - 1939

Shea Kate 1864 - 1920

Shea Marie M 1894 - 1947

Shea Mary Abigail Dec 1, 1926 - Mar 15, 2009

Shea Michael 1812 - 1872 Ellan Horine 1804 - 1884

Shea Theresa Ann Dec 3, 1967 daughter of Daniel J and Mary
Ann

Shea Thomas 1888 - 1953

Shea William 1828 - 1849

Sheanan Dennis died May 1881

Sheehan Bridget died Oct 31, 1938 Mary S Doyle died Feb 5,
1929 Mayme Doyle died Dec 17, 1922

Sheehan Dennis Dec 2, 1863 - Feb 4, 1945 Thomas Feb 28,
1858 - Aug 20, 1906

Sheehan John G 1844 - 1921 CW

Sheehan Josephine Jan 29, 1856 - Aug 12, 1897 Nellie Sept 9,
1861 - Feb 17, 1893

Sheehan Katherine C died Mar 27, 1943

Sheehan Martin May 21, 1821 - July 9, 1909 Ellen July 18,

1827 - July 22, 1895
Sheehy Ann Wallace 1925 - 1986
Sheehy Anna K 1880 - 1922
Sheehy Anne Mae 1888 - 1973
Sheehy Elizabeth 1858 - 1917
Sheehy John 1880 - 1953
Sheehy John T 1872 - 1928
Sheehy Lucille Miner 1899 - 1961
Sheehy Mary Elizabeth Apr 21, 1898 - Jan 30, 1970
Sheehy Mary Rose May 19, 1920 - May 10, 1976
Sheehy Richard William 1893 - 1963
Sheehy Thomas 1854 - 1915
Shelhan John F died Dec 2, 1926
Shelton Dorothy A Sept 22, 1908 - July 16, 1952
Shelton James Lee Feb 28, 1896 - Feb 7, 1973
Shelton Miller F Apr 10, 1907 - Mar 21, 1969
Shelton Miller F Apr 10, 1907 - Mar 21, 1969 WWII
Shely Isadore 1898 - 1965
Shephard Veronica McMahon May 27, 1911 - Sept 1, 1938
Sherlock Billie 1868 - 1941
Sherlock Leo T Feb 20, 1898 - Oct 23, 1973
Sherlock Michael 1870 - 1956 Elizabeth 1880 - 1940
Sherlock Paul A Sept 1, 1915 - Apr 8, 2000 Frances C Oct 10,
    1913 - July 18, 1988 Joan Sherlock Shepherd Oct 7,
    1936 - May 5, 1987
Sherlock Patrick 1833 - 1916 Catherine 1847 - 1900 Mary
    1872 - 1906
July 29, 1906 Leader
The funeral services of Miss Mary Ann Sherlock, 34 years of
    age, who died at the home of her father, Patrick
    Sherlock, on the Iron Works road, Saturday morning,
    will take place at St. Paul's Catholic Church Monday
    morning. Burial in Catholic Cemetery.

Sherlock Thomas Leo Oct 1, 1930 Wilma Reynolds Sept 11,

1933 Thomas Joseph July 27, 1961 - July 31, 1983
Shields Alice C 1861 - 1917
Shinn Robert Carter died May 1946 Billye Benckart died Jan
    7, 1975
Shipley David A July 28, 1957 - Apr 17, 1973
Shirley Elwood Oct 23, 1923 - Mar 18, 2007 Dorothy G Dec
    22, 1924
Shirley Elwood Oct 23, 1923 - Mar 18, 2007 WWII
Shropshire James T Dec 10, 1922 - May 12, 1971 Susan S Feb
    17, 1923 - July 12, 1985
Shuey Earl Albert 1918 - 1974 Frances 1919
Shuey Mary Jo 1950 - 1975
Shumaker Ann P Feb 13, 1894 - Sept 3, 1935
Shumaker Harrison B Jr. 1927 - 1930
Silvestri Harry 1901 - 1978 Anna 1900 - 1997
Simmons Mollie Winkle 1890 - 1931
Simmons W E Aug 29, 1909 - June 13, 1985
Simon Jerome Linus Oct 18, 1922 -Oct 22, 2002 Ann Geneva
    Sept 22, 1922
Simon Wayne J Apr 20, 1949 - May 12, 1981
Simpson F C 1872 - 1899
Singleton Nora McCullough 1900 - 1984
Sipe Margaret C nee Bietz 1922 - 1991
Skain Unknown
Skain John Sept 30, 1868 - Apr 30, 1945
Skain John William
Skain Nellie H Apr 8, 1873 - Feb 4, 1951
Skees Hilary R Dec 26, 1920 - June 15, 1969 Eileen Kelley
    May 6, 1927 - Jan 17, 2003
Skees Stephanie Marie Jan 30, 1953 - Oct 27, 198?
Slattery Edward 1866 - 1933 Katherine Knox 1863 - 1928
    Robert 1898 - 1946
Slattery Margaret Mary 1903 - 1980
Slavin Ellen 1849 - 1904
Oct 15, 1904 Morning Herald

The funeral services of Mrs. Ellen Slavin, who died Thursday, will be held at St. Paul's Catholic Church this morning at 9 o'clock, the interment to be in the family lot in the Catholic Cemetery.

Slavin James E Apr 24, 1857 - Sept 27, 1922
Slavin James Jr. 1868 - 1949
Slavin James Sr. 1832 - 1905
Slavin Joanna A June 14, 1868 - Sept 12, 1948
Slavin John P June 20, 1860 - July 22, 1929
Slavin Katie

Jan 22, 1906 Leader
Katherine Lavin, 69, died at Walnut Hills, January 18, of complicated diseases. Burial in Catholic Cemetery.

Slavin Margaret 1876 - 1915
Slavin Mary C Mar 14, 1868 - May 8, 1924
Slavin Pat 1881 - 1941

Jan 8, 1906 Leader
Thomas Lyons Slavin, 5 years, died January 5, of scarlet fever. Burial in Catholic Cemetery January 6.

Jan 21, 1906 Leader
The funeral services of Mrs. Thomas Lavin, of Walnut Hill, this county, took place Saturday morning at St. Paul's Church, Rev. James P. Barry officiating. The internment was in the Catholic Cemetery, this city.

Slavin Tom 1885 - 1955
Slavin William A 1887 - 1959

Nov 16, 1907 Lexington Herald-leader
Services for William Sleath who died form heart disease will

be held form his residence tomorrow afternoon at 3
o'clock and interment will be in the Catholic
Cemetery.

Smith Annie Cromwell 1874 - 1909
Smith Annie McCarthy 1877 - 1909
Smith Annie Saunier 1890 - 1958 wife of Adam H Smith

Apr 27, 1909 Leader
The funeral of Mrs. Annie Cromwell Smith will take place
from the residence of her husband, and the services
will be held at St. Paul's Church with requiem mass
Wednesday morning. The interment will follow in the
family lot in the Catholic Cemetery.

Smith Arthur Augustus 1910 - 1962
Smith Benjamin B Aug 20, 1879 - Oct 17, 1959
Smith Bridget died Dec 28, 1937
Smith Bryant May 13, 1853 - Feb 23, 1912 Kate June 26,
1855 - Mar 18, 1913
Smith Charles D "Speedy" 1892 - 1959

May 26, 1914 Leader
The funeral services of Mr. Edward Smith were held at the St.
Paul's Catholic Church this morning, and were
attended by a great number of the young man's friends.
Interment followed in the Catholic Cemetery.

Smith Frances Miner Oct 12, 1901 - Mar 10, 1957
Smith Isabell Riley 1878 - 1947
Smith J Reid 1909 - 1966 Mark E 1902 - 1962
Smith James Edward July 1915 - Aug 23, 1962 WWII
Smith James F 1912 - 1973 Mary Rita 1919 - 1980
Smith James Leland Sept 27, 1904 - June 28, 1931
Smith Johanna McGrath 1888 - 1954

Smith John D 1871 - 1945
Smith John J Apr 22, 924 - Oct 15, 1953 WWI
Smith John T 1902 - 1965 Shirley W 1914 - 1996
Smith Luke A 1886 - 1939
Smith Luther Tutas May 1956 - Apr 12, 1922
Smith M Sgt Adam H 1875 - 1958
Smith Mary Frances Jan 17, 1917 - Apr 25, 2008 WWII
Smith Mayme Gillispie 1888 - 1952
Smith Norman Pitt Apr 27, 1905 - Nov 24, 1947 Agnes Hogan
        Apr 30, 1906 - Oct 3, 1991
Smith Patrick Hogan Oct 23, 1947 - Aug 27, 2006 Jean
        Hendricks Nov 22, 1947 married Apr 12, 1969
Smith Thomas J 1888 - 1942
Smitha Edwina Bryan 1870 - 1964
Smithers Agnes L 1913 - Hubert C 1903 - 1959
Smreker Rupert Anthony June 14, 1908 - Feb 5, 1993 Hattie
        Ielene Feb 13, 1911- Mar 14, 1999
Soard John N Sr. Sept 11, 1897 - Jan 25, 1965 Lillie M Oct
        19, 1900 - Apr 5, 1983
Soard Joretta Monson 1931 - 1954 wife of Wallace D
Soard Lena May 18, 1903 - June 15, 1965
Soard Roy July 4, 1899 - June 15, 1957
Southwood Brent C Mar 26, 1915 - Jan 3, 2000 Edith Mosier
        Oct 17, 1918
Sparks John Calvert Oct 23, 1923 - Nov 25, 1985 Jane
        Mulholland July 5, 1921 - Mar 16, 2009
Spears
Spears Dan K Nov 14, 1943 - Mar 15, 2004
Spellman Patrick Family
May 12, 1903 Leader
The funeral services of Miss Mary Spellman will be held at
        Saint Paul's Church Friday morning. The interment
        will be in the family lot in the Catholic Cemetery.

Spencer Franz Joseph 1868 - 1944 Georgette F 1868 - 1947

Spencer Henry R 1924 - 1995 Lucille Haney 1911 - 1963
Spengler Frank J 1895 - 1974 Lillian Hall 1903 - 1987
Spengler Loyal Joseph 1906 - 1945
Spicer Edward T Sept 25, 1950
Spicer Elizabeth Apr 3, 1961
Spicer J Albert Nov 6, 1918
Spicer Mary Elizabeth Sept 27, 1847 - Jan 23, 1914
Spicer Susan Mary Dec 30, 1959

Mar 29, 1897 Morning Herald
The funeral service of Mrs. Johanna G. Spillman will be held
    at St. Paul's Church Tuesday morning at 9 o'clock.
    Interment in the Catholic Cemetery.

Spink Ella R 1861 - 1942
Spradling Ann Starck 1913
Springer Robert F 1938 Joan C 1940 - 2003
Stafford Frank D 1895 - 1966 Lucile Mahoney 1905 - 19
Stagg Carolina Schwitz Nov 14, 1886 - May 4, 1953 wife of
    Stanley M
Stagg William Stanley Oct 6, 1914 - Jan 26, 1986
Stakelin Rose Mary Keller July 23, 1913 - Dec 11, 1979
Stallard John Anthony May 13, 1920 - Oct 5, 2009 Nettie Sue
    Jan 27, 1918 - Feb 11, 1996
Stallard W M 1891 - 1982 Ann Eva 1892 - 1942
Stanton Edward C Aug 10, 1922 - Oct 16, 2002 Hildegard M
    May 14, 1928 - Sep 29, 2009
Stapp John A 1914 - 196? Mary M ? - 2006
Starck Anne McKenna 1879 - 1971 wife of William Starck
Starck James J 1912 - 1977
Starck Mary Louise 1909 infant daughter of W and A Mck
    Starck
Starck William 1874 - 1949
Stefany William Apr 26, 1912 - Nov 25, 2004 Helen Freese
    Sept 11, 1913 - Dec 14, 1983

Stella William 1855 - 1935 Michael 1851 - 1918 Louise 1862
- 1920
Stemmier Edward M died June 14, 1942
Stemmler Ellen O died Nov 7, 1953
Stencel Alfred A Sept 7, 1897 - Jan 17 16, 1945 WWI
Stengel Alfred A Sept 7, 1897 - Jan 17 16, 1945 Chornie B
Feb 20, 1906 - Jan 2, 1992
Stevens Imogene O Apr 1930 - June 3, 1986
Stevens Jacob 1862 - 1943
Stevens Jesse T Feb 1895 - Feb 5, 1953 WWI
Stevens John Keller "Jackie" 1934 - 1944
Stevens Katherine Burke 1903 - 1974
Stevens Leo 1900 - 1937
Stevens Margaret Dunleavy Apr 24, 1904 - June 30, 2001
Stevens Susie M 1865 - 1937
Stevens Uma Rutledge died 1992
Stevens Walter D 1897 - 1951
Stevens William E Jr. Feb 15, 1927 - Nov 26, 1988
Stevens William L Sept 8, 1897 - Mar 31, 1982
Stevenson
Stewart Charles L May 14, 1869 - Apr 18, 1958 Margaret
O'Brien Oct 4, 1883 - Sept 20, 1961
Stewart Connie B Dec 30, 1925 - Nov 23, 1944 Killed in
Action
Stewart Cornelius B 1888 - 1930
Stewart Isaac N 1884 - 1967 Marie E 1883 - 1955
Stewart Kenneth H 1926 - 1930
Stewart Ray McKinley June 22, 897 - Oct 11, 1962 Frances
Jeter Apr 7, 1909 - May 6, 1980
Stewart Vincent M 1921 Laura J 1925 - 1931
Stewart William B 1871 - 1943 Mary Matlack 1877 - 1937
Sticks William 1885 - 1968 Josephine 1887
Stickwith Louisa 1853 - Sept 18, 1906 wife of John
Still Edward 1872 - 1941 Anna Price 1880 - 1929
Stivers Larry R 1948 - 1998

Stivers Robert 1924 - 1969 Robert K 1953 - 1963 Marilyn
    1923 - 1988
Stoeckinger Jo Ann July 7, 1939 - Jan 30, 2002
Stoeckinger Joan Nov 1935 - May 13, 2000
Stoeckinger John Malcolm May 1, 1933 - ?
Stoeckinger Joseph A June 14, 1891 - Dec 15, 1966 Margaret
    C Aug 15, 1902 - Dec 25, 1996
Stoeckinger Joseph A June 18, 1928 - Aug 8, 1951
Stoeser John 1857 - 1935 Mary C 1868 - 1959
Stokley Nell Holt Jan 21, 1900 - Jan 1, 1984
Storner John Frederick Feb 15, 1922 - Dec 9, 1995 WWII
Stough - Smith
Stout Henry H Jr. Apr 7, 1919 - June 21, 1998 Sara May 10,
    1918 - May 10, 2007
Strader Elizabeth J Murphy 1883 - 1940 wife of Stewart W
    Strader
Strader Stewart W 1882 - 1948
Streiff Frank 1870 - 1941 Mabel 1875 - 1937
Streiff Fred Dec 26, 1912 - Mar 24, 1993
Streiff Joseph J 1903 - 1962
Streine John 1835 - 1922 Elizabeth McDonald 1850 - 1879
Strine Mary Chevalier 1847 - 1913
Strom Sue Ann Brown Apr 30, 1930 - Mar 7, 1996
Sulier Ruth C Sept 15, 1910 - Jan 18, 1991 John B J Jan 11,
    1908 -July 30, 2003
Sulla Seraeina Pace 1923 - 2000 Ferinando N 1920 - 1985
Sullivan - To every thing there is a season --- A time to be
    born and a time to die
Sullivan Albert Frances
Sullivan Bartholomew 1888 - 1924
Sullivan Catherine
Sullivan Children Patrick 1855 - 1876 Mrs. Nettie Heafey
    1880 - 1896 John J 1858 - 1897
Sullivan Denis 1821 - 1907 Ellen 1819 - 1911
Mar 6, 1911 Leader

Mrs. Ellen Sullivan, aged 92 years, died at the home of her daughter, Mrs. Mary C. Stewart. Burial will take place in the Catholic Cemetery.

Sullivan Edward A 1881 - 1949
Sullivan Ellen C 1897 - 1972
Sullivan Ellen Z 1895 - 1965
Sullivan Emily Aug 31, 1836 - Mar 25, 1916
Sullivan Emmett Eugene Feb 8, 1906 - Nov 8, 1954
Sullivan Eugene J 1860 - 1906 Margaret M 1860 - 1912
Sullivan Francea X 1889 - 1974
Sullivan Francis R 1934 - 1979
Sullivan Francis T June 22, 1913 - Nov 14, 1949 WWII
Sullivan Galena S 1897 - 1973
Sullivan Geo M Aug 16, 1864 - Jan 7, 1954
Sullivan Gerald May 14, 1909 - Jan 1, 2007 Margaret June 24, 1907 - Mar 6, 2005
Sullivan James T Apr 18, 1860 - Aug 22, 1927
Sullivan Jere E Apr 7, 1914 Virginia Johnson Mar 10, 1913 - Mar 28, 1989
Sullivan Jere P 1865 - 1934
Sullivan John G Chris 1908 - 1959 Laura B Halsey 1914 - 1999
Sullivan John Jeremiah Sr. July 26, 1904 - Feb 6, 1964 Elanore O'Brien July 9, 1911 - Dec 25, 1988
Sullivan John L 1866 - 1901 Annie 1867 - 1925 John L Jr. 1898 - 1924
Sullivan John P 1900 - 1955
Sullivan John S 1858 - 1897
May 25, 1897 Morning Herald
John Sullivan - The remains of the deceased were held at St. Paul's Catholic Church yesterday morning, burial was in the Catholic Cemetery.

Sullivan Joseph A Feb 16, 1878 - Nov 21, 1935

Sullivan Julia 1857 - 1922

Sullivan Katherine Maloney 1886 - 1953

Sullivan Kathryn F 1895 - 1977 James M 1875 - 1948

Sullivan Louise 1905 - 1964

Sullivan Margaret 1911 - ?

Sullivan Margaret F Roche 1860 - 1932 wife of John J

Sullivan Mary C Apr 28, 1903 - Mar 26, 1988

Sullivan Mary G Jan 7, 1943

Sullivan Mary Smith Died Jan 7, 1935

Sullivan Michael Sept 29, 1826 - Feb 10, 1905

Sullivan Michael William Mar 10, 1945 - July 26, 2000

Sullivan Nellie Mar 7, 1846 - May 8, 1916

Sullivan Nellie Dundon 1870 - 1939

Sullivan Neville C 1893 - 1979

Sullivan Pearle Irene Mar 20, 1884 - Sept 4, 1962

Sullivan Thomas Marshall July 14, 1930 - Feb 7, 2003 Esther
        Stickney May 19, 1930 - Jan 8, 1986

Sullivan Virginia J Mar 10, 1913 - Mar 28, 1989

Sullivan William Harrison 1894 - 1950

Sullivan Wm D Apr 26, 1867 - Dec 25, 1912

Sumpter Rosaloa K Nov 13, 1917 - Nov 24, 2005

Sun Eileen

Sun Jessie

Sun Jessie Marie June 19, 1907 - June 19, 1980 Eileen May
        1902 - May 12, 1989

Sunley William B Dec 7, 1890 - Sept 30, 1955 Mary H Aug
        27, 1890 - June 30, 1983

Sutton Ernest Ellis June 7, 1898 - Jan 5, 1966 Justina Heinl
        Sept 25, 1900 - May 21, 1970

Sutton Gordon George Dec 16, 1926 - May 1, 1978 Elizabeth
        Jeter Apr 9, 1925

Sutton Gordon George Dec 16, 1926 - May 1, 1978 WWII

Sutton William Klair Dec 11, 1924 - Sept 16, 1991

Swanson Dorothy L May 13, 1940 - Dec 12, 1998 daughter of
        George & Alice

Sweeney
Sweeney A Craig 1916 - 1943
Sweeney Catherine 1821 - 1891
Sweeney Emma Jackson May 24, 1906 - Aug 10, 1977
Sweeney James Stephen May 14, 1884 - May 6, 1955
Sweeney John 1846 - 1908
Sweeney John J June 18, 1902 - Nov 7, 1957
Sweeney John Francis June 11, 1881 - Dec 1952 Martha
    Valiria Sept 17, 1889 - Oct 12, 1954
Sweeney Mary Trainor Dec 31, 19?5
Sweeney Michael 1811 - 1893
Sweeney Michael 1876 - 1953
Sweeney Peter Apr 30, 192?
Sweeney Philip Joseph Feb 25, 1966
Sweeney Rose O
Sweeny Charles 1910 - 1968
Sweeny John 1875 - 1959 Katherine 1880 - 1959
Sweeny John Thomas 1907 - 1972 Florence Foster 1911 -
    1994

Jan 26, 1909 Lexington Herald
The funeral services of Martin E Sweeney, who died at his
    home, Sunday will take place at St. Paul's Catholic
    Church this afternoon at 2 o'clock and interment being
    in the Catholic Cemetery.

Sweeny Martin 1905 - 1956 Marie
Sweeny Mary A Kennedy 1882 - 1956 wife of Michael J
Swieterman Julius H 1899 - 1977 Alvira 1900 - 1997
Swift Calk Catherine B 1903 - 1984
Swift Elizabeth A June 2, 1924 - Mar 15, 2005
Swift Mary McCarthy July 10, 1926 - Mar 26, 2007
Swift Morrison V 1900 - 1957 Virginia B 1900 - 1952
Swift Morrison V Jr. July 26, 1925 - Jan 22, 1985
Swigert Margaret 1855 - 1896

Talbott George H 1887 - 1955
Talbott Thelma M 1895 - 1987
Tate Clifford J Sept 10, 1902 - Mar 4, 1975 Mary Bivin Aug
    23, 1904 - June 11, 1980
Taylor Dr Richard May 3, 1846 - May 10, 1882
Taylor Katherine Kelley Dec 31, 1898 - June 20, 1961
Taylor Mary Kelly 1852 - 1926
Taylor Richard K 1877 - 1948
Taylor W Denham 1910 - 1981 Frances G 1912 - 1984
Tearney Thomas died Nov 1860 John son of T & M died Aug
    14, 1864 age 7
Terney Ann O'Connell 1905 - 1934
Terney James Francis 1905 - 1987
Thomas 1878 - 1911
Thomas Edwin W Aug 18, 1918 - Mar 19, 2004
Thomas Edwin W Jr. Apr 30, 1942 - Oct 7, 1955
Thomas Frank D Sept 28, 1946 - Sept 21, 1996
Thomas Henry
Thomas in Gormely area
Thomas James Kenney Dec 25, 1915 - June 19, 1997 Sandra
    Gayle
Thomas Joseph Jr. Alonzo William
Thomas Lester C Jan 24, 1899 - Jan 26, 1975 Frances R Feb
    16, 1900 - Apr 2, 1993
Thomas Mary Elizabeth Oct 21, 1919 - July 8, 1985
Thomason Florence Hall Jan 26, 1915 - Feb 13, 1957
Thompson H J 1880 - 1987
Thompson Charles Dewey Aug 21, 1898 - Jan 31, 1984
Thompson Charles R 1906 - 1988 Henry A 1949 - 1960 Helen
    C 1918 - 2003
Thompson Gladys Louise Oct 12, 1936 - Apr 4, 1946
Thompson Mary Charles Sept 13, 1927 - Sept 7, 1998
Thompson Mary Welsh Sept 18, 1902 - Dec 3, 2000
Thompson William Matthew Jan 31, 1931 - Apr 6, 1988
    Grace Blair Nov 16, 1936

Thompson William Matthew 1931 - 1988 US Navy

Thornton Catherine Rhorer 1867 - 1963 wife of M F

Thornton Charles A Jan 25, 1895 - July 26, 1984 Clara M July 2, 1892 - Nov 24, 1966

Thornton Cornelius 1896 - Mar 24, 1985 WWI

Thornton Hannah C 1877 - 1972 Joseph D 1899 - 1958

Thornton Helen Catherine Nov 7, 1914 - Nov 25, 1989

Thornton James A June 24, 1929 - Feb 25, 1965 WWII

Thornton James A June 24, 1929 - Feb 25, 1965

Thornton James E Dec 1, 1894 - July 22, 1990 Anna Frances June 20, 1894 - Oct 4, 1987

Thornton James W Jr. Apr 18, 1913 - Nov 18, 1981

Thornton M F 1864 - 1939

Thornton M Katherine May 10, 1911 - July 6, 1997

Thornton Mary Josephine Nov 13, 1909 - July 7, 1982

Thornton Mary Louise May 25, 1926 - Nov 28, 1995

Thornton W B 1904 - 1957

Thorton John 1892 Cornelius 1906 Daniel1924 James J 1936 Kate 1913 Henry 1901 Thomas E 1948

Thorton Josephine S died Apr 25, 1956 William B died Jan 9, 1934

Thurston William O July 9, 1914 - May 11, 1968 WWII

Thurston William Ovid July 9, 1914 - May 11, 1968 Margaret Papa June 12, 1916 - Dec 11, 1992

Thyen Bernard A Nov 16, 1917 - July 2, 1979 Lois July 31, 1911 - Aug 29, 1973

Tiedt G Michael 1945 - 1950 Gordon M 1906 - 1981 Louise M 1908 - 1993

Tiemeyer Bernard E Apr 7, 1911 - Oct 2, 2006 Rosella P June 27, 1915

Tiemeyer Shawn Marie 1966 Edward Bernard 1940 Norma Nov 19??

Tierney Mary died Apr 23, 1892 aged 67

Tierney Thos A died Feb 1911

Feb 19, 1911 Leader

The burial of Mr. Thomas A. Tierney, aged 52, the well
known horseman who died at the residence of his aunt,
Mrs. Mary Flynn, on East Third Street last Saturday
night, took place Monday morning at the Catholic
Cemetery.

Tillman Harold Francis Sept 29, 1906 - Oct 30, 1973
Tillman Mary Fritz Sept 20, 1917 - Apr 23,1980
Timmins Joseph 1825 - 1919 Mary Herne 1851 - 1924
    William Joseph 1885 - 1938 Francis Saunier 1888 -
    1924
Timmins Joseph Francis 1924 - 1975
Timmons Daniel Joseph Jr. July 1, 2003
Toben Bernard E Apr 6, 1914 - July 27, 1976
Toben Irene F Apr 5, 1916 - July 31, 1967
Tomlinson Jean 1911 - 1965
Tomlinson Laura Jean 1951
Tonner Matt J 1861 - 1909
Tonner Matt Sr.. 1835 - 1910
Tonner Nellie W 1869 - 1946
Toohey Francis N July 1, 1927 - June 2, 1946
Toohey John died June 27, 1820 Maggie died Oct 1884
Toohey John 1825 - 1898 Margaret 1847 - 1892 son of Lucy
    Redding and Norbert B
Toohey John 1825 - 1898 his wife Margaret 1847 - 1892
Toohey Norbert B 1904 - 1917
Toohey Susie died Dec 22, 1878aged 27
Toschi John 1860 - 1911
Toth - Anderson
Toth Louis A Aug 23, 1909 - Nov 25, 2000 Catherine
    McKenna Toth Mar 23, 1909 - Oct 24, 1988
Tracey Arthur E Oct 10, 1910 - May 1, 1967 Mary M Aug 30,
    1912 - June 26, 1975
Trainor John J 1845 - 1923
Trammell Infant daughter of Plummer and Louise Oct 1965

Travis Ellen W Aug 28, 1879 - Sept 12, 1942
Travis John Aug 4, 1876 - May 6, 1947
Traylinek Anton 1890 - 1998 Elizabeth 1903 - Nov 9, 1993
Traynor Augusta S 1876 - 1963
Traynor John H 1872 - 1925
Traynor Rose L 1906 - 1990
Treacy Bernard J 1842 - 1897 Mary E 1842 - 1914
Oct 14, 1897 Morning Herald
B J Treacy dies of his injuries early last night in a Boston
    Hospital.

Treacy Francis O'Conner died Apr 8, 1876 aged 39

Oct 15, 1905 Morning Herald
The funeral for J Treacy will be held at St. Paul's Church
    Sunday afternoon at 2:15 o'clock. Interment in the
    family lot in the Catholic Cemetery.

Treacy James F 1884 - 1959 Anna M 1882 - 1947
Treacy Margaret Josephine June 19, 1906 - Dec 9, 1987
Treacy Mary Lynn 1914 - 1915
Treacy William J June 14, 1868 - Jan 1915 Elizabeth W Oct
    28, 1879 - Mar 1963
Treiber George 1906 - 1931
Treiber Leonard 1859 - 1939
Treiber Mary Schweibold 1871 - 1948 wife of Leonard
Tuchcial 1888 - 1944
Tucker May Glass 1893 - 19 Freeman 1890 - 1954
Tully Annie died Feb 1918
Tully Leander 1861 - 1916
Turk Elva Sibbald 1912 - 1972
Turnery Joseph died July 26, 1878 age 27
Tussey Cliff C JR 1918 - Mary Gabbard 1921 - 1969
Tuttle Landon S 1915 - 1965 Mary F 1913 - 1995
Twyman Dec 5, 1808 - Apr 17, 1896

Twyman 1853 - 1932
Twyman Lewwllyn T died Mar 18, 1928
Twyman Frances L Oct 1860 - Nov 23, 1933
Twyman Greenwell 1835 - 18
Twyman John Bonner 1884 - 1913
Tyler William R Jr. Dec 22, 1936 - Nov 11, 1981 Roberta P
    May 2, 1935
Tylorenz Henry Dec 27, 1887 - Feb 21, 1913
Tyrrell Bessie 1885 - 1954
Tyrrell James 1855 - 1904
Jan 18, 1904 Leader
The funeral services of Patrolman James Tyrrell were held
    yesterday afternoon at St. Paul's Church. Twenty-two
    uniformed patrolmen, in charge of Lieuts. Overley and
    Harkins, acted as escort for the hearse. The interment
    was in the Catholic Cemetery.

Tyrrell James H 1829 - 1901 Elizabeth 1811 - 1858
Tyrrell Margaret 1858 - 1939
Tyrrell Margaret 1887 - 1941
Tywman Unknown died Dec 8, 188?
Underwood Carol Jo Scully Feb 9, 1955 - Feb 1, 2002
Underwood Louis C 1920 - 1936 John C 1899 - 1991
Unser William Fred 1860 - 1937 Mary Elizabeth 1865 - 1957
Updike Edwin Burgess III June 6, 1920 - Sept 6, 1948
Upington John V 1873 - 1917 Carriage Builder
Upington John V 1841 - 1917 Harriet 1869 - 1884 John V Jr.
    and Charlotte 1875 - 1875
Upington John V 1921 - 1996
Urfer Len 1913 - 1965 Rosemary 1917 - 1993
Valone Louis L 1907 - 1971 Carmilia S 1903 - 1970
Van Outer Henry June 23, 1915 - Nov 4, 1979 Frances Dec 7,
    ? - Aug 12, ?
Van Outer Robert H Oct 29, 1941 - Nov 14, 1998
Vanderheiden Kay Christy Feb 20, 1957 - July 25, 1957

Varrone Hugo May 29, 1911 - Nov 17, 1963
Varrone Hugo M Feb 3, 1951 - Feb 14, 1956
Varrone Olga Angelucci Oct 27, 1911 - June 18, 1999
Vaughan May E 1882 - 1914 Carlos D 1884 - 19
Venn May Scully June 6, 1876 - Sept 28, 1978
Vernie Ricardo WWII
Vernier Margaret E 1905 - 1985
Vernier Pietro 1898 - 1971
Vertuca Carl Mar 1, 1912 - Oct 8, 1981
Vertuca Vincenzo Dec 6, 1879 - Nov 2, 1966
Vertuga Leda Angela June 10, 1950 - Apr 23, 1966
Vertuga Margaret Nov 14, 1917 - Jan 15, 1955
Vertuga Marie Roberti July 6, 1883 - Apr 24, 1929
Vest Charles Lloyd Jul 6, 1926 - Oct 9, 1984 WWII
Via Dolorosa
Vidal Frederick Alexander Sept 9, 1928 - June 10, 1982
Villeminot P Edward Nov 13, 1872 - Sept 18, 1953
Villeminot P Edward Jr. July 1, 1906 - Sept 7, 1997
Vish Rebecca Fister Nov 14, 1968 - Nov 12, 1999
Vissing Theresa M July 3, 1939 - Oct 10, 1996
Vonderheide
Vonderheide Elizabeth O Mar 28, 1900 - Nov 12, 1985
Vonderheide Ira L Aug 19, 1897 - Mar 14, 1972
Wagers Robert Ryan Feb 16, 1963 - Oct 25, 2003 Melissa
        Durs Aug 18, 1864
Wagers Sam Parkes 1896 - 1952 Mary J McKee 1898 - 1961
Wagers Samuel Parkes Jr. Oct 2, 1923 - Oct 28, 1990
Wagner Chas O 1886 - 1950 Addie B 1890 - 1963
Wagner Florence Ruh 1894 - 1957
Wagner Leonard S 1892 - 1959
Walker Magg
Walker Charles L 1880 - 1952 Grace M 1890 - 1963
Walker Gerald E 1907 - 1980 Nona N 1904 - 1990
Walker James
Walker Josephine 1874 - 1949

Walker Kate 1857 - 1939
Walker Margaret died Jan 8, 1912 aged 83
Walker Robert L Sr. 1865 - 1959
Walker Robert Lee Jr. 1905 - 1986
Walker Rufus Lee 1902 - 1972 Josephine H 1907 - 1996
Walker Wilhelmina Apr 27, 1898 - Feb 25, 1959
Wall Helen Apr 14, 1894 - Nov 27, 1983 Claire Liske Sept 7,
    1897 - Oct 28, 1982
Wallace James Bernard Mar 1, 1876 - May 1972 Pauline
    Worland Apr 28, 1883 - Oct 26, 1973
Wallace Louise Feb 28, 1911 - Feb 5, 1982
Wallace Paul A Apr 7, 1912 - Apr 21, 1927
Wallace Raymond Feb 17, 1919 - Jan 29, 1943 WWII
Walsh Ellen July 16, 1856 - Apr 11, 1918
Walsh Geraldine Fitzgerald Jan 12, 1910 - Nov 13, 1997
Walter Eugene F Aug 7, 1929 - Apr 2, 1982 Frances A Dec 7,
    1932
Walter Leslie III
Walz
Walz Kathleen Marie Dec 4, 1953 daughter of Raymond C &
    Roberta N
Walz Mari A Dec 10, 1946 - Mar 5, 1973
Walz Roberta N Jan 9, 1918 - July 1, 2002
Wamsley Annie 1881 - 1960
Ward - He will raise you up on eagle's wings
Ward Francis James Nov 27, 1912
Ward George Francis died Jul 2, 1992 WWII
Ward John Peter Sr. July 10, 1890 - June 10, 1969 Florence A
    Dec 17, 1882 - May 1967
Waren Betty 1929 - 2001 Minnie 1895 - 1932 Doris 1934
Warren
Warren Hubert Cronin Dec 28, 1919 - Oct 1981
Warren Joseph Garcia Nov 12, 2000 - May 3, 2004
Warren Joseph E Sr. Jan 25, 1912 - June 11, 1976
Warren Karen Marie Sept 30, 1955 - Feb 24, 1972

Warren Kathleen Forman Aug 30, 1913 - Aug 8, 1964
Wasserman David Austin Feb 21, 1975 - Nov 22, 1992
Waters Mary Krieger Dec 3, 1919
Wathen Mark T Feb 10, 1890 - Mar 22, 1992 Katherine A
    Sept 3, 1895 - Aug 29, 1985 married June 17, 1925
Wathen Mary Stevens 1904 - 1938
Weaver Amile 1866 - 1940 Katie 1874 - 1953
Weaver Charles 1899 - 1973 Katherine Midden 1901 - 1973
Weaver William J June 20, 1905 - Mar 21, 1981 Violette S
    July 13, 1900 - June 2, 1978
Webb Union B May 21, 1922 - Sept 13, 1984 Ruth S Oct 11,
    1922 - Jan 9, 2004
Webb Union B Jr. May 21, 1922 - Sept 13, 1984 US Army Air
    Corps
Webber Charles L 1886 - 1943 Mary Fallon 1888 - 1949
Webber Nell Mitchell 1898 - 1982 Charles W 1898 - 1951

Nov 1, 1911 Leader
Mr. J. L. Webb arrived here Saturday night from his home in
    Louisville with the bodies of his wife and son. The
    sons who was six years of age died at the Louisville
    city Hospital Thursday night. The wife and mother
    died at St. Mary Elizabeth Hospital Saturday morning.
    The burial will be in the Catholic Cemetery.

Weber John 1877 - 1910
Weber Peter 1834 - 1917 Katherine 1839 - 1917
Wedding - Greenwald, Ralph E Wedding May 9, 1917 - Sept
    30, 1967 Arthur A Greenwald Sept 29, 1915 - Sept 1,
    2003 Norma J Brouilette Wedding Greenwald Mar 2,
    1920 - May 26, 2009
Wehle Elsie Milliette Jan 13 - Feb 15, 2001
Wehle Frank Edward Mar 30, 1914 - July 3, 1983
Wehle Frank A Dec 13, 1879 - June 11, 1911
Wehle Frances Dowling Oct 11, 1887 - Mar 5, 1977

Wehle Herbert M 1915 - 1917
Wehle Jane Dowling Apr 19, 1917 - Jan 13, 2001
Wehle Margaret Dowling Aug 2, 1925
Wehle Ruth Dowling Dec 22, 1911 - Oct 31, 2000
Wehrle James F Jan 4, 1911 - Aug 6, 2002 Betty Brophy Feb
    13, 1911 - Aug 18, 1999
Wehrle John B Jr. Sept 5, 1928 - Oct 25, 1998 Lydia W June
    4, 1930
Wehrle John E 1832 - 1902 Kunigunda 1834 - 1900
Dec 30, 1902 Morning Herald
The funeral of John E Wherle occurred at St. Paul's Church at
    11 o'clock yesterday morning and the burial followed
    in the Catholic Cemetery.

Wehrle Marcus A 1887 - 1894
Wehrle William M 1897 - 1903
Wehtzel Charles A Oct 23, 1906 - Jan 2, 1983
Weisenberger
Weisenberger Lillian E 1880 - 1973
Weisenberger Margaret L Mahoney 1870 - 1924 wife of Phil J
Weisenberger Phil L 1868 - 1936
Weissinger Robert J 1912 - 1957
Weissinger Virginia S Jan 25, 1910
Weitzel A Klair 1887 - 1936
Weitzel Adeline E Dec 29, 1907 - Oct 12, 2001 daughter of
    Jerome B & Laetitia K
Weitzel Anthony Aug 7, 1862 - Oct 14, 1944
Weitzel Charles B 1883 - 1949
Weitzel Charles J 1922 - 1968 son of A K & Francina
Weitzel Edna C May 10, 1900 - Apr 11, 1922
Weitzel Francina 1895 - 1923 wife of A K
Weitzel Henry 1832 - 1904
Weitzel Jerome B 1859 - 1917
Weitzel Kathryn 1880 - 1927
Weitzel Laetita Klair 1872 - 1962 wife of Jerome B

Weitzel Leona O Oct 22, 1862 - Apr 5, 1910
Weitzel Louis Jan 21, 1821 - Apr 14, 1903
Weitzrel Elizabeth Klair 1862 - 1895 wife of Jerome B
Welch Anna V died Dec 16, 1948
Welch Earnest 1882 - 1957 Catherine H 1878 - 1951
Welch Edward Lawrence Jan 6, 1908 - Mar 9, 1980 Mary
    Burke Jan 26, 1908 - July 31, 1979
Welch Elizabeth Madigan Jan 9, 1892 - Aug 27, 1964 wife of
    Richard L
Welch Ernest A III Sept 22, 1938 - Sept 24, 1944
Welch Ernest Augustus 1910 - 1978 Virginia Adleta 1915 -
    1991
Welch Eugene J Nov 21, 1921 - Oct 4, 1995
Welch James Joseph Sr. Jan 16, 1912 - Mar 27, 1986 Jessie
    Mae July 20, 1911 - Apr 25, 1964
Welch James T Jr. Mar 11, 1911 - Aug 13, 1985 Thecla N
    July 30, 1913 - Sept 13, 2006
Welch James William 1879 - 1951
Welch Jean Marie born Jan 18, 1938
Welch Johanna died May 18, 1862 daughter of Jas and B
    Welch age 18
Welch John 1877
Welch John Matthew July 12, 1919 - Sept 3, 1966
Welch L Conrad Dec 16, 1939 - Sept 25, 1944
Welch Lawrence 1833 - 1917
Welch Loreta R died 1959
Welch Margaret June 7, 1885 - Feb 17, 1967
Welch Martha E 1918
Welch Mary Moynahan 1882 - 1982 James Thomas 1875 -
    1967
Welch Mary R 1858 - 1918
Welch Mary Thecla Apr 3, 1940 - Apr 4, 1996
Welch Mary Virginia Benckart Apr 8, 1920 - Oct 24, 1990
Welch Michael V May 28, 1946 Dahlia M Nov 18, 1941 - Feb
    12, 1999

Welch Paul E 1912 - 1916
Welch Paul P 1916 - 1917
Welch Richard L Jan 27, 1885 - Aug 14, 1936
Welch Robert Emmett 1874 - 1914
Nov 7, 1914   Leader
The funeral services of Robert E. Welch will be held Sunday
    afternoon at St. Paul's Catholic Church, followed by
    interment in the Catholic Cemetery.

Welch Rosemary 1887 - 1901
Weldon George L 1908 - 1977 Garnette G 1912
Weldon George L Oct 3, 1908 - May 20, 1977 Maj US Army
Welsh Anna Mae B 1890 - 1977
Welsh Bartholomew J 1856 - 1896
May 22, 1896 Leader
All that was mortal of Bartholomew J. Welsh was laid to rest
    among the evergreens at the Catholic Cemetery this
    morning. The funeral services were held at the
    Catholic Church, and from there the funeral procession
    moved to the Cemetery. It was one of the largest
    funerals ever seen in this city.

May 23, 1896 Morning Herald
The Body of Auditor Bartholomew J. Welch was buried in the
    Catholic Cemetery yesterday morning

Welsh Edna Agnes 1902 - 1980
Welsh Father 1837 - 1909
Welsh Garrett Aug 19, 1874 - Feb 25, 1931
Welsh Garrett died 1918
Welsh James 1865 - 1941
Welsh John E 1904 - 1962 Edith B 1908 - 1982
Welsh John M 1871 - 1898
Welsh King 1887 - 1917
Welsh Mary

Welsh Mary 1872 - 1950

Welsh Mary died 1928

Welsh Mary Ferrell May 4, 1875 - Feb 26, 1945

Welsh Mother 1842 - 1921

Welsh Nannie died 1951

Welsh Sarah King 1865 - 1932

Welsh Thomas

Welsh Thomas A Feb 14, 1894 - Oct 17, 1964 WWI

Welsh W P Apr 1862 - June 14, 1884

Welsh Anna 1837 - 1911

Wessels

Wessling

Wessling Francis W Oct 11, 1902 - Jan 11, 1982

Wessling Raymond C Feb 28, 1896 - Apr 25, 1964

West Albert J Mar 28, 1909 - Nov 24 198? Ann Price Sept 17, 1926

West Estelle J July 25, 1897 - July 28, 1982

West Leo 1904 - 1983

West Oliver H Oct 20, 1868 - Apr 3, 1945 Margaret S June 2, 1879 - Sept 16, 1937

West Rosa L 1899 - 1965

Westley Bruce May 26, 1915 - Apr 2, 1990 Rosemary N Jan 14, 1914 - Nov 20, 2009 Paul M Sept 11, 1951 - Dec 7, 1998

Westley Bruce H May 26, 1915 - Apr 1990

Westscott Frank Robert 1898 - 1944

May 9, 1906 Leader

The funeral services of James A. Westscott, the four-year-old son of Mr. And Mrs. J. W. Westscott of Clay City, Ky., will take place at the St. Paul's Catholic Church Thursday morning. The burial will be in the Catholic Cemetery.

Westscott John Matthew 1896 - 1924

Westscott John W Jan 28, 1864 - Oct 4, 1941 Katherine K
    Mar 3, 1867 - Mar 28, 1944
Westscott Lydia Elizabeth 1891 - 1921
Westscott Paul T 1907 - 1984 Christine L Naive 1908 - 1983
Wetzel 1845 - 1928
Whalen James 1835 - 19??
Whalen John Joseph Mary 1919
Whalen Susanna B 1903 - 1989 John O 1906 - 1987 Mary C
    1909 - 1986
Whalen William 1877 - 1901
Whitaker Mary K July 17, 1894 - Nov 29, 1976
White
White John F Aug 16, 1906 - Aug 4, 1942
White Michael J Sept 30, 1866 - June 5, 1925
White Robert J 1900 - 1971 Anna Mae 1922 - 1970
White Sylvester B 1819 - 1906 Nora Ann 1933 - 1907 James
    L B 1858 - 1934 Lema C 1870 - 1907 William T 1864
    - 1902 Mary A C 1861 John S age 7 John C age 4

May 14, 1906 Leader
Thomas W. White, 87, died May 8 of senile exhaustion. Burial
    in Catholic Cemetery.

Wieman
Wientjes Raphael E Sept 23, 1918 - May 18, 1999 Juanita F
    July 12, 1923 - Apr 21, 1984
Wiley Elizabeth Apr 14, 1885 - Sept 26, 1938
Wilford Vernon R Jr. Dec 10, 1947
Wilkosz Clarence J 1922 - 2003 Genevieve M 1925
Wilkosz Clarence J Jan 18, 1922 - Feb 27, 2003 WWII
Willett Dr James B 1940 - 1998
Willett J William 1915 - 1982 Catherine M 1918
Willett Joseph E 1907 - 1969 Virginia M 1916
Willettop Rev WM T May 6, 1824 aged about 34 first Native
    priest of Ky.

William Mary Ellen Sheehy 1921 - 1997
William Thomas J 1865 - 1935
Williams Bettye M Aug 11, 1943 - Nov 8, 2000
Williams Charles J May 10, 1936 - May 22, 2005 US Air
    Force
Williams Charles M died June 30, 1874
Williams Charles P 1906 - 1971 Margaret S 1915 - 1998
Williams Florence Cloud Apr 26, 1911 - June 27, 1952 and
    infant wife of Charles P
Williams Frances Mar 8, 1919 - Feb 5, 1971 Tilford May 22,
    1910
Williams James Doty July 8, 1963 - Oct 19, 1980
Williams Margaret Baker 1903 - 1935
Williams Nannie S Peinz 1875 - 1943
Williams Steven Edward Aug 11-18, 1958 son of D L &
    Helen
Williams John G 1862 - 1939 Caroline K 1877 - 1954
Williams Catherine 1860 - 1928
Willmont Curtis Simeonth May 30, 1919 - May 16, 1974
    Aimle K Murray Aug 28, 1920 - Dec 29, 2005
Willmott Curtis S May 30, 1919 - May 16, 1974 WWII
Wilson Charles W 1878 - 1963
Wilson John Allen 1904 - 1967 Natalie Wides 1907 - 1984
Wilson Kirby Woods Jan 21, 1904 - Feb 6, 1989
Wilson Leonard Shouse Dec 13, 1907 - Aug 31, 1984
Wilson Margaret B 1877 - 1964
Wilson Mary Jane Jan 19, 1877 - June 24, 1940
Wilson Oscar R 1898 - 1969 Katherine 1900 - 1982
Wilson Oscar R WWI 1898 - July 1969
Wilson Patricia Traynor 1913 - 1992
Wilson Raymond P Aug 18, 1915 - Mar 28, 1978 Angeline T
    Jan 2, 1914 - Apr 12, 1973
Wilson Thomas J 1875 - 1940
Winders Herbert J 1929 - May 12, ?
Witt George R Sr. 1903 - 1931

Witten Stoy Graham Feb 15, 1910 - Aug 5, 1979 Anne
Ricketts Sept 1922 - May 199?
Wombwell Barbara Futrell 1926 - 2008
Wombwell Joseph H 1895 - 1931
Wombwell Joseph Henry Jr. 1925 - 1995
Wombwell Josephine Burkley 1896 - 1967
Wood Charles 1927 - 1984 Mary E Clarke 1887 - 1981
Charles O 1886 - 1983
Wood Florence Garland 1907 - 1980
Wood George A 1894 - 1982
Wood Mary Jan 9, 1893 - Apr 8, 1997
Woods Charles Nov 21, 1926 - Apr 17, 1999 Margaret Henry
Dec 11, 1928 - May 10, 1986
Woods George Dougherty 1843 Catherine N Woods 1846 -
1918
Woods John (JC) Sept 29, 1910 - Dec 28, 1980 Mary C Apr
20, 1915
Woods Margaret G 1867 - 1960
Woods Margaret Magee 1908 - 1935
Worland Catherine died Oct 2, 1885 age 28 Elizabeth Kearney
Feb 12, 1856 - July 16, 1816
Worland Mary A 1883
Worland Sara C 1836 - 1917 Anna E 1837 - 1915
Worland Thomas L Dec 19, 1805 - Feb 16, 1889 Thos C July
6, 1860
Wright Kate Hanly May 22, 1874 - Jan 14, 1964
Wright Katie Haney 1877 aged 26 wife of A W
Wright Patrick Sept 19, 1954 - Nov 20, 1954
Wurtenberger Harold W Nov 1, 1922 - Jan 21, 1990 Patty Rae
Sept 8, 1934
Wurtenberger Harold W Nov 1, 1922 - Jan 21, 1990 US Army
Wurtenberger Joseph F 1921 - 2002 Mary Jane G 1918 - 1982
Wurtenberger Joseph F Jan 7, 1921 - Oct 15, 2002 WWII
Wurtenberger Josephine B Apr 5, 1898 - Apr 21, 1979 Holy
Mary pray for us

Wylie Charles Geoffrey Feb 11, 1963 - Aug 31, 1980 son of
    Kathryn Rupert Gentry
Yarnell Nancy C died Jan 17, 1990
Yeaple Chester Oct 3, 1903 - Jan 1, 1989 Ethel R Mar 3, 1907
    - Oct 14, 1980
Yelicic Mary Ellis died July 6, 1924
Yelicic Pete died May 23, 1922
Young Francis 195?
Young Lucy Spalding 1860 - 1937
Young Milton 1891 - 1974
Young Milton 1918
Young Thomas Brown 1901 - 1958
Zaccarelli Albina (Alba) S May 6, 1909 - Dec 15, 1994
Zaccarelli James Michael Aug 6, 1956 - Jan 26, 1987
Zaccarelli Louise B Dec 4, 1917 - Jan 31, 1982
Zaccarelli Michele L Dec 27, 1907
Zaccarelli Olga E Sept 16, 1912
Zaccarelli Robert E Oct 14, 1946 - Feb 16, 1988
Zaccarelli Virginia L June 18, 1948 - Jan 8, 1966
Zaccarelli William E Oct 22, 1945 - Apr 17, 1958
Zaccaria Angelo 1895 - 1967 Maria G 1897 - 1994
Zechella Marilyn Miller 1928 - 1984

www.ingramcontent.com/pod-product-compliance
Lightning Source LLC
Chambersburg PA
CBHW070912270326
41927CB00011B/2540